Oxford School Spelling Dictionary

Robert Allen

Education Consultant Michele Chapman

D1454967

OXFORD
UNIVERSITY PRESS

OXFORD
UNIVERSITY PRESS

Great Clarendon Street, Oxford OX2 6DP

Oxford University Press is a department of the University of Oxford.
It furthers the University's objective of excellence in research,
scholarship, and education by publishing worldwide in

Oxford NewYork

Auckland Bangkok Buenos Aires Cape Town Chennai
Dar es Salaam Delhi Hong Kong Istanbul Karachi Kolkata
Kuala Lumpur Madrid Melbourne Mexico City Mumbai Nairobi
São Paulo Taipei Tokyo Toronto

Oxford is a registered trade mark of Oxford University Press
in the UK and in certain other countries

The moral rights of the author have been asserted
Database right Oxford University Press (maker)

First published 2001
This edition 2004

Database right Oxford University Press (maker)

British Library cataloguing in Publication Data available

Part of a 6-part set. Not to be sold separately.

ISBN 0-19-911201-0 (complete set)

ISBN 0-19-911263-0 *Oxford School Spelling Dictionary* (when part of this set)

10 9 8 7 6 5 4 3 2 1

Printed in the UK by Cox and Wyman

Introduction

The *Oxford School Spelling Dictionary* is a special dictionary
designed to help students with their spelling. Generally speaking
there are three main areas of spelling difficulty for users of English
whatever their age.

- Some words are difficult because they have unusual or
  unpredictable features. **Eighth**, **guard**, and **niece** are often
  spelt wrongly because they have awkward letter sequences.
  Disappear and **embarrass** are confusing because some
  letters are doubled while others are not. Words such as
  desperate and **separate** seem inconsistent because one
  has an **e** in the middle where the other has an **a** for no
  apparent reason.

- Then there are words that are easily confused. **Vain**, **vein**,
  and **vane** sound the same but have very different meanings.
  Some words change their spelling according to how they
  are used. For example, **dependant** as a *noun* is spelt with
  an **a**, but as an *adjective*, it is spelt with an **e**.

- The third type of difficulty arises when suffixes and endings
  are added to words. It is not easy to remember to keep an
  e in **changeable**, to replace **y** with **i** in **happily**, and not
  to double the **p** in **galloping**.

With increased interest in spelling, reading, and writing in
schools today we hope that the *Oxford School Spelling Dictionary*
will provide a valuable tool offering useful strategies for dealing with
spelling difficulties. We also hope that it will support teachers and
parents whose task is to enable young writers to become confident,
accurate spellers and to express themselves with a voice of their own.

How to use this book

Entries

Words are listed alphabetically in **bold** and the part of speech or word class (e.g. *noun*, *verb*, *adjective*) follows in italic. If the word has endings (called inflections), these are also listed below the headword.

Decide on the first sound of the word you are looking for. Some first sounds can be confusing. If you cannot find the word you are looking for, use the **Try also** tips which will guide you to other possible spellings.

Footnotes

Some words have footnotes attached to them. These identify words that you need to check that you have the right meaning. For example, at **bite** you will find a footnote to tell you that there is another word that sounds like it but is spelt a different way, **!byte**. Words that sound the same but are spelt differently are called homophones. Some footnotes also give extra information on usage and grammar.

Panels

There are about 250 panels which highlight particular problems. For example, you may want to know which words are spelt **-able** like **bendable**, and which ones are spelt **-ible** like **accessible**. Or you may want to know how you form plurals of nouns ending in **-f** such as **calf** or **roof**. Use these information panels to build your knowledge of spelling rules and practices.

It may be useful to keep a spelling jotter for new words. When using a new word, say it aloud several times before you write it down. When you go on to use it in your writing, try not to copy it but to write the word from memory.

Try also

Entry word

Panel

selfishness
selfless *adjective*
selflessly
self-service
★ sell *verb*
sells
selling
sold
semaphore
semen

semi-
semi- makes words
meaning 'half', e.g.
semi-automatic,
semi-skimmed.
A few words are spelt
joined up, e.g.
semicircle,
semicolon, but most
of them have hyphens.

semibreve *noun*
semibreves
semicircle *noun*
semicircles
semicircular
semicolon *noun*
semicolons
semi-detached
semi-final *noun*
semi-finals
semi-finalist *noun*
semi-finalists
semitone *noun*
semitones
semolina
senate
senator *noun*
senators

send *verb*
sends
sending
sent
senior *adjective* and
noun
seniors
seniority
sensation *noun*
sensations
sensational *adjective*
sensationally
sense *noun*
senses
sense *verb*
senses
sensing
sensed
senseless *adjective*
senselessly
sensible *adjective*
sensibly
sensitive *adjective*
sensitively
sensitivity *noun*
sensitivities
sensitize *verb*
sensitizes
sensitizing
sensitized
sensor *noun*
sensors
☆ sent see send
sentence *noun*
sentences
sentence *verb*
sentences
sentencing
sentenced
sentiment *noun*
sentiments

sentimental
adjective
sentimentally
sentimentality
sentinel *noun*
sentinels
sentry *noun*
sentries
separable
separate *adjective*
separately
separate *verb*
separates
separating
separated
separation *noun*
separations
September *noun*
Septembers
septic
sequel *noun*
sequels
sequence *noun*
sequences
sequin *noun*
sequins
serene *adjective*
serenely
serenity
sergeant *noun*
sergeants
sergeant major
noun
sergeant majors
○ serial *noun*
serials
series *noun*
series
serious *adjective*
seriously

Inflections

Word
class
(part of
speech)

★ To sell something means 'to exchange it for money'. ! cell.
☆ You use sent in e.g. *he was sent home*. ! cent, scent.
○ A serial is a story or programme in separate parts. ! cereal.

Footnote

Do not confuse with

Aa

-a
Most nouns ending in -a, e.g. amoeba, gala, have plurals ending in -as, e.g. amoebas, galas. A few technical words have plurals ending in -ae, e.g. antennae.

aback

abacus *noun*
abacuses

abandon *verb*
abandons
abandoning
abandoned

abbey *noun*
abbeys

abbot *noun*
abbots

abbreviate *verb*
abbreviates
abbreviating
abbreviated

abbreviation *noun*
abbreviations

abdomen *noun*
abdomens

abdominal

abduct *verb*
abducts
abducting
abducted

abide *verb*
abides
abiding
abided

ability *noun*
abilities

ablaze

able *adjective*
abler
ablest

-able and -ible
You add -able to a verb to make an adjective that means 'able to be done', e.g. bendable means 'able to be bent'. Some adjectives that have this meaning end in -ible, e.g. accessible, convertible and incredible. You cannot use -ible to make new words as you can with -able.

ably

abnormal
abnormally

abnormality *noun*
abnormalities

aboard

abode *noun*
abodes

abolish *verb*
abolishes
abolishing
abolished

abolition

abominable

aboriginal

Aborigines

abort *verb*
aborts
aborting
aborted

abortion *noun*
abortions

abound *verb*
abounds
abounding
abounded

about

above

abrasive

abreast

abroad

abrupt

abscess *noun*
abscesses

abseil *verb*
abseils
abseiling
abseiled

absence *noun*
absences

absent

absentee *noun*
absentees

absent-minded
absent-mindedly

absolute
absolutely

absorb *verb*
absorbs
absorbing
absorbed

absorbent

absorption

abstract *adjective*
and *noun*
abstracts

abstract *verb*
abstracts
abstracting
abstracted

absurd
  absurdly
absurdity noun
  absurdities
abundance
abundant
abuse verb
  abuses
  abusing
  abused
abuse noun
  abuses
abusive
  abusively
abysmal
abyss noun
  abysses
academic
academy noun
  academies
accelerate verb
  accelerates
  accelerating
  accelerated
acceleration
accelerator noun
  accelerators
accent noun
  accents
accent verb
  accents
  accenting
  accented
* **accept** verb
  accepts
  accepting
  accepted
acceptable
acceptance
access noun
  accesses

access verb
  accesses
  accessing
  accessed
accessibility
accessible
accession noun
  accessions
accessory noun
  accessories
accident noun
  accidents
accidental
  accidentally
acclaim verb
  acclaims
  acclaiming
  acclaimed
accommodate verb
  accommodates
  accommodating
  accommodated
accommodation
accompaniment
  noun
  accompaniments
accompanist noun
  accompanists
accompany verb
  accompanies
  accompanying
  accompanied
accomplish verb
  accomplishes
  accomplishing
  accomplished
accomplished
accomplishment
  noun
  accomplishments
accord noun
  accords

according
  accordingly
accordion noun
  accordions
account noun
  accounts
account verb
  accounts
  accounting
  accounted
accountancy
accountant noun
  accountants
accumulate verb
  accumulates
  accumulating
  accumulated
accumulation
accuracy
accurate
  accurately
accusation noun
  accusations
accuse verb
  accuses
  accusing
  accused
accustomed
ace noun
  aces
ache noun
  aches
ache verb
  aches
  aching
  ached
achieve verb
  achieves
  achieving
  achieved

- -

★ To accept something is to take it. ! except.

achievement
achievements

acid noun
acids

acidic

acidity noun

acknowledge verb
acknowledges
acknowledging
acknowledged

acknowledgement
noun
acknowledgements

acne

acorn noun
acorns

acoustic

acoustics

acquaint verb
acquaints
acquainting
acquainted

acquaintance noun
acquaintances

acquire verb
acquires
acquiring
acquired

acquisition noun
acquisitions

acquit verb
acquits
acquitting
acquitted

acquittal noun
acquittals

acre noun
acres

acrobat noun
acrobats

acrobatic adjective
acrobatically

acrobatics

acronym noun
acronyms

across adverb and
preposition

act noun
acts

act verb
acts
acting
acted

action noun
actions

activate verb
activates
activating
activated

active

activity noun
activities

actor noun
actors

actress noun
actresses

actual
actually

acupuncture

acute

Adam's apple noun
Adam's apples

adapt verb
adapts
adapting
adapted

adaptable

adaptation

adaptor noun
adaptors

add verb
adds
adding
added

adder noun
adders

addict noun
addicts

addicted

addiction noun
addictions

addictive

addition noun
additions

additional

additive noun
additives

address noun
addresses

address verb
addresses
addressing
addressed

adenoids

adequate

adhere verb
adheres
adhering
adhered

adhesive noun
adhesives

adhesion

adhesive

Adi Granth

adjacent

adjective noun
adjectives

ad - ae

adjourn *verb*
adjourns
adjourning
adjourned
adjournment
adjudicate *verb*
adjudicates
adjudicating
adjudicated
adjudication
adjudicator
adjust *verb*
adjusts
adjusting
adjusted
adjustment *noun*
adjustments
administer *verb*
administers
administering
administered
administration
noun
administrations
administrative
administrator
admirable
admirably
admiral *noun*
admirals
admiration
admire *verb*
admires
admiring
admired
admirer *noun*
admirers
admission *noun*
admissions
admit *verb*
admits

admitting
admitted
admittance
admittedly
ado
adolescence
adolescent *noun*
adolescents
adopt *verb*
adopts
adopting
adopted
adoption
adoptive
adorable
adorably
adoration
adore *verb*
adores
adoring
adored
adorn *verb*
adorns
adorning
adorned
adornment
adrenalin
adrift
adult *noun*
adults
adulterer
adultery
advance *noun*
advances
advance *verb*
advances
advancing
advanced
advanced
advantage *noun*

advantages
advantageous
★ **Advent**
adventure *noun*
adventures
adventurous
adjective
adventurously
adverb *noun*
adverbs
adversary *noun*
adversaries
adverse
adversity *noun*
adversities
advertise *verb*
advertises
advertising
advertised
advertisement
noun
advertisements
advice
advisable
advise *verb*
advises
advising
advised
adviser *noun*
advisers
advisory
advocate *noun*
advocates
advocate *verb*
advocates
advocating
advocated
aerial *adjective* and
noun
aerials

★ Use a capital A when you mean the period before Christmas.

aero-
You use *aero-* to make words to do with the air or aircraft, e.g. **aerobatics**. If the word is a long one you spell it with a hyphen, e.g. **aero-engineering**.

aerobatic
aerobatics
aerobics
aeronautical
aeronautics
aeroplane *noun*
aeroplanes
aerosol *noun*
aerosols
aesthetic
aesthetically
affair *noun*
affairs
★ **affect** *verb*
affects
affecting
affected
affection *noun*
affections
affectionate
affectionately
afflict *verb*
afflicts
afflicting
afflicted
affliction
afflictions
affluence
affluent
afford *verb*
affords

affording
afforded
afforestation
afloat *adjective* and *adverb*
afraid
afresh
African *adjective* and *noun*
Africans
aft
after
afternoon *noun*
afternoons
afterwards
again
against
age *noun*
ages
age *verb*
ages
ageing
aged
aged
agency *noun*
agencies
agenda *noun*
agendas
agent *noun*
agents
aggravate *verb*
aggravates
aggravating
aggravated
aggravation
aggression
aggressive
aggressively
aggressor
aggressors

agile
agility
agitate *verb*
agitates
agitating
agitated
agitation
agitator *noun*
agitators
agnostic *noun*
agnostics
ago
agonizing
agony *noun*
agonies
agree *verb*
agrees
agreeing
agreed
agreeable
agreement *noun*
agreements
agriculture
agricultural
aground
ahead
ahoy
aid *noun*
aids
aid *verb*
aids
aiding
aided
☆ **Aids**
ailing
ailment *noun*
ailments
aim *verb*
aims
aiming
aimed

★ Affect means 'to make something change'. ! effect.
☆ Use a capital A when you mean the disease.

aim *noun*
aims

aimless
aimlessly

★ air *noun*
airs

air *verb*
airs
airing
aired

airborne

air-conditioned

air-conditioning

aircraft *noun*
aircraft

Airedale *noun*
Airedales

airfield *noun*
airfields

air force *noun*
air forces

airgun *noun*
airguns

airline *noun*
airlines

airlock *noun*
airlocks

airmail

airman *noun*
airmen

airport *noun*
airports

airship *noun*
airships

airstream *noun*
airstreams

airtight

airy *adjective*
airier
airiest
airily

☆ aisle *noun*
aisles

ajar

○ akela *noun*
akelas

alarm *verb*
alarms
alarming
alarmed

alarm *noun*
alarms

alas

albatross *noun*
albatrosses

album *noun*
albums

alcohol

alcoholic *adjective*
and *noun*
alcoholics

alcoholism

alcove *noun*
alcoves

✳ ale *noun*
ales

alert *verb*
alerts
alerting
alerted

alert *adjective* and
noun
alerts

algebra

algebraic

alias *noun*
aliases

alibi *noun*
alibis

alien *adjective* and
noun
aliens

alienate *verb*
alienates
alienating
alienated

alienation

alight

alike

alive

alkali *noun*
alkalis

alkaline

alkalinity

Allah

allegation *noun*
allegations

allege *verb*
alleges
alleging
alleged

allegedly

allegiance *noun*
allegiances

allegorical

allegory *noun*
allegories

allergic

allergy *noun*
allergies

alley *noun*
alleys

alliance *noun*
alliances

allied

alligator *noun*
alligators

. . . .

★ You can use a plural in the phrase *to put on airs*.
☆ An **aisle** is a passage in a church or cinema. ! **isle**.
○ **Akela** is a Scout leader.
✳ You can use a plural when you mean 'different types of ale'.

allot *verb*
allots
allotting
allotted

allotment *noun*
allotments

allow *verb*
allows
allowing
allowed

allowance *noun*
allowances

alloy *noun*
alloys

all right

all-round

all-rounder

ally *noun*
allies

ally *verb*
allies
allying
allied

almighty

almond *noun*
almonds

almost

aloft

alone

along

alongside

★ **aloud**

alphabet *noun*
alphabets

alphabetical
alphabetically

alpine

already

Alsatian *noun*
Alsatians

also

☆ **altar** *noun*
altars

✪ **alter** *verb*
alters
altering
altered

alteration

alternate

alternate *verb*
alternates
alternating
alternated

alternately

alternation

alternating current

alternative *noun*
alternatives

alternative

alternator *noun*
alternators

although *conjunction*

altitude *noun*
altitudes

altogether

aluminium

always

amalgamate *verb*
amalgamates
amalgamating
amalgamated

amalgamation

amateur *adjective and noun*
amateurs

amateurish

amaze *verb*
amazes
amazing
amazed

amazement

ambassador *noun*
ambassadors

amber

ambiguity
ambiguities

ambiguous
ambiguously

ambition *noun*
ambitions

ambitious
ambitiously

amble *verb*
ambles
ambling
ambled

ambulance *noun*
ambulances

ambush *noun*
ambushes

ambush *verb*
ambushes
ambushing
ambushed

amen

amend *verb*
amends
amending
amended

amendment

amenity *noun*
amenities

American *adjective and noun*
Americans

amiable
amiably

amicable
amicably

✲ **amid**

• •

★ **Aloud** means 'in a voice that can be heard'. **!** allowed.
☆ An **altar** is a raised surface in religious ceremonies. **!** alter.
✪ **Alter** means to change something. **!** altar.
✲ You can also spell this word **amidst**.

amidships
ammonia
ammunition
amnesty *noun*
amnesties
amoeba *noun*
amoebas
★ among
amount *noun*
amounts
amount *verb*
amounts
amounting
amounted
amphibian *adjective*
and *noun*
amphibians
amphibious
ample *adjective*
ampler
amplest
amply
amplification
amplifier *noun*
amplifiers
amplify *verb*
amplifies
amplifying
amplified
amputate *verb*
amputates
amputating
amputated
amputation
amuse *verb*
amuses
amusing
amused
amusement *noun*
amusements
amusing

☆ an
anaemia
anaemic
anaesthetic *noun*
anaesthetics
anaesthetist
anaesthetize *verb*
anaesthetizes
anaesthetizing
anaesthetized
anagram *noun*
anagrams
analogous
◎ analogue
analogy *noun*
analogies
analyse *verb*
analyses
analysing
analysed
analysis *noun*
analyses
analytical
anarchism
anarchist *noun*
anarchists
anarchy
anatomical
anatomy

-ance and -ence
Most nouns ending in
-*ance* come from
verbs, e.g.
disturbance,
endurance. Some
nouns end in -*ence*,
e.g. dependence,
obedience, and you
need to be careful not
to misspell these.

ancestor *noun*
ancestors
ancestral
ancestry *noun*
ancestries
anchor *noun*
anchors
anchorage *noun*
anchorages
ancient
anemone *noun*
anemones
angel *noun*
angels
angelic
anger
angle *noun*
angles
angle *verb*
angles
angling
angled
angler *noun*
anglers
Anglican *adjective*
and *noun*
Anglicans
Anglo-Saxon
adjective and *noun*
Anglo-Saxons
angry *adjective*
angrier
angriest
angrily
anguish
angular
animal *noun*
animals
animated
animation

• •

★ You can also spell this word *amongst*.
☆ You use *an* instead of *a* before a word beginning with a vowel, e.g. *an apple*, or
   before an abbreviation that sounds as though it begins with a vowel, e.g. *an*
   MP.
◎ You will sometimes see the spelling *analog*, especially when it is about
   computers.

animosity noun
animosities
aniseed
ankle noun
ankles
annex verb
annexes
annexing
annexed
annexation
annexe noun
annexes
annihilate verb
annihilates
annihilating
annihilated
annihilation
anniversary noun
anniversaries
announce verb
announces
announcing
announced
announcer
announcement noun
announcements
annoy verb
annoys
annoying
annoyed
annoyance noun
annoyances
annual adjective
annually
annual noun
annuals
★ **anonymity**
anonymous
anonymously
anorak noun
anoraks

anorexia
anorexic
another
answer noun
answers
answer verb
answers
answering
answered

-ant and -ent
Many adjectives end
in -ant, e.g.abundant,
important. Some
adjectives end in -ent,
e.g. dependent
(dependant is a
noun), permanent,
and you need to be
careful not to misspell
these.

antagonism
antagonistic
antagonize verb
antagonizes
antagonizing
antagonized
Antarctic adjective
and noun
anteater noun
anteaters
☆ **antelope** noun
antelope or
antelopes
antenna noun
antennas
anthem noun
anthems
anthill noun
anthills
anthology noun
anthologies

anthracite
anthropologist
anthropology

anti-
anti- at the beginning
of a word makes a
word meaning
'against something'
or 'stopping
something', e.g.
antifreeze means 'a
liquid that stops
water from freezing'.
If the word you are
adding anti- to begins
with a vowel, you use
a hyphen, e.g.
anti-aircraft.

antibiotic noun
antibiotics
anticipate verb
anticipates
anticipating
anticipated
anticipation
anticlimax noun
anticlimaxes
anticlockwise
adverb and adjective
anticyclone noun
anticyclones
antidote noun
antidotes
antifreeze
○ **antipodes**
antiquated
antique adjective and
noun
antiques
antiseptic noun
antiseptics

· ·

★ The noun from **anonymous**.
☆ You use **antelope** when you mean a lot of animals and **antelopes** when you
  mean several you are thinking about separately.
○ A word Europeans use for Australia and New Zealand.

antler noun
antlers

anus noun
anuses

anvil noun
anvils

anxiety noun
anxieties

anxious
anxiously

anybody

anyhow

anyone

anything

anyway

anywhere

apart

apartment noun
apartments

apathetic

apathy

ape noun
apes

aphid noun
aphids

apiece

apologetic
apologetically

apologize verb
apologizes
apologizing
apologized

apology noun
apologies

apostle noun
apostles

apostrophe noun
apostrophes

appal verb
appals

appalling
appalled

appalling

apparatus noun
apparatuses

apparent
apparently

appeal verb
appeals
appealing
appealed

appeal noun
appeals

appear verb
appears
appearing
appeared

appearance noun
appearances

appease verb
appeases
appeasing
appeased

appeasement

appendicitis

★ appendix
appendixes or
appendices

appetite noun
appetites

appetizing

applaud verb
applauds
applauding
applauded

applause

apple noun
apples

appliance noun
appliances

applicable

applicant noun
applicants

application noun
applications

applied

apply verb
applies
applying
applied

appoint verb
appoints
appointing
appointed

appointment noun
appointments

appraisal
appraisals

appraise verb
appraises
appraising
appraised

appreciate verb
appreciates
appreciating
appreciated

appreciation

appreciative

apprehension noun

apprehensive

apprentice noun
apprentices

apprenticeship

approach verb
approaches
approaching
approached

approach noun
approaches

approachable

appropriate

. . . .

★ You use appendixes when you mean organs of the body and appendices when
you mean parts of a book.

approval
approve *verb*
  approves
  approving
  approved
approximate
  approximately
apricot *noun*
  apricots
April
apron *noun*
  aprons
aptitude *noun*
  aptitudes
aquarium *noun*
  aquariums
aquatic
aqueduct *noun*
  aqueducts
★ Arab *noun*
  Arabs
★ Arabian *adjective*
☆ Arabic
☆ arabic
arable
arbitrary
arbitrate *verb*
  arbitrates
  arbitrating
  arbitrated
arbitration
arbitrator
◐ arc *noun*
  arcs
arcade *noun*
  arcades
arch *noun*
  arches
arch *verb*
  arches

arching
arched
archaeology
archaeological
archaeologist
archbishop *noun*
  archbishops
archer *noun*
  archers
archery
architect *noun*
  architects
architecture

-archy
-archy at the end of a
word means 'rule or
government', e.g.
anarchy (= a lack of
rule) and monarchy
(= rule by a king or
queen). The plural
forms is *-archies*, e.g.
monarchies.

Arctic
are
area *noun*
  areas
arena *noun*
  arenas
aren't *abbreviation*
argue *verb*
  argues
  arguing
  argued
argument *noun*
  arguments
arid
aridity
arise *verb*
  arises

arising
arose
arisen
aristocracy *noun*
  aristocracies
aristocrat *noun*
  aristocrats
aristocratic
arithmetic
arithmetical
★ ark *noun*
  arks
arm *noun*
  arms
arm *verb*
  arms
  arming
  armed
armada *noun*
  armadas
armadillo *noun*
  armadillos
armaments
armchair *noun*
  armchairs
armful *noun*
  armfuls
armistice *noun*
  armistices
armour
armoured
armpit *noun*
  armpits
army *noun*
  armies
aroma *noun*
  aromas
aromatic
arose see arise
around

. . . .

★ You use **Arab** when you mean a person or the people, and **Arabian** when you
    mean the place, e.g. *the Arabian desert.*
☆ You use **Arabic** when you mean the language, and **arabic** when you mean
    numbers, e.g. *arabic numerals.*
◐ **Arc** means a curve. ! **ark.**
★ **Ark** means a boat. ! **arc.**

ar - as

arouse *verb*
arouses
arousing
aroused

arrange *verb*
arranges
arranging
arranged

arrangement

array *noun*
arrays

arrears

arrest *verb*
arrests
arresting
arrested

arrest *noun*
arrests

arrival

arrive *verb*
arrives
arriving
arrived

arrogance

arrogant

arrow *noun*
arrows

arsenal *noun*
arsenals

arsenic

arson

artefact *noun*
artefacts

artery *noun*
arteries

artful
artfully

arthritic

arthritis

article *noun*
articles

articulate *adjective*

articulate *verb*
articulates
articulating
articulated

artificial
artificially

artillery *noun*
artilleries

artist *noun*
artists

artiste *noun*
artistes

artistic

artistry

asbestos

ascend *verb*
ascends
ascending
ascended

ascent *noun*
ascents

★ **ash** *noun*
ashes

ashamed

ashen

ashore

ashtray *noun*
ashtrays

Asian *adjective* and
noun
Asians

aside

ask *verb*
asks
asking
asked

asleep

aspect *noun*
aspects

☆ **asphalt**

aspirin *noun*
aspirins

ass *noun*
asses

assassin *noun*
assassins

assassinate *verb*
assassinates
assassinating
assassinated

assassination *noun*
assassinations

assault *verb*
assaults
assaulting
assaulted

assault *noun*
assaults

assemble *verb*
assembles
assembling
assembled

assembly *noun*
assemblies

assent

assert *verb*
asserts
asserting
asserted

assertion

assertive

assess *verb*
assesses
assessing
assessed

assessment

assessor

★ The tree and the burnt powder.
☆ Note that this word is not spelt *ash-*.

asset noun
  assets
assign verb
  assigns
  assigning
  assigned
assignment noun
  assignments
assist verb
  assists
  assisting
  assisted
assistance
assistant noun
  assistants
associate verb
  associates
  associating
  associated
associate noun
  associates
association noun
  associations
assorted
assortment
assume verb
  assumes
  assuming
  assumed
assumption noun
  assumptions
assurance noun
  assurances
assure verb
  assures
  assuring
  assured
asterisk noun
  asterisks
asteroid noun
  asteroids

asthma
asthmatic adjective
  and noun
  asthmatics
astonish verb
  astonishes
  astonishing
  astonished
astonishment
astound verb
  astounds
  astounding
  astounded
astride
astrologer
astrological
astrology
astronaut noun
  astronauts
astronomer
astronomical
astronomy

-asy
Not many words end
in -asy. The most
important are
ecstasy, fantasy,
idiosyncrasy. There
are a lot of words
ending in -acy,
however, e.g.
accuracy.

★ **ate** see eat
atheist noun
  atheists
atheism
athlete noun
  athletes
athletic

athletics
atlas noun
  atlases
atmosphere noun
  atmospheres
atmospheric
atoll noun
  atolls
atom noun
  atoms
atomic
atrocious
  atrociously
atrocity noun
  atrocities
attach verb
  attaches
  attaching
  attached
attached
attachment noun
  attachments
attack verb
  attacks
  attacking
  attacked
attack noun
  attacks
attain verb
  attains
  attaining
  attained
attainment
attempt verb
  attempts
  attempting
  attempted
attempt noun
  attempts

★ **Ate** is the past tense of eat e.g. I ate an apple. ! **eight.**

at - av

attend verb
attends
attending
attended
attendance noun
attendances
attendant noun
attendants
attention
attentive
attic noun
attics
attitude noun
attitudes
attract verb
attracts
attracting
attracted
attraction noun
attractions
attractive
auburn
auction noun
auctions
auctioneer
audibility
audible
audience noun
audiences

audio-
audio- makes words with 'sound' or 'hearing' in their meaning. Some of them have hyphens, e.g. **audio-visual** (= to do with hearing and seeing).

audiovisual
audition noun
auditions

auditorium noun
auditoriums
August
aunt noun
aunts
★ **auntie** noun
aunties
☆ **au pair** noun
au pairs
○ **aural**
austere
austerity
Australian adjective and noun
Australians
authentic
authentically
authenticity
author noun
authors
authority noun
authorities
authorize verb
authorizes
authorizing
authorized
autistic

auto-
auto- at the beginning of a word means 'self', e.g. **autobiography** (= a biography of yourself), **automatic** (= done by itself). But some words beginning with auto- are to do with cars, e.g. **autocross** (= car racing across country).

autobiography noun
autobiographies
autograph noun
autographs
automate verb
automates
automating
automated
automatic
automatically
automation
automobile noun
automobiles
autumn noun
autumns
autumnal
auxiliary adjective and noun
auxiliaries
availability
available
avalanche noun
avalanches
avenue noun
avenues
average adjective and noun
averages
average verb
averages
averaging
averaged
avert verb
averts
averting
averted
aviary noun
aviaries
aviation
avid

★ You can also spell this word *aunty*.
☆ **Au pair** means a young person from another country who works in your house.
○ **Aural** means 'to do with hearing'. ! *oral*.

avoid *verb*
  avoids
  avoiding
  avoided

avoidance

await *verb*
  awaits
  awaiting
  awaited

awake *adjective*

awake *verb*
  awakes
  awaking
  awoke
  awoken

awaken *verb*
  awakens
  awakening
  awakened

award *noun*
  awards

award *verb*
  awards
  awarding
  awarded

aware

awareness

awash

away

awe

awed

awful
  awfully

★ **awhile**

awkward

awoke see **awake**
awoken see **awake**

axe *noun*
  axes

axe *verb*
  axes
  axing
  axed

axis *noun*
  axes

axle *noun*
  axles

Aztec *noun*
  Aztecs

azure *adjective*

Bb

babble *verb*
  babbles
  babbling
  babbled

baboon *noun*
  baboons

baby *noun*
  babies

babyish

babysit *verb*
  babysits
  babysitting
  babysat

babysitter *noun*
  babysitters

bachelor *noun*
  bachelors

back *noun*
  backs

back *verb*
  backs
  backing
  backed

backache *noun*
  backaches

backbone *noun*
  backbones

background *noun*
  backgrounds

backing

backlash *noun*
  backlashes

backlog *noun*
  backlogs

backside *noun*
  backsides

backstroke

backward *adjective*
  and *adverb*

backwards *adverb*

backwater *noun*
  backwaters

backyard *noun*
  backyards

bacon

bacteria

bacterial

bad *adjective*
  worse
  worst
  badly

baddy *noun*
  baddies

badge *noun*
  badges

badger *noun*
  badgers

badger *verb*
  badgers
  badgering
  badgered

badminton

★ Awhile means 'for a short time', e.g. *Wait here awhile*. You spell it as two words in e.g. *a short while*.

baffle *verb*
  baffles
  baffling
  baffled

bag *noun*
  bags

bag *verb*
  bags
  bagging
  bagged

bagel *noun*
  bagels

baggage

baggy *adjective*
  baggier
  baggiest

bagpipes

★ bail *noun*
  bails

☆ bail *verb*
  bails
  bailing
  bailed

Bairam *noun*
  Bairams

Baisakhi

bait *noun*

bait *verb*
  baits
  baiting
  baited

bake *verb*
  bakes
  baking
  baked

baker *noun*
  bakers

bakery *noun*
  bakeries

baking powder

balance *noun*
  balances

balance *verb*
  balances
  balancing
  balanced

balcony *noun*
  balconies

bald *adjective*
  balder
  baldest

◐ bale *noun*
  bales

✳ bale *verb*
  bales
  baling
  baled

ballad *noun*
  ballads

ballerina *noun*
  ballerinas

ballet *noun*
  ballets

ballistic *adjective*

balloon *noun*
  balloons

ballot *noun*
  ballots

ballpoint *noun*
  ballpoints

ballroom *noun*
  ballrooms

balsa

bamboo *noun*
  bamboos

ban *verb*
  bans
  banning
  banned

banana *noun*
  bananas

band *noun*
  bands

band *verb*
  bands
  banding
  banded

bandage *noun*
  bandages

bandit *noun*
  bandits

bandstand *noun*
  bandstands

bandwagon *noun*
  bandwagons

bandy *adjective*
  bandier
  bandiest

bang *noun*
  bangs

bang *verb*
  bangs
  banging
  banged

banger *noun*
  bangers

banish *verb*
  banishes
  banishing
  banished

banishment

banisters

banjo *noun*
  banjos

bank *noun*
  banks

bank *verb*
  banks
  banking
  banked

banknote *noun*
  banknotes

. . . .

★ **Bail** means 'money paid to let a prisoner out of prison' and 'a piece of wood put on the stumps in cricket'. ! **bale**.
☆ **Bail** means 'to pay money to let a prisoner out of prison' and 'to scoop water out of a boat'. ! **bale**.
◐ **Bale** means 'a large bundle'. ! **bail**.
✳ **Bale** means 'to jump out of an aircraft'. ! **bail**.

bankrupt
bankruptcy
banner *noun*
 banners
banquet *noun*
 banquets
baptism *noun*
 baptisms
★ Baptist *noun*
 Baptists
baptize *verb*
 baptizes
 baptizing
 baptized
bar *noun*
 bars
bar *verb*
 bars
 barring
 barred
barb *noun*
 barbs
barbarian *noun*
 barbarians
barbaric
barbarism
barbarity *noun*
 barbarities
barbarous *adjective*
barbecue *noun*
 barbecues
barber *noun*
 barbers
bar code *noun*
 bar codes
bard *noun*
 bards
☆ bare *adjective*
 barer
 barest
bareback

barely
bargain *noun*
 bargains
bargain *verb*
 bargains
 bargaining
 bargained
barge *noun*
 barges
barge *verb*
 barges
 barging
 barged
baritone *noun*
 baritones
bark *noun*
 barks
bark *verb*
 barks
 barking
 barked
barley
barman *noun*
 barmen
bar mitzvah *noun*
 bar mitzvahs
barnacle *noun*
 barnacles
barnyard *noun*
 barnyards
barometer *noun*
 barometers
barometric
baron *noun*
 barons
baroness *noun*
 baronesses
baronial
barrack *verb*
 barracks
 barracking

barracked
◐ barracks *plural noun*
barrage *noun*
 barrages
barrel *noun*
 barrels
barren
barricade *noun*
 barricades
barricade *verb*
 barricades
 barricading
 barricaded
barrier *noun*
 barriers
barrister *noun*
 barristers
barrow *noun*
 barrows
barter *verb*
 barters
 bartering
 bartered
✻ base *noun*
 bases
base *verb*
 bases
 basing
 based
baseball *noun*
 baseballs
basement *noun*
 basements
bash *verb*
 bashes
 bashing
 bashed
bash *noun*
 bashes
bashful
 bashfully

★ You use a capital B when you mean a member of the Christian Church.
☆ Bare means 'naked' or 'not covered'. ! bear.
◐ Barracks is plural but sometimes has a singular verb, e.g. *The Barracks is over there.*
✻ Base means 'a place where things are controlled'. ! bass.

basic
basically

basin noun
basins

basis noun
bases

bask verb
basks
basking
basked

basket noun
baskets

basketball noun
basketballs

basketful noun
basketfuls

★ **bass** noun
basses

bassoon noun
bassoons

bastard noun
bastards

bat noun
bats

bat verb
bats
batting
batted

batch noun
batches

bath noun
baths

bath verb
baths
bathing
bathed

bathe verb
bathes
bathing
bathed

bathroom noun
bathrooms

☆ **baton** noun
batons

batsman noun
batsmen

battalion noun
battalions

○ **batten** noun
battens

batter verb
batters
battering
battered

batter noun

battery noun
batteries

battle noun
battles

battlefield noun
battlefields

battlements

battleship noun
battleships,

bawl verb
bawls
bawling
bawled

bay noun
bays

bayonet noun
bayonets

bazaar noun
bazaars

✳ **beach** noun
beaches

beacon noun
beacons

bead noun
beads

beady adjective
beadier
beadiest

beagle noun
beagles

beak noun
beaks

beaker noun
beakers

beam noun
beams

beam verb
beams
beaming
beamed

✲ **bean** noun
beans

✲ **bear** verb
bears
bearing
bore
borne

✲ **bear** noun
bears

bearable

beard noun
beards

bearded

bearing noun
bearings

beast noun
beasts

beastly

beat verb
beats
beating
beat
beaten

beat noun
beats

beautiful
beautifully

- -

★ **Bass** means 'a singer with a low voice'. ! **base**.
☆ A **baton** is a stick used by a conductor in an orchestra. ! **batten**.
○ A **batten** is a flat strip of wood. ! **baton**.
✳ **Beach** means 'sandy part of the seashore'. ! **beech**.
✲ A **bean** is a vegetable. ! **been**.
✲ To **bear** something is to carry it and a **bear** is an animal. ! **bare**.

beautify verb
  beautifies
  beautifying
  beautified
beauty noun
  beauties
beaver noun
  beavers
becalmed
became see become
because
beckon verb
  beckons
  beckoning
  beckoned
become verb
  becomes
  becoming
  became
  become
bedclothes
bedding
bedlam
bedraggled
bedridden
bedroom noun
  bedrooms
bedside
bedspread noun
  bedspreads
bedstead noun
  bedsteads
bedtime
bee noun
  bees
★ **beech** noun
  beeches
beef
beefburger noun
  beefburgers

beefeater noun
  beefeaters
beefy adjective
  beefier
  beefiest
beehive noun
  beehives
beeline
☆ **been** see be
beer noun
  beers
beet noun
  beet or beets
beetle noun
  beetles
beetroot noun
  beetroot
before
beforehand
beg verb
  begs
  begging
  begged
began see begin
beggar noun
  beggars
begin verb
  begins
  beginning
  began
  begun
beginner noun
  beginners
beginning noun
  beginnings
begrudge verb
  begrudges
  begrudging
  begrudged
begun see begin
behalf

behave verb
  behaves
  behaving
  behaved
behaviour
behead verb
  beheads
  beheading
  beheaded
behind adverb and
  preposition
behind noun
  behinds
beige noun
being noun
  beings
belch verb
  belches
  belching
  belched
belch noun
  belches
belfry noun
  belfries
belief noun
  beliefs
believe verb
  believes
  believing
  believed
believable
believer
bellow verb
  bellows
  bellowing
  bellowed
bellows
belly noun
  bellies

. . . .
★ **Beech** means 'a tree'. ! **beach**.
☆ You use **been** in e.g. I've been to the zoo. ! **bean**.

belong *verb*
  belongs
  belonging
  belonged

belongings

beloved

below

belt *noun*
  belts

belt *verb*
  belts
  belting
  belted

bench *noun*
  benches

bend *verb*
  bends
  bending
  bent

bend *noun*
  bends

beneath

benefaction

benefactor *noun*
  benefactors

benefit *noun*
  benefits

beneficial
  beneficially

benevolence

benevolent

bent see bend

bequeath *verb*
  bequeaths
  bequeathing
  bequeathed

bequest

★ bereaved

bereavement

☆ bereft

beret *noun*
  berets

berry *noun*
  berries

berserk

berth *noun*
  berths

beside

besides

besiege *verb*
  besieges
  besieging
  besieged

bestseller *noun*
  bestsellers

bet *noun*
  bets

bet *verb*
  bets
  betting
  bet
  betted

betray *verb*
  betrays
  betraying
  betrayed

betrayal

better *adjective* and
  adverb

better *verb*
  betters
  bettering
  bettered

between

◐ beware *verb*

bewilder *verb*
  bewilders
  bewildering
  bewildered

bewilderment

bewitch *verb*
  bewitches

bewitching
  bewitched

beyond

bi-
bi- at the beginning of
a word means 'two',
e.g. bicycle (= a
machine with two
wheels), bilateral
(= having two sides).

bias *noun*
  biases

biased

bib *noun*
  bibs

Bible *noun*
  Bibles

biblical

bicycle *noun*
  bicycles

bid *noun*
  bids

bid *verb*
  bids
  bidding
  bid

bide *verb*
  bides
  biding
  bided

big *adjective*
  bigger
  biggest

bigamist

bigamous

bigamy

bike *noun*
  bikes

bikini *noun*
  bikinis

. . . .

★ You use **bereaved** when you mean a person with a close relative who has died.
  ! bereft.

☆ You use **bereft** when you mean 'deprived of something', e.g. *bereft of hope*.
  ! bereaved.

◐ **Beware** has no other forms.

bile

bilge *noun*
  bilges

bilingual

billiards

billion *noun*
  billions

billionth

billow *noun*
  billows

billow *verb*
  billows
  billowing
  billowed

billy goat *noun*
  billy goats

binary

bind *verb*
  binds
  binding
  bound

bingo

binoculars

bio-
bio- at the beginning of a word means 'life', e.g. **biography** (= a story of a person's life), **biology** (= the study of living things).

biodegradable

biographer

biographical

biography *noun*
  biographies

biological

biologist

biology

bionic

biosphere

birch *noun*
  birches

bird *noun*
  birds

birdseed

Biro *noun*
  Biros

birth *noun*
  births

birth control

birthday *noun*
  birthdays

birthmark *noun*
  birthmarks

birthplace *noun*
  birthplaces

biscuit *noun*
  biscuits

bisect *verb*
  bisects
  bisecting
  bisected

bishop *noun*
  bishops

bison *noun*
  bison

bit *noun*
  bits

bit see **bite**

bitch *noun*
  bitches

bitchy *adjective*
  bitchier
  bitchiest

bite *verb*
  bites
  biting
  bit
  bitten

★ **bite** *noun*
  bites

bitter

black *adjective*
  blacker
  blackest

black *noun*
  blacks

blackberry *noun*
  blackberries

blackbird *noun*
  blackbirds

blackboard *noun*
  blackboards

blacken *verb*
  blackens
  blackening
  blackened

blackmail *verb*
  blackmails
  blackmailing
  blackmailed

blackout *noun*
  blackouts

blacksmith *noun*
  blacksmiths

bladder *noun*
  bladders

blade *noun*
  blades

blame *verb*
  blames
  blaming
  blamed

blame *noun*

blancmange *noun*
  blancmanges

blank *adjective* and *noun*
  blanks

blanket *noun*
  blankets

• •

★ A bite is an act of biting. **!** byte.

blare *verb*
blares
blaring
blared

blaspheme *verb*
blasphemes
blaspheming
blasphemed

blasphemous

blasphemy

blast *noun*
blasts

blast *verb*
blasts
blasting
blasted

blast-off

blaze *noun*
blazes

blaze *verb*
blazes
blazing
blazed

blazer *noun*
blazers

bleach *noun*
bleaches

bleach *verb*
bleaches
bleaching
bleached

bleak *adjective*
bleaker
bleakest

bleary *adjective*
blearier
bleariest
blearily

bleat *noun*
bleats

bleat *verb*
bleats
bleating
bleated

bleed *verb*
bleeds
bleeding
bled

bleep *noun*
bleeps

blemish *noun*
blemishes

blend *verb*
blends
blending
blended

blend *noun*
blends

bless *verb*
blesses
blessing
blessed

blessing *noun*
blessings

★ **blew** see blow

blight *noun*
blights

blind *adjective*
blinder
blindest

blind *verb*
blinds
blinding
blinded

blind *noun*
blinds

blindfold *noun*
blindfolds

blindfold *verb*
blindfolds
blindfolding
blindfolded

blindfold

blink *verb*
blinks
blinking
blinked

bliss

blissful
blissfully

blister *noun*
blisters

blitz *noun*
blitzes

blizzard *noun*
blizzards

bloated

block *noun*
blocks

block *verb*
blocks
blocking
blocked

blockade *noun*
blockades

blockage *noun*
blockages

blond *adjective*
blonder
blondest

☆ **blonde** *noun*
blondes

blood

bloodhound *noun*
bloodhounds

bloodshed

bloodshot

bloodstream

bloodthirsty
adjective
bloodthirstier
bloodthirstiest

- -

★ You use **blew** in e.g. *the wind blew hard*. ! **blue**.
☆ You use **blonde** when you are talking about a girl or woman.

bloody adjective
  bloodier
  bloodiest
bloom verb
  blooms
  blooming
  bloomed
bloom noun
  blooms
blossom noun
  blossoms
blossom verb
  blossoms
  blossoming
  blossomed
blot noun
  blots
blot verb
  blots
  blotting
  blotted
blotch noun
  blotches
blotchy adjective
  blotchier
  blotchiest
blouse noun
  blouses
blow noun
  blows
blow verb
  blows
  blowing
  blew
  blown
blowlamp noun
  blowlamps
blowtorch noun
  blowtorches
blue adjective
  bluer
  bluest

★ **blue** noun
  blues
bluebell noun
  bluebells
bluebottle noun
  bluebottles
blueprint noun
  blueprints
bluff verb
  bluffs
  bluffing
  bluffed
bluff noun
  bluffs
blunder verb
  blunders
  blundering
  blundered
blunder noun
  blunders
blunt adjective
  blunter
  bluntest
blur verb
  blurs
  blurring
  blurred
blur noun
  blurs
blush verb
  blushes
  blushing
  blushed
bluster verb
  blusters
  blustering
  blustered
blustery
boa constrictor
  noun
  boa constrictors

☆ **boar** noun
  boars
◉ **board** noun
  boards
board verb
  boards
  boarding
  boarded
boarder noun
  boarders
board game noun
  board games
boast verb
  boasts
  boasting
  boasted
boastful
  boastfully
boat noun
  boats
boating
bob verb
  bobs
  bobbing
  bobbed
bobble noun
  bobbles
bobsled noun
  bobsleds
bobsleigh noun
  bobsleighs
bodice noun
  bodices
bodily
body noun
  bodies
bodyguard noun
  bodyguards

· ·

★ **Blue** is the colour. ! blew.
☆ A **boar** is a wild pig. ! bore.
◉ A **board** is a piece of wood. ! bored.

boggy adjective
boggier
boggiest

bogus

boil verb
boils
boiling
boiled

boil noun
boils

boiler noun
boilers

boisterous
boisterously

bold adjective
bolder
boldest

bollard noun
bollards

bolster verb
bolsters
bolstering
bolstered

bolster noun
bolsters

bolt noun
bolts

bolt verb
bolts
bolting
bolted

bomb noun
bombs

bomb verb
bombs
bombing
bombed

bombard verb
bombards
bombarding
bombarded

bombardment

bomber noun
bombers

bond noun
bonds

bondage

bone noun
bones

bonfire noun
bonfires

bonnet noun
bonnets

bonus noun
bonuses

bony adjective
bonier
boniest

boo verb
boos
booing
booed

booby noun
boobies

book noun
books

book verb
books
booking
booked

bookcase noun
bookcases

booklet noun
booklets

bookmaker noun
bookmakers

bookmark noun
bookmarks

boom noun
booms

boom verb
booms
booming
boomed

boomerang noun
boomerangs

boost verb
boosts
boosting
boosted

booster noun
boosters

boot noun
boots

boot verb
boots
booting
booted

booth noun
booths

border noun
borders

borderline

bore verb
bores
boring
bored

★ **bore** noun
bores

boredom

boring

☆ **born**

✿ **borne** see bear

borough noun
boroughs

borrow verb
borrows
borrowing
borrowed

bosom noun
bosoms

- -

★ **Bore** means 'something boring'. **! boar.**

☆ You use **born** in e.g. *He was born in June.* **! borne.**

✿ You use **borne** in e.g. *She has borne three children* and *The cost is borne by the government.* **! born.**

boss *noun*
bosses

boss *verb*
bosses
bossing
bossed

bossy *adjective*
bossier
bossiest

botanical

botanist

botany

both

bother *verb*
bothers
bothering
bothered

bother *noun*

bottle *noun*
bottles

bottle *verb*
bottles
bottling
bottled

bottleneck *noun*
bottlenecks

bottom *noun*
bottoms

bottomless

★ **bough** *noun*
boughs

bought

boulder *noun*
boulders

bounce *verb*
bounces
bouncing
bounced

bounce *noun*
bounces

bouncing

bouncy *adjective*
bouncier
bounciest

bound *verb*
bounds
bounding
bounded

bound *adjective* and *noun*
bounds

bound see **bind**

boundary *noun*
boundaries

bounds

bouquet *noun*
bouquets

bout *noun*
bouts

boutique *noun*
boutiques

☆ **bow** *noun*
bows

◐ **bow** *verb*
bows
bowing
bowed

bowels

bowl *noun*
bowls

bowl *verb*
bowls
bowling
bowled

bow-legged

bowler *noun*
bowlers

bowling

bowls

bow tie *noun*
bow ties

box *noun*
boxes

box *verb*
boxes
boxing
boxed

boxer *noun*
boxers

Boxing Day *noun*

boy *noun*
boys

boycott *verb*
boycotts
boycotting
boycotted

boyfriend *noun*
boyfriends

boyhood

boyish

bra *noun*
bras

brace *noun*
braces

bracelet *noun*
bracelets

braces

bracken

bracket *noun*
brackets

bracket *verb*
brackets
bracketing
bracketed

brag *verb*
brags
bragging
bragged

★ A **bough** is a part of a tree. ! **bow**.
☆ A **bow** is a knot with loops and rhymes with 'go'. A **bow** is also the front of a
 ship or a bending of the body and rhymes with 'cow'.
◐ To **bow** is to bend the body and rhymes with 'cow'.

braid noun
braids
braille
brain noun
brains
brainy adjective
brainier
brainiest
★ **brake** noun
brakes
bramble noun
brambles
branch noun
branches
branch verb
branches
branching
branched
brand noun
brands
brand verb
brands
branding
branded
brandish verb
brandishes
brandishing
brandished
brand-new
brandy noun
brandies
brass
brassière noun
brassières
brassy adjective
brassier
brassiest
brave adjective
braver
bravest

brave noun
braves
bravery
brawl noun
brawls
brawn
brawny adjective
brawnier
brawniest
bray verb
brays
braying
brayed
brazen
brazier noun
braziers
☆ **breach** noun
breaches
bread
breadth noun
breadths
breadwinner noun
breadwinners
○ **break** verb
breaks
breaking
broke
broken
break noun
breaks
breakable
breakage noun
breakages
breakdown noun
breakdowns
breaker noun
breakers
breakfast noun
breakfasts
breakneck

breakthrough noun
breakthroughs
breakwater noun
breakwaters
breast noun
breasts
breaststroke
breath noun
breaths
breathalyse
breathalyses
breathalysing
breathalysed
breathalyser noun
breathalysers
breathe verb
breathes
breathing
breathed
breather noun
breathers
breathless
breathtaking
bred see breed
✳ **breech** noun
breeches
breeches
breed verb
breeds
breeding
bred
breed noun
breeds
breeder noun
breeders
breeze noun
breezes
breezy adjective
breezier
breeziest
brethren

★ A brake is what makes a car stop. **! break.**
☆ A breach is a gap or a breaking of a rule. **! breech.**
○ To break something is to make it go into pieces. **! brake.**
✳ A breech is a part of a gun. **! breach.**

brevity

brew verb
brews
brewing
brewed

brewer noun
brewers

brewery noun
breweries

★ **briar** noun
briars

bribe noun
bribes

bribe verb
bribes
bribing
bribed

bribery

brick noun
bricks

bricklayer noun
bricklayers

bride noun
brides

☆ **bridal**

bridegroom noun
bridegrooms

bridesmaid noun
bridesmaids

bridge noun
bridges

○ **bridle** noun
bridles

brief adjective
briefer
briefest

brief noun
briefs

brief verb
briefs
briefing
briefed

briefcase noun
briefcases

brigade noun
brigades

brigadier noun
brigadiers

brigand noun
brigands

bright adjective
brighter
brightest

brighten verb
brightens
brightening
brightened

brilliance

brilliant

brim noun
brims

brimming

brine

bring verb
brings
bringing
brought

brink

brisk adjective
brisker
briskest

bristle noun
bristles

bristly
bristlier
bristliest

British

Briton noun
Britons

brittle adjective
brittler
brittlest

❋ **broach** verb
broaches
broaching
broached

broad adjective
broader
broadest
broadly

broadcast noun
broadcasts

broadcast verb
broadcasts
broadcasting
broadcast

broadcaster

broaden verb
broadens
broadening
broadened

broad-minded

broadside noun
broadsides

brochure noun
brochures

brogue noun
brogues

broke see **break**
broken see **break**
bronchitis

bronze

❋ **brooch** noun
brooches

brood noun
broods

brood verb
broods
brooding
brooded

- -

★ **Briar** means 'a prickly bush' and 'a pipe'. You will sometimes see it spelt *brier*.
☆ **Bridal** means 'to do with a **bride**'. ! **bridle**.
○ A **bridle** is part of a horse's harness. ! **bridal**.
❋ **Broach** means 'to mention something'. ! **brooch**.
❋ A **brooch** is an ornament you wear. ! **broach**.

broody adjective
broodier
broodiest

brook noun
brooks

broom noun
brooms

broomstick noun
broomsticks

broth noun
broths

brother noun
brothers

brotherly

brother-in-law noun
brothers-in-law

brought see bring

brow noun
brows

brown adjective
browner
brownest

★ **brownie** noun
brownies

☆ **Brownie** noun
Brownies

browse verb
browses
browsing
browsed

bruise noun
bruises

bruise verb
bruises
bruising
bruised

brunette noun
brunettes

brush noun
brushes

brush verb
brushes
brushing
brushed

Brussels sprout noun
Brussels sprouts

brutal
brutally

brutality
brutalities

brute noun
brutes

bubble noun
bubbles

bubble verb
bubbles
bubbling
bubbled

bubble gum

bubbly adjective
bubblier
bubbliest

buccaneer noun
buccaneers

buck noun
bucks

buck verb
bucks
bucking
bucked

bucket noun
buckets

bucketful noun
bucketfuls

buckle noun
buckles

buckle verb
buckles
buckling
buckled

bud noun
buds

Buddhism

Buddhist

budding

budge verb
budges
budging
budged

budgerigar noun
budgerigars

budget noun
budgets

budget verb
budgets
budgeting
budgeted

budgie noun
budgies

buff

buffalo noun
buffalo or
buffaloes

buffer noun
buffers

buffet noun
buffets

bug noun
bugs

bug verb
bugs
bugging
bugged

bugle noun
bugles

bugler

build verb
builds
building
built

. . . .

★ A brownie is a chocolate cake.
☆ A Brownie is a junior Guide.

builder *noun*
  builders
building *noun*
  buildings
built-in
built-up
bulb *noun*
  bulbs
bulge *noun*
  bulges
bulge *verb*
  bulges
  bulging
  bulged
bulk
bulky *adjective*
  bulkier
  bulkiest
bull *noun*
  bulls
bulldog *noun*
  bulldogs
bulldoze *verb*
  bulldozes
  bulldozing
  bulldozed
bulldozer *noun*
  bulldozers
bullet *noun*
  bullets
bulletin *noun*
  bulletins
bulletproof
bullfight *noun*
  bullfights
bullfighter
bullion
bullock *noun*
  bullocks
bull's-eye *noun*
  bull's-eyes

bully *verb*
  bullies
  bullying
  bullied
bully *noun*
  bullies
bulrush *noun*
  bulrushes
★ **bulwark** *noun*
  bulwarks
☆ **bulwarks** *plural noun*
bum *noun*
  bums
bumble-bee *noun*
  bumble-bees
bump *verb*
  bumps
  bumping
  bumped
bump *noun*
  bumps
bumper *adjective*
  and noun
  bumpers
bumpy *adjective*
  bumpier
  bumpiest
bunch *noun*
  bunches
bundle *noun*
  bundles
bundle *verb*
  bundles
  bundling
  bundled
bung *verb*
  bungs
  bunging
  bunged

bung *noun*
  bungs
bungalow *noun*
  bungalows
bungle *verb*
  bungles
  bungling
  bungled
bungler
bunk *noun*
  bunks
bunk bed *noun*
  bunk beds
bunker *noun*
  bunkers
bunny *noun*
  bunnies
bunsen burner *noun*
  bunsen burners
buoy *noun*
  buoys
buoyancy
buoyant
burden *noun*
  burdens
burdensome
◉ **bureau** *noun*
  bureaux
burglar *noun*
  burglars
burglary *noun*
  burglaries
burgle *verb*
  burgles
  burgling
  burgled
burial *noun*
  burials
burly *adjective*
  burlier
  burliest

• •

★ A bulwark is a strong wall.
☆ Bulwarks are the sides of a ship.
◉ Bureau is a French word used in English. It means 'a writing desk' or 'an office'.

★ **burn** verb
burns
burning
burnt or burned

burn noun
burns

burner noun
burners

burning

burp noun
burps

burp verb
burps
burping
burped

burr noun
burrs

burrow noun
burrows

burrow verb
burrows
burrowing
burrowed

burst verb
bursts
bursting
burst

burst noun
bursts

bury verb
buries
burying
buried

bus noun
buses

bus stop noun
bus stops

bush noun
bushes

bushy adjective
bushier
bushiest

busily

business noun
businesses

businesslike

busker noun
buskers

bust verb
busts
busting
bust

bust noun
busts

bust adjective

bustle verb
bustles
bustling
bustled

busy adjective
busier
busiest

busybody noun
busybodies

☆ **but**

butcher noun
butchers

butchery

butler noun
butlers

⊙ **butt** noun
butts

✳ **butt** verb
butts
butting
butted

butter

buttercup noun
buttercups

butterfingers noun
butterfingers

butterfly noun
butterflies

butterscotch noun
butterscotches

buttocks

button noun
buttons

button verb
buttons
buttoning
buttoned

buttonhole noun
buttonholes

buttress noun
buttresses

buy verb
buys
buying
bought

buy noun
buys

buyer

buzz noun
buzzes

buzz verb
buzzes
buzzing
buzzed

buzzard noun
buzzards

buzzer noun
buzzers

✳ **by** preposition

✳ **bye** noun
byes

bye-bye

by-election noun
by-elections

by-law noun
by-laws

- -

★ You use **burned** in e.g. *I burned the cakes.* You use **burnt** in e.g. *I can smell burnt cakes.* You use **burned** or **burnt** in e.g. *I have burned/burnt the cakes.*

☆ You use **but** in e.g. *I like fish but I'm not hungry.* ! **butt**.

⊙ A **butt** is a barrel or part of a gun. ! **but**.

✳ **Butt** means 'to hit with your head'. ! **but**.

✳ You use **by** in e.g. *a book by J. K. Rowling.* ! **bye**.

✳ You use **bye** in e.g. *bye for now.* ! **by**.

bypass noun
bypasses
by-product noun
by-products
bystander noun
bystanders
★ **byte** noun

Cc

CAB abbreviation
cab noun
cabs
cabaret noun
cabarets
cabbage noun
cabbages
cabin noun
cabins
cabinet noun
cabinets
cable noun
cables
cackle verb
cackles
cackling
cackled
cackle noun
cackles
cactus noun
cacti
☆ **caddie** noun
caddies
○ **caddy** noun
caddies ·
cadet noun
cadets

cadge verb
cadges
cadging
cadged
cafe noun
cafes
cafeteria noun
cafeterias
caffeine
caftan noun
caftans use **kaftan**
cage noun
cages
cagey adjective
cagier
cagiest
cagoule noun
cagoules
cake noun
cakes
caked
calamine
calamitous
calamity noun
calamities
calcium
calculate verb
calculates
calculating
calculated
calculation
calculator noun
calculators
calendar noun
calendars
★ **calf** noun
calves
calico
call noun
calls

call verb
calls
calling
called
calling noun
callings
callipers
callous
calm adjective
calmer
calmest
calmly
calmness
calorie noun
calories
✳ **calves** see **calf**
calypso noun
calypsos
camcorder noun
camcorders
came see **come**
camel noun
camels
camera noun
cameras
cameraman
camouflage
camp noun
camps
camp verb
camps
camping
camped
campaign noun
campaigns
camper noun
campers

. . . .

★ A **byte** is a unit in computing. ! **bite**.
☆ A **caddie** is a person who helps a golfer. ! **caddy**.
○ A **caddy** is a container for tea. ! **caddie**.
✳ **Calf** means 'a young cow' and 'a part of your leg'.
✳ **Calves** is the plural of calf. ! **carves**.

campaign verb
campaigns
campaigning
campaigned

campsite noun
campsites

campus noun
campuses

can verb
could

★ **can** verb
cans
canning
canned

can noun
cans

canal noun
canals

canary noun
canaries

cancel verb
cancels
cancelling
cancelled

cancellation noun
cancellations

cancer noun
cancers

candidate noun
candidates

candle noun
candles

candlelight

candlestick noun
candlesticks

candy noun
candies

candyfloss

cane noun
canes

cane verb
canes
caning
caned

canine

cannabis

canned music

cannibal noun
cannibals

cannibalism

☆ **cannon** noun
cannon or cannons

cannonball noun
cannonballs

cannot

canoe noun
canoes

canoe verb
canoes
canoeing
canoed

canoeist

○ **canon** noun
canons

canopy noun
canopies

can't verb

canteen noun
canteens

canter verb
canters
cantering
cantered

canton noun
cantons

✳ **canvas** noun
canvases

✱ **canvass** verb
canvasses
canvassing
canvassed

canyon noun
canyons

cap verb
caps
capping
capped

cap noun
caps

capable
capably

capability

capacity noun
capacities

cape noun
capes

caper verb
capers
capering
capered

caper noun
capers

capital noun
capitals

capitalism

capitalist

capsize verb
capsizes
capsizing
capsized

capsule noun
capsules

captain noun
captains

caption noun
captions

captivating

captive adjective and noun
captives

★ This verb **can** means 'to put food in a can', and it has normal forms.
☆ A **cannon** is a gun. ! **canon**. You use **cannons** in e.g. *There are ten cannons on the walls* and **cannon** in e.g. *They use all their cannon.*
○ A **canon** is a member of the clergy. ! **cannon**.
✳ **Canvas** means 'a strong cloth'. ! **canvass**.
✱ **Canvass** means 'to ask people for their support'. ! **canvas**.

captivity

captor noun
captors

capture verb
captures
capturing
captured

capture noun

car noun
cars

caramel noun
caramels

carat noun
carats

caravan noun
caravans

carbohydrate noun
carbohydrates

carbon

car-boot sale noun
car-boot sales

carburettor noun
carburettors

carcass noun
carcasses

card noun
cards

cardboard

cardigan noun
cardigans

cardinal noun
cardinals

cardphone noun
cardphones

care noun
cares

care verb
cares
caring
cared

career noun
careers

career verb
careers
careering
careered

carefree

careful adjective
carefully

careless adjective
carelessly
carelessness

caress verb
caresses
caressing
caressed

caress noun
caresses

caretaker noun
caretakers

cargo noun
cargoes

Caribbean

caricature noun
caricatures

carnation noun
carnations

carnival noun
carnivals

carnivore noun
carnivores

carnivorous

carol noun
carols

caroller

carolling

carp noun
carp

carpenter noun
carpenters

carpentry

carpet noun
carpets

carriage noun
carriages

carriageway noun
carriageways

carrier noun
carriers

carrot noun
carrots

carry verb
carries
carrying
carried

cart noun
carts

cart verb
carts
carting
carted

carthorse noun
carthorses

cartilage

carton noun
cartons

cartoon noun
cartoons

cartoonist

cartridge noun
cartridges

cartwheel noun
cartwheels

★ **carve** verb
carves
carving
carved

cascade noun
cascades

case noun
cases

★ You use **carves** in e.g. *He carves the meat with a knife.* ! **calves.**

cash verb
cashes
cashing
cashed

cash noun

cashier noun
cashiers

cash register noun
cash registers

cask noun
casks

casket noun
caskets

casserole noun
casseroles

cassette noun
cassettes

cast verb
casts
casting
cast

cast noun
casts

castanets plural
noun

castaway noun
castaways

castle noun
castles

castor noun
castors

castor sugar

casual adjective
casually

casualty noun
casualties

cat noun
cats

catalogue noun
catalogues

catalyst noun
catalysts

catamaran noun
catamarans

catapult noun
catapults

catastrophe noun
catastrophes

catastrophic

catch verb
catches
catching
caught

catch noun
catches

catching

catchphrase noun
catchphrases

catchy adjective
catchier
catchiest

category noun
categories

cater verb
caters
catering
catered

caterer noun
caterers

caterpillar noun
caterpillars

cathedral noun
cathedrals

Catherine wheel
noun
Catherine wheels

cathode noun
cathodes

Catholic adjective
and noun
Catholics

catkin noun
catkins

Cat's-eye noun
Cat's-eyes

cattle

caught see **catch**

cauldron noun
cauldrons

cauliflower noun
cauliflowers

cause verb
causes
causing
caused

cause noun
causes

caution noun
cautions

cautious adjective
cautiously

cavalier noun
cavaliers

cavalry noun
cavalries

cave noun
caves

cave verb
caves
caving
caved

caveman noun
cavemen

cavern noun
caverns

cavity noun
cavities

CD

CD-ROM noun

cease verb
ceases
ceasing
ceased

ceasefire noun
ceasefires

ceaseless adjective
ceaselessly

cedar noun
cedars

ceiling noun
ceilings

celebrate verb
celebrates
celebrating
celebrated

celebration noun
celebrations

celebrity noun
celebrities

celery

★ **cell** noun
cells

cellar noun
cellars

cello noun
cellos

cellular

celluloid

cellulose

Celsius

Celt noun
Celts

Celtic

cement

cemetery noun
cemeteries

censor verb
censors
censoring
censored

☆ **censor** noun
censors

censorship

censure verb
censures
censured
censuring

○ **censure** noun

census noun
censuses

✻ **cent** noun
cents

centenary noun
centenaries

centigrade

centimetre noun
centimetres

centipede noun
centipedes

central adjective
centrally

centre noun
centres

centrifugal force

centurion noun
centurions

century noun
centuries

ceramic adjective

ceramics plural noun

• **cereal** noun
cereals

ceremony noun
ceremonies

ceremonial adjective
ceremonially

certain

certainly

certainty noun
certainties

certificate noun
certificates

certify verb
certifies
certifying
certified

chaffinch noun
chaffinches

chain noun
chains

chair noun
chairs

chairlift noun
chairlifts

chairman noun
chairmen

chairperson noun
chairpersons

chalet noun
chalets

chalk noun
chalks

chalky adjective
chalkier
chalkiest

challenge verb
challenges
challenging
challenged

challenge noun
challenges

challenger noun
challengers

chamber noun
chambers

champagne

champion noun
champions

championship noun
championships

★ A **cell** is a small room or a part of an organism. ! **sell**.
☆ A **censor** is someone who makes sure books and films are suitable for people to see. ! **censure**.
○ **Censure** means 'harsh criticism'. ! **censor**.
✻ A **cent** is a coin used in America. ! **scent, sent**.
• A **cereal** is something you eat. ! **serial**.

chance noun
chances

chancel noun
chancels

chancellor noun
chancellors

Chancellor of the Exchequer

chandelier noun
chandeliers

change verb
changes
changing
changed

change noun
changes

changeable

channel noun
channels

chant noun
chants

chant verb
chants
chanting
chanted

chaos

chaotic adjective
chaotically

chap noun
chaps

chapatti noun
chapattis

chapel noun
chapels

chapped

chapter noun
chapters

char verb
chars
charring
charred

character noun
characters

characteristic adjective
characteristically

characteristic noun
characteristics

characterize verb
characterizes
characterizing
characterized

charades plural noun

charcoal

charge verb
charges
charging
charged

charge noun
charges

chariot noun
chariots

charioteer noun
charioteers

charitable adjective
charitably

charity noun
charities

charm verb
charms
charming
charmed

charm noun
charms

charming

chart noun
charts

charter noun
charters

charter verb
charters
chartering
chartered

charwoman noun
charwomen

chase verb
chases
chasing
chased

chase noun
chases

chasm noun
chasms

chassis noun
chassis

chat verb
chats
chatting
chatted

chat noun
chats

chatty adjective
chattier
chattiest

★ **château** noun
châteaux

chatter verb
chatters
chattering
chattered

chauffeur noun
chauffeurs

chauvinism

chauvinist

☆ **cheap** adjective
cheaper
cheapest

cheat verb
cheats
cheating
cheated

cheat noun
cheats

· ·

★ **Château** is a French word used in English. It means 'a castle or large house'.

☆ **Cheap** means 'not costing much'. ! **cheep**.

check *verb*
checks
checking
checked

check *noun*
checks

checkmate *noun*
checkmates

checkout *noun*
checkouts

check-up *noun*
check-ups

cheek *noun*
cheeks

cheek *verb*
cheeks
cheeking
cheeked

cheeky *adjective*
cheekier
cheekiest
cheekily

★ **cheep** *verb*
cheeps
cheeping
cheeped

cheer *verb*
cheers
cheering
cheered

cheer *noun*
cheers

cheerful *adjective*
cheerfully

cheerio

cheese *noun*
cheeses

cheesy *adjective*
cheesier
cheesiest

cheetah *noun*
cheetahs

chef *noun*
chefs

chemical *adjective*
chemically

chemical *noun*
chemicals

chemist *noun*
chemists

chemistry

cheque *noun*
cheques

chequebook *noun*
chequebooks

chequered

cherish *verb*
cherishes
cherishing
cherished

cherry *noun*
cherries

chess

chest *noun*
chests

chestnut *noun*
chestnuts

chest of drawers
noun
chests of drawers

chew *verb*
chews
chewing
chewed

chewy *adjective*
chewier
chewiest

☆ **chic**

chick *noun*
chicks

chicken *noun*
chickens

chicken *verb*
chickens
chickening
chickened

chickenpox

chief *adjective*
chiefly

chief *noun*
chiefs

chieftain *noun*
chieftains

chilblain *noun*
chilblains

child *noun*
children

childhood *noun*
childhoods

childish

childminder *noun*
childminders

childproof

chill *noun*
chills

chill *verb*
chills
chilling
chilled

✪ **chilli** *noun*
chillies

✳ **chilly** *adjective*
chillier
chilliest

chime *noun*
chimes

chime *verb*
chimes
chiming
chimed

chimney *noun*
chimneys

. . . .

★ **Cheep** is the noise a bird makes. **! cheap.**
☆ **Chic** is a French word and means 'smart or elegant'. There is no word *chicly.*
✪ A **chilli** is a type of hot pepper, added to meat or vegetable dishes. **! chilly.**
✳ You use **chilly** to describe cold, bleak weather or atmosphere. **! chilli.**

chimpanzee noun
  chimpanzees
chin noun
  chins
china
chink noun
  chinks
chip noun
  chips
chip verb
  chips
  chipping
  chipped
chirp verb
  chirps
  chirping
  chirped
chirpy adjective
  chirpier
  chirpiest
chisel noun
  chisels
chisel verb
  chisels
  chiselling
  chiselled
chivalrous adjective
  chivalrously
chivalry
chlorine
chlorophyll
choc ice noun
  choc ices
chock-a-block
chock-full
chocolate noun
  chocolates
choice noun
  choices
choir noun
  choirs

choirboy noun
  choirboys
choirgirl noun
  choirgirls
choke verb
  chokes
  choking
  choked
choke noun
  chokes
cholera
cholesterol
choose verb
  chooses
  choosing
  chose
  chosen
choosy adjective
  choosier
  choosiest
chop verb
  chops
  chopping
  chopped
chop noun
  chops
chopper noun
  choppers
choppy adjective
  choppier
  choppiest
chopsticks
choral
★ **chord** noun
  chords
chore noun
  chores
chorister noun
  choristers
chorus noun
  choruses

chose see **choose**
chosen see **choose**
christen verb
  christens
  christening
  christened
christening
Christian adjective
  and noun
  Christians
Christianity
Christmas noun
  Christmases
chrome
chromium
chromosome noun
  chromosomes
chronic adjective
  chronically
chronicle noun
  chronicles
chronological
  adjective
  chronologically
chronology
chrysalis noun
  chrysalises
chrysanthemum
  noun
  chrysanthemums
chubby adjective
  chubbier
  chubbiest
chuck verb
  chucks
  chucking
  chucked
chuckle verb
  chuckles
  chuckling
  chuckled

. . . .

★ A **chord** is a number of musical notes played together. ! **cord**.

chuckle *noun*
chuckles

chug *verb*
chugs
chugging
chugged

chum *noun*
chums

chummy *adjective*
chummier
chummiest

chunk *noun*
chunks

chunky *adjective*
chunkier
chunkiest

church *noun*
churches

churchyard *noun*
churchyards

churn *noun*
churns

churn *verb*
churns
churning
churned

★ chute *noun*
chutes

chutney *noun*
chutneys

cider *noun*
ciders

cigar *noun*
cigars

cigarette *noun*
cigarettes

cinder *noun*
cinders

cine camera *noun*
cine cameras

cinema *noun*
cinemas

cinnamon

circle *noun*
circles

circle *verb*
circles
circling
circled

circuit *noun*
circuits

circular *adjective and noun*
circulars

circulate *verb*
circulates
circulating
circulated

circulation *noun*
circulations

circumference *noun*
circumferences

circumstance *noun*
circumstances

circus *noun*
circuses

cistern *noun*
cisterns

citizen *noun*
citizens

citizenship

citric acid

citrus

city *noun*
cities

civic

civil

civilian *noun*
civilians

civilization *noun*
civilizations

civilize *verb*
civilizes
civilizing
civilized

clad

claim *verb*
claims
claiming
claimed

claim *noun*
claims

claimant *noun*
claimants

clam *noun*
clams

clamber *verb*
clambers
clambering
clambered

clammy *adjective*
clammier
clammiest

clamp *noun*
clamps

clamp *verb*
clamps
clamping
clamped

clan *noun*
clans

clang *verb*
clangs
clanging
clanged

clanger *noun*
clangers

clank *verb*
clanks
clanking
clanked

★ A chute is a funnel for sending things down. **!** shoot.

clap verb
claps
clapping
clapped

clap noun
claps

clapper noun
clappers

clarification

clarify verb
clarifies
clarifying
clarified

clarinet noun
clarinets

clarinettist

clarity

clash verb
clashes
clashing
clashed

clash noun
clashes

clasp verb
clasps
clasping
clasped

clasp noun
clasps

class noun
classes

class verb
classes
classing
classed

classic noun
classics

classic

classical adjective
classically

classification

classified

classify verb
classifies
classifying
classified

classmate noun
classmates

classroom noun
classrooms

clatter noun

clatter verb
clatters
clattering
clattered

★ **clause** noun
clauses

☆ **claw** noun
claws

○ **claw** verb
claws
clawing
clawed

clay

clayey

clean adjective
cleaner
cleanest
cleanly

clean verb
cleans
cleaning
cleaned

cleaner noun
cleaners

cleanliness

cleanse verb
cleanses
cleansing
cleansed

cleanser

clear adjective
clearer
clearest
clearly

clear verb
clears
clearing
cleared

clearance noun
clearances

clearing noun
clearings

clef noun
clefs

clench verb
clenches
clenching
clenched

clergy

clergyman noun
clergymen

clergywoman noun
clergywomen

clerical

clerk noun
clerks

clever adjective
cleverer
cleverest

cliché noun
clichés

click noun
clicks

client noun
clients

cliff noun
cliffs

cliffhanger noun
cliffhangers

climate noun
climates

. . . .

★ A **clause** is a part of a sentence or contract. **! claws**.
☆ **Claws** are the hard sharp nails that some animals have on their feet. **! clause**.
○ To **claw** is to scratch, maul, or pull a person or thing.

climatic

climax noun
 climaxes

climb verb
 climbs
 climbing
 climbed

climb noun
 climbs

climber noun
 climbers

cling verb
 clings
 clinging
 clung

clingfilm

clinic noun
 clinics

clink verb
 clinks
 clinking
 clinked

clip verb
 clips
 clipping
 clipped

clip noun
 clips

clipboard noun
 clipboards

clipper noun
 clippers

clippers plural noun

clipping noun
 clippings

cloak noun
 cloaks

cloakroom noun
 cloakrooms

clobber verb
 clobbers
 clobbering
 clobbered

clock noun
 clocks

clockwise

clockwork

clog verb
 clogs
 clogging
 clogged

clog noun
 clogs

cloister noun
 cloisters

clone noun
 clones

clone verb
 clones
 cloning
 cloned

close verb
 closes
 closing
 closed

close adjective and
noun
 closer
 closest
 closely

close noun
 closes

close-up noun
 close-ups

closure noun
 closures

clot noun
 clots

clot verb
 clots
 clotting
 clotted

cloth noun
 cloths

clothe verb
 clothes
 clothing
 clothed

clothes

clothing

cloud noun
 clouds

cloud verb
 clouds
 clouding
 clouded

cloudless

cloudy adjective
 cloudier
 cloudiest

clout verb
 clouts
 clouting
 clouted

clove noun
 cloves

clover

clown noun
 clowns

clown verb
 clowns
 clowning
 clowned

club noun
 clubs

club verb
 clubs
 clubbing
 clubbed

cluck verb
 clucks
 clucking
 clucked

clue noun
clues

clueless

clump noun
clumps

clumsiness

clumsy adjective
clumsier
clumsiest
clumsily

clung see cling

cluster noun
clusters

clutch verb
clutches
clutching
clutched

clutch noun
clutches

clutter verb
clutters
cluttering
cluttered

clutter noun

co-
co- makes words meaning 'together', e.g. a **co-pilot** is another pilot who sits together with the chief pilot. You often need a hyphen, e.g. **co-author, co-driver**, but some words are spelt joined up, e.g. **cooperate, coordinate**.

coach verb
coaches
coaching
coached

coach noun
coaches

coal

★ **coarse** adjective
coarser
coarsest
coarsely

coast noun
coasts

coast verb
coasts
coasting
coasted

coastal

coastguard noun
coastguards

coastline

coat noun
coats

coat verb
coats
coating
coated

coating noun
coatings

coax verb
coaxes
coaxing
coaxed

cobalt

cobbled

cobbler noun
cobblers

cobbles plural noun

cobblestone noun
cobblestones

cobra noun
cobras

cobweb noun
cobwebs

cock noun
cocks

cock verb
cocks
cocking
cocked

cockerel noun
cockerels

cocker spaniel noun
cocker spaniels

cockle noun
cockles

cockney noun
cockneys

cockpit noun
cockpits

cockroach noun
cockroaches

cocky adjective
cockier
cockiest

cocoa noun
cocoas

coconut noun
coconuts

cocoon noun
cocoons

☆ **cod** noun
cod

code noun
codes

code verb
codes
coding
coded

coeducation

coeducational

coffee noun
coffees

coffin noun
coffins

★ **Coarse** means 'rough' or 'crude'. ! **course**.
☆ You use **cod** for the plural: *The sea is full of cod.*

cog noun
cogs

cohort noun
cohorts

coil verb
coils
coiling
coiled

coil noun
coils

coin noun
coins

coin verb
coins
coining
coined

coinage noun
coinages

coincide verb
coincides
coinciding
coincided

coincidence noun
coincidences

coincidentally

coke

cola noun
colas

colander noun
colanders

cold adjective
colder
coldest
coldly

cold noun
colds

cold-blooded

coldness

coleslaw

collaborate verb
collaborates
collaborating
collaborated

collaboration

collaborator

collage noun
collages

collapse verb
collapses
collapsing
collapsed

collapse noun
collapses

collapsible

collar noun
collars

collate verb
collates
collating
collated

colleague noun
colleagues

collect verb
collects
collecting
collected

collection noun
collections

collective

collector

college noun
colleges

collide verb
collides
colliding
collided

collie noun
collies

collision noun
collisions

colloquial adjective
colloquially

colon noun
colons

★ **colonel** noun
colonels

colonial

colonist noun
colonists

colony noun
colonies

colossal adjective
colossally

colour noun
colours

colour verb
colours
colouring
coloured

colour-blind

coloured

colourful adjective
colourfully

colouring

colourless

colt noun
colts

column noun
columns

coma noun
comas

comb noun
combs

comb verb
combs
combing
combed

combat noun
combats

combat verb
combats
combating
combated

★ A **colonel** is an army officer. ! **kernel.**

combatant noun
combatants

combination noun
combinations

combine verb
combines
combining
combined

combine noun
combines

combustion

come verb
comes
coming
came

comeback noun
comebacks

comedian noun
comedians

comedy noun
comedies

comet noun
comets

comfort verb
comforts
comforting
comforted

comfort noun
comforts

comfortable
adjective
comfortably

comic adjective and
noun
comics

comical adjective
comically

comma noun
commas

command verb
commands
commanding
commanded

command noun
commands

commander noun
commanders

commandment
noun
commandments

commando noun
commandos

commemorate verb
commemorates
commemorating
commemorated

commemoration

commence verb
commences
commencing
commenced

commencement

commend verb
commends
commending
commended

commendable

commendation

comment verb
comments
commenting
commented

comment noun
comments

commentary noun
commentaries

commentate

commentator noun
commentators

commerce

commercial
adjective
commercially

commercial noun
commercials

commercialized

commit verb
commits
committing
committed

commitment noun
commitments

committee noun
committees

commodity noun
commodities

common adjective
commoner
commonest

common noun
commons

commonplace

commonwealth
noun
commonwealths

commotion noun
commotions

communal adjective
communally

commune noun
communes

communicate verb
communicates
communicating
communicated

communication
noun
communications

communicative

communion noun
communions

communism

communist noun
communists

community noun
communities

commute

commuter noun
commuters

compact adjective
compactly

compact noun
compacts

compact disc noun
compact discs

companion noun
companions

companionship

company noun
companies

comparable
adjective
comparably

comparative
adjective
comparatively

comparative noun
comparatives

compare verb
compares
comparing
compared

comparison noun
comparisons

compartment noun
compartments

compass noun
compasses

compassion

compassionate
adjective
compassionately

compatible adjective
compatibly

compel verb
compels
compelling
compelled

compensate verb
compensates
compensating
compensated

compensation noun
compensations

compère noun
compères

compete verb
competes
competing
competed

competence

competent adjective
competently

competition noun
competitions

competitive
adjective
competitively

competitor noun
competitors

compilation noun
compilations

compile verb
compiles
compiling
compiled

compiler noun
compilers

complacent
adjective
complacently

complain verb
complains
complaining
complained

complaint noun
complaints

★ **complement** noun
complements

☆ **complementary**

complete adjective
completely

complete verb
completes
completing
completed

completion

complex adjective
and noun
complexes

complexion noun
complexions

complexity noun
complexities

complicated

complication noun
complications

○ **compliment** noun
compliments

✳ **complimentary**

component noun
components

compose verb
composes
composing
composed

composer noun
composers

composition noun
compositions

compost

compound noun
compounds

★ A **complement** is a thing that completes something. ! compliment.
☆ Something **complementary** completes something. ! complimentary.
○ A **compliment** is something good you say about someone. ! complement.
✳ Something **complimentary** praises someone. ! complementary.

comprehend *verb*
comprehends
comprehending
comprehended

comprehension
noun
comprehensions

comprehensive
adjective
comprehensively

comprehensive
noun
comprehensives

compress *verb*
compresses
compressing
compressed

compression

comprise *verb*
comprises
comprising
comprised

compromise *noun*
compromises

compromise *verb*
compromises
compromising
compromised

compulsory

computation

compute *verb*
computes
computing
computed

computer *noun*
computers

comrade *noun*
comrades

comradeship

con *verb*
cons
conning
conned

concave

conceal *verb*
conceals
concealing
concealed

concealment

conceit

conceited

conceive *verb*
conceives
conceiving
conceived

concentrate *verb*
concentrates
concentrating
concentrated

concentrated

concentration *noun*
concentrations

concentric

concept *noun*
concepts

conception *noun*
conceptions

concern *verb*
concerns
concerning
concerned

concern *noun*
concerns

concerning

concert *noun*
concerts

concertina *noun*
concertinas

concerto *noun*
concertos

concession *noun*
concessions

concise *adjective*
concisely

conclude *verb*
concludes
concluding
concluded

conclusion *noun*
conclusions

concrete *adjective*
and *noun*

concussion

condemn *verb*
condemns
condemning
condemned

condemnation

condensation

condense *verb*
condenses
condensing
condensed

condition *noun*
conditions

condom *noun*
condoms

conduct *verb*
conducts
conducting
conducted

conduct *noun*

conduction

conductor *noun*
conductors

cone *noun*
cones

confectioner *noun*
confectioners

confectionery

confer verb
confers
conferring
conferred

conference noun
conferences

confess verb
confesses
confessing
confessed

confession noun
confessions

confetti

confide verb
confides
confiding
confided

confidence noun
confidences

confident adjective
confidently

confidential
adjective
confidentially

confine verb
confines
confining
confined

confinement

confirm verb
confirms
confirming
confirmed

confirmation

confiscate verb
confiscates
confiscating
confiscated

confiscation noun
confiscations

conflict verb
conflicts
conflicting
conflicted

conflict noun
conflicts

conform verb
conforms
conforming
conformed

conformity

confront verb
confronts
confronting
confronted

confrontation noun
confrontations

confuse verb
confuses
confusing
confused

confusion noun
confusions

congested

congestion

congratulate verb
congratulates
congratulating
congratulated

congratulations
plural noun

congregation noun
congregations

congress noun
congresses

congruence

congruent

conical

conifer noun
conifers

coniferous

conjunction noun
conjunctions

conjure verb
conjures
conjuring
conjured

conjuror noun
conjurors

★ **conker** noun
conkers

connect verb
connects
connecting
connected

connection noun
connections

conning tower noun
conning towers

☆ **conquer** verb
conquers
conquering
conquered

conqueror noun
conquerors

conquest noun
conquests

conscience

conscientious
adjective
conscientiously

conscious adjective
consciously

consciousness

conscription

consecutive
adjective
consecutively

consensus

consent verb
consents
consenting
consented

. . . .

★ A **conker** is the fruit of a horse chestnut tree. ! **conquer.**
☆ To **conquer** means 'to invade or take over'. ! **conker.**

consent noun
consequence noun
  consequences
consequently
conservation
conservationist
conservative
★ **Conservative** noun
  Conservatives
conservatory noun
  conservatories
conserve verb
  conserves
  conserving
  conserved
consider verb
  considers
  considering
  considered
considerable
  adjective
  considerably
considerate
  adjective
  considerately
consideration noun
  considerations
consist verb
  consists
  consisting
  consisted
consistency noun
  consistencies
consistent adjective
  consistently
consolation noun
  consolations
console verb
  consoles
  consoling
  consoled

consonant noun
  consonants
conspicuous
  adjective
  conspicuously
conspiracy noun
  conspiracies
conspirator
conspire verb
  conspires
  conspiring
  conspired
constable noun
  constables
constancy
constant adjective
  constantly
constant noun
  constants
constellation noun
  constellations
constipated
constipation
constituency noun
  constituencies
constituent noun
  constituents
constitute verb
  constitutes
  constituting
  constituted
constitution noun
  constitutions
constitutional
construct verb
  constructs
  constructing
  constructed
construction noun
  constructions

constructive
consul noun
  consuls
consult verb
  consults
  consulting
  consulted
consultant noun
  consultants
consultation noun
  consultations
consume verb
  consumes
  consuming
  consumed
consumer noun
  consumers
consumption
contact noun
  contacts
contact verb
  contacts
  contacting
  contacted
contagious
contain verb
  contains
  containing
  contained
container noun
  containers
contaminate verb
  contaminates
  contaminating
  contaminated
contamination
contemplate verb
  contemplates
  contemplating
  contemplated
contemplation

★ Use a capital C when you mean a member of the political party.

contemporary
adjective and noun
contemporaries

contempt

contemptible
adjective
contemptibly

contemptuous
adjective
contemptuously

contend verb
contends
contending
contended

contender noun
contenders

content adjective and noun

contented adjective
contentedly

contentment

contents plural noun

contest verb
contests
contesting
contested

contest noun
contests

contestant noun
contestants

context noun
contexts

continent noun
continents

continental

continual adjective
continually

continuation

continue verb
continues
continuing
continued

continuous adjective
continuously

continuity

contour noun
contours

contraception

contraceptive noun
contraceptives

contract verb
contracts
contracting
contracted

contract noun
contracts

contraction noun
contractions

contractor noun
contractors

contradict verb
contradicts
contradicting
contradicted

contradiction noun
contradictions

contradictory

contraflow noun
contraflows

contraption noun
contraptions

contrary adjective and noun

contrast verb
contrasts
contrasting
contrasted

contrast noun
contrasts

contribute verb
contributes
contributing
contributed

contribution noun
contributions

contributor noun
contributors

contrivance noun
contrivances

contrive verb
contrives
contriving
contrived

control verb
controls
controlling
controlled

control noun
controls

controller noun
controllers

controversial
adjective
controversially

controversy noun
controversies

conundrum noun
conundrums

convalescence

convalescent

convection

convector noun
convectors

convenience noun
conveniences

convenient adjective
conveniently

convent noun
convents

convention noun
conventions

conventional
adjective
  conventionally
converge verb
  converges
  converging
  converged
conversation noun
  conversations
conversational
adjective
  conversationally
converse verb
  converses
  conversing
  conversed
converse noun
conversion noun
  conversions
convert verb
  converts
  converting
  converted
convert noun
  converts
convertible
convex
convey verb
  conveys
  conveying
  conveyed
conveyor belt noun
  conveyor belts
convict verb
  convicts
  convicting
  convicted
convict noun
  convicts
conviction noun
  convictions

convince verb
  convinces
  convincing
  convinced
convoy noun
  convoys
cook verb
  cooks
  cooking
  cooked
cook noun
  cooks
cooker noun
  cookers
cookery
cool adjective
  cooler
  coolest
  coolly
cool verb
  cools
  cooling
  cooled
cooler
coolness
coop noun
  coops
cooperate verb
  cooperates
  cooperating
  cooperated
cooperation
cooperative
coordinate verb
  coordinates
  coordinating
  coordinated
coordinate noun
  coordinates
coordination
coordinator noun
  coordinators

coot noun
  coots
cop verb
  cops
  copping
  copped
cop noun
  cops
cope verb
  copes
  coping
  coped
copier noun
  copiers
copper noun
  coppers
copper sulphate
copy verb
  copies
  copying
  copied
copy noun
  copies
coral
★ **cord** noun
  cords
cordial adjective
  cordially
cordial noun
  cordials
cordiality
corduroy
core noun
  cores
corgi noun
  corgis
cork noun
  corks
corkscrew noun
  corkscrews

★ A **cord** is a piece of thin rope. **! chord.**

cormorant noun
cormorants

corn noun
corns

corned beef

corner noun
corners

corner verb
corners
cornering
cornered

cornet noun
cornets

cornfield noun
cornfields

cornflakes

cornflour

cornflower noun
cornflowers

Cornish

Cornish pasty noun
Cornish pasties

corny adjective
cornier
corniest

coronation noun
coronations

coroner noun
coroners

corporal noun
corporals

corporal adjective

corporation noun
corporations

★ **corps** noun
corps

☆ **corpse** noun
corpses

corpuscle noun
corpuscles

corral noun
corrals

correct adjective
correctly

correct verb
corrects
correcting
corrected

correction noun
corrections

correctness

correspond verb
corresponds
corresponding
corresponded

correspondence

correspondent noun
correspondents

corridor noun
corridors

corrode verb
corrodes
corroding
corroded

corrosion

corrosive

corrugated

corrupt

corruption

corset noun
corsets

cosmetics plural noun

cosmic

cosmonaut noun
cosmonauts

cost verb
costs
costing
cost

cost noun
costs

costly adjective
costlier
costliest

costume noun
costumes

cosy adjective
cosier
cosiest

cosy noun
cosies

cot noun
cots

cottage noun
cottages

cotton

couch noun
couches

cough verb
coughs
coughing
coughed

cough noun
coughs

could see can

couldn't

○ **council** noun
councils

✳ **councillor** noun
councillors

✱ **counsel** noun
counsels

counsel verb
counsels
counselling
counselled

✳ **counsellor** noun
counsellors

★ A **corps** is a unit of soldiers. ! **corpse**.
☆ A **corpse** is a dead body. ! **corps**.
○ A **council** is a group of people who run the affairs of a town. ! **counsel**.
✳ A **councillor** is a member of a council. ! **counsellor**.
✱ **Counsel** means 'advice'. ! **council**.
✳ A **counsellor** is someone who gives advice. ! **councillor**.

count verb
counts
counting
counted

count noun
counts

countdown noun
countdowns

countenance noun
countenances

counter-
counter- makes words
meaning 'opposite',
e.g. a **counter-claim**
is a claim someone
makes in response to
a claim from someone
else. You often need a
hyphen, but some
words are spelt joined
up, e.g. **counteract,
counterbalance.**

counter noun
counters

counterfeit

countess noun
countesses

countless

country noun
countries

countryman noun
countrymen

countryside

countrywoman
noun
countrywomen

county noun
counties

couple noun
couples

couple verb
couples
coupling
coupled

coupling noun
couplings

coupon noun
coupons

courage

courageous
adjective
courageously

courgette noun
courgettes

courier noun
couriers

★ **course** noun
courses

court noun
courts

court verb
courts
courting
courted

courteous adjective
courteously

courtesy noun
courtesies

court martial noun
courts martial

courtship

courtyard noun
courtyards

cousin noun
cousins

cove noun
coves

cover verb
covers
covering
covered

cover noun
covers

coverage

cover-up noun
cover-ups

cow noun
cows

coward noun
cowards

cowardice

cowardly

cowboy noun
cowboys

cowslip noun
cowslips

cox noun
coxes

coxswain noun
coxswains

coy adjective
coyly

coyness

crab noun
crabs

crack verb
cracks
cracking
cracked

crack noun
cracks

cracker noun
crackers

crackle verb
crackles
crackling
crackled

crackling

cradle noun
cradles

craft noun
crafts

- -

★ You use **course** in e.g. *a French course.* **! coarse.**

craftsman noun
craftsmen

craftsmanship

crafty adjective
craftier
craftiest
craftily

craftiness

crag noun
crags

craggy adjective
craggier
craggiest

cram verb
crams
cramming
crammed

cramp verb
cramps
cramping
cramped

cramp noun
cramps

crane noun
cranes

crane verb
cranes
craning
craned

crane-fly noun
crane-flies

crank verb
cranks
cranking
cranked

crank noun
cranks

cranky adjective
crankier
crankiest

cranny noun
crannies

crash verb
crashes
crashing
crashed

crash noun
crashes

crate noun
crates

crater noun
craters

crave verb
craves
craving
craved

crawl verb
crawls
crawling
crawled

crawl noun
crawls

crayon noun
crayons

craze noun
crazes

craziness

crazy adjective
crazier
craziest
crazily

creak verb
creaks
creaking
creaked

creak noun
creaks

creaky adjective
creakier
creakiest

cream noun
creams

creamy adjective
creamier
creamiest

crease verb
creases
creasing
creased

crease noun
creases

create verb
creates
creating
created

creation noun
creations

creative adjective
creatively

creativity

creator noun
creators

creature noun
creatures

crèche noun
crèches

credibility

credible adjective
credibly

credit verb
credits
crediting
credited

credit noun

creditable adjective
creditably

creditor noun
creditors

creed noun
creeds

creek noun
creeks

creep verb
creeps
creeping
crept

creep noun
creeps

creeper noun
creepers

creepy adjective
creepier
creepiest

cremate verb
cremates
cremating
cremated

cremation noun
cremations

crematorium noun
crematoria

creosote

crêpe noun
crêpes

crept see **creep**

crescendo noun
crescendos

crescent noun
crescents

cress

crest noun
crests

crevice noun
crevices

crew noun
crews

crib verb
cribs
cribbing
cribbed

crib noun
cribs

★ **cricket** noun
crickets

cricketer noun
cricketers

cried see **cry**

crime noun
crimes

criminal adjective
and noun
criminals

crimson

crinkle verb
crinkles
crinkling
crinkled

crinkly adjective
crinklier
crinkliest

cripple verb
cripples
crippling
crippled

cripple noun
cripples

crisis noun
crises

crisp adjective
crisper
crispest

crisp noun
crisps

criss-cross adjective

critic noun
critics

critical adjective
critically

criticism noun
criticisms

criticize verb
criticizes
criticizing
criticized

croak verb
croaks
croaking
croaked

croak noun
croaks

☆ **crochet**

crock noun
crocks

crockery

crocodile noun
crocodiles

crocus noun
crocuses

croft noun
crofts

crofter

croissant noun
croissants

crook noun
crooks

crook verb
crooks
crooking
crooked

crooked

croon verb
croons
crooning
crooned

crop noun
crops

crop verb
crops
cropping
cropped

. . . .

★ **Cricket** means 'a game' and 'an insect like a grasshopper'.
☆ **Crochet** is a kind of needlework. ! **crotchet**.

cross-
cross- makes words meaning 'across', e.g. a *cross-channel ferry* is one that goes across the English Channel. You usually need a hyphen, but some words are spelt joined up, e.g. **crossroads** and **crosswind**.

cross adjective
crossly
cross verb
crosses
crossing
crossed
cross noun
crosses
crossbar noun
crossbars
crossbow noun
crossbows
cross-country
cross-examine verb
cross-examines
cross-examining
cross-examined
cross-examination noun
cross-examinations
cross-eyed
crossing noun
crossings
cross-legged
crossness
crossroads noun
crossroads
cross-section noun
cross-sections

crosswise
crossword noun
crosswords
★ **crotchet** noun
crotchets
crouch verb
crouches
crouching
crouched
crow noun
crows
crow verb
crows
crowing
crowed
crowbar noun
crowbars
crowd noun
crowds
crowd verb
crowds
crowding
crowded
crown noun
crowns
crown verb
crowns
crowning
crowned
crow's-nest noun
crow's-nests
crucial adjective
crucially
crucifix noun
crucifixes
☆ **crucifixion** noun
crucifixions
crucify verb
crucifies
crucifying
crucified

crude adjective
cruder
crudest
cruel adjective
crueller
cruellest
cruelly
cruelty noun
cruelties
cruise verb
cruises
cruising
cruised
cruise noun
cruises
cruiser noun
cruisers
crumb noun
crumbs
crumble verb
crumbles
crumbling
crumbled
crumbly adjective
crumblier
crumbliest
crumpet noun
crumpets
crumple verb
crumples
crumpling
crumpled
crunch noun
crunches
crunch verb
crunches
crunching
crunched
crunchy adjective
crunchier
crunchiest

★ A **crotchet** is a note in music. ! **crochet**.
☆ Use a capital C when you are talking about Christ.

crusade noun
crusades
crusader noun
crusaders
crush verb
crushes
crushing
crushed
crush noun
crushes
crust noun
crusts
crustacean noun
crustaceans
crutch noun
crutches
cry verb
cries
crying
cried
cry noun
cries
crypt noun
crypts
crystal noun
crystals
crystalline
crystallize verb
crystallizes
crystallizing
crystallized
cub noun
cubs
cubbyhole noun
cubbyholes
cube noun
cubes
cube verb
cubes
cubing
cubed

cubic
cubicle noun
cubicles
cuboid noun
cuboids
cuckoo noun
cuckoos
cucumber noun
cucumbers
cud
cuddle verb
cuddles
cuddling
cuddled
cuddly
★ **cue** noun
cues
cuff verb
cuffs
cuffing
cuffed
cuff noun
cuffs
cul-de-sac noun
cul-de-sacs or
culs-de-sac
culminate verb
culminates
culminating
culminated
culmination
culprit noun
culprits
cult noun
cults
cultivate verb
cultivates
cultivating
cultivated
cultivation

cultivated
culture noun
cultures
cultural adjective
culturally
cultured
cunning
cup noun
cups
cup verb
cups
cupping
cupped
cupboard noun
cupboards
cupful noun
cupfuls
curate noun
curates
curator noun
curators
☆ **curb** verb
curbs
curbing
curbed
curd noun
curds
curdle verb
curdles
curdling
curdled
cure verb
cures
curing
cured
cure noun
cures
curfew noun
curfews

★ A **cue** is a signal for action or a stick used in snooker. ! **queue**.
☆ To **curb** a feeling is to restrain it. ! **kerb**.

curiosity noun
curiosities

curious adjective
curiously

curl verb
curls
curling
curled

curl noun
curls

curly adjective
curlier
curliest

★ **currant** noun
currants

currency noun
currencies

☆ **current** noun
currents

current adjective
currently

curriculum noun
curriculums or
curricula

curry verb
curries
currying
curried

curry noun
curries

curse verb
curses
cursing
cursed

curse noun
curses

cursor noun
cursors

curtain noun
curtains

curtsy verb
curtsies
curtsying
curtsied

curtsy noun
curtsies

curvature noun
curvatures

curve verb
curves
curving
curved

curve noun
curves

cushion noun
cushions

cushion verb
cushions
cushioning
cushioned

custard

custom noun
customs

customary adjective
customarily

customer noun
customers

customize noun
customizes
customizing
customized

cut verb
cuts
cutting
cut

cut noun
cuts

cute adjective
cuter
cutest

cutlass noun
cutlasses

cutlery

cutlet noun
cutlets

cut-out noun
cut-outs

cut-price

cutter noun
cutters

cutting noun
cuttings

cycle noun
cycles

cycle verb
cycles
cycling
cycled

cyclist noun
cyclists

cyclone noun
cyclones

cyclonic

♻ **cygnet** noun
cygnets

cylinder noun
cylinders

cylindrical

cymbal noun
cymbals

cynic noun
cynics

cynical adjective
cynically

cynicism

cypress noun
cypresses

. . . .

★ A **currant** is a small dried grape. ! **current**.
☆ A **current** is a flow of water, air, or electricity. ! **currant**.
♻ A **cygnet** is a young swan. ! **signet**.

Dd

dab verb
dabs
dabbing
dabbed

dab noun
dabs

dabble verb
dabbles
dabbling
dabbled

dachshund noun
dachshunds

dad noun
dads

daddy noun
daddies

daddy-long-legs noun
daddy-long-legs

daffodil noun
daffodils

daft adjective
dafter
daftest

dagger noun
daggers

dahlia noun
dahlias

daily adjective and adverb

daintiness

dainty adjective
daintier
daintiest
daintily

dairy noun
dairies

daisy noun
daisies

dale noun
dales

Dalmatian noun
Dalmatians

dam noun
dams

★ **dam** verb
dams
damming
dammed

damage verb
damages
damaging
damaged

damage noun

damages plural noun

☆ **Dame** noun
Dames

○ **dame** noun
dames

✳ **damn** verb
damns
damning
damned

damned

damp adjective and noun
damper
dampest

dampen verb
dampens
dampening
dampened

damson noun
damsons

dance verb
dances
dancing
danced

dance noun
dances

dancer noun
dancers

dandelion noun
dandelions

dandruff

danger noun
dangers

dangerous adjective
dangerously

dangle verb
dangles
dangling
dangled

dappled

dare verb
dares
daring
dared

dare noun
dares

daredevil noun
daredevils

daring

dark adjective and noun
darker
darkest

darken verb
darkens
darkening
darkened

darkness

darkroom noun
darkrooms

darling noun
darlings

darn verb
darns
darning
darned

- -

★ **Dam** means 'to build a dam across water'. **! damn.**
☆ Use a capital D when it is a title, e.g. *Dame Jane Smith*.
○ Use a small d when you mean a pantomime woman played by a man.
✳ **Damn** means 'to say that something is very bad'. **! dam.**

dart *noun*
darts

dartboard *noun*
dartboards

dash *verb*
dashes
dashing
dashed

dash *noun*
dashes

dashboard *noun*
dashboards

★ **data** *plural noun*

database *noun*
databases

date *noun*
dates

date *verb*
dates
dating
dated

daughter *noun*
daughters

dawdle *verb*
dawdles
dawdling
dawdled

dawn *noun*
dawns

dawn *verb*
dawns
dawning
dawned

day *noun*
days

daybreak

daydream *verb*
daydreams
daydreaming
daydreamed

daylight

day-to-day

daze *verb*
dazes
dazing
dazed

daze *noun*

dazzle *verb*
dazzles
dazzling
dazzled

de-
de- makes verbs with
an opposite meaning,
e.g. **deactivate** means
'to stop something
working'. You need a
hyphen when the
word begins with an e
or *i*, e.g. **de-escalate**,
de-ice.

dead

deaden *verb*
deadens
deadening
deadened

dead end *noun*
dead ends

deadline *noun*
deadlines

deadlock

deadly *adjective*
deadlier
deadliest

deaf *adjective*
deafer
deafest

deafness

deafen *verb*
deafens
deafening
deafened

deal *verb*
deals
dealing
dealt

deal *noun*
deals

dealer *noun*
dealers

dean *noun*
deans

☆ **dear** *adjective*
dearer
dearest

death *noun*
deaths

deathly

debatable

debate *noun*
debates

debate *verb*
debates
debating
debated

debris

debt *noun*
debts

debtor *noun*
debtors

debug *verb*
debugs
debugging
debugged

début *noun*
débuts

decade *noun*
decades

decay *verb*
decays
decaying
decayed

★ **Data** is strictly a plural noun, but is often used as a singular noun: *Here is the data.*

☆ **Dear** means 'loved' or 'expensive'. ! **deer**.

de

decay noun
deceased
deceit
deceitful adjective
 deceitfully
deceive verb
 deceives
 deceiving
 deceived
December
decency
decent adjective
 decently
deception noun
 deceptions
deceptive
decibel noun
 decibels
decide verb
 decides
 deciding
 decided
deciduous
decimal noun
 decimals
decimalization
decimalize verb
 decimalizes
 decimalizing
 decimalized
decipher verb
 deciphers
 deciphering
 deciphered
decision noun
 decisions
decisive adjective
 decisively
deck noun
 decks

deckchair noun
 deckchairs
declaration noun
 declarations
declare verb
 declares
 declaring
 declared
decline verb
 declines
 declining
 declined
decode verb
 decodes
 decoding
 decoded
decompose verb
 decomposes
 decomposing
 decomposed
decorate verb
 decorates
 decorating
 decorated
decoration noun
 decorations
decorative
decorator noun
 decorators
decoy noun
 decoys
decrease verb
 decreases
 decreasing
 decreased
decrease noun
 decreases
decree noun
 decrees

decree verb
 decrees
 decreeing
 decreed
decrepit
dedicate verb
 dedicates
 dedicating
 dedicated
dedication
deduce verb
 deduces
 deducing
 deduced
deduct verb
 deducts
 deducting
 deducted
deductible
deduction noun
 deductions
deed noun
 deeds
deep adjective
 deeper
 deepest
 deeply
deepen verb
 deepens
 deepening
 deepened
deep-freeze noun
 deep-freezes
★ **deer** noun
 deer
deface verb
 defaces
 defacing
 defaced
default noun
 defaults

★ A deer is an animal. ! dear.

defeat verb
defeats
defeating
defeated

defeat noun
defeats

defect noun
defects

defect verb
defects
defecting
defected

defective adjective
defectively

defence noun
defences

defenceless

defend verb
defends
defending
defended

defendant noun
defendants

defender noun
defenders

defensible

defensive adjective
defensively

defer verb
defers
deferring
deferred

deferment

defiance

defiant adjective
defiantly

deficiency noun
deficiencies

deficient

deficit noun
deficits

defile verb
defiles
defiling
defiled

define verb
defines
defining
defined

definite adjective
definitely

definition noun
definitions

deflate verb
deflates
deflating
deflated

deflect verb
deflects
deflecting
deflected

deflection

deforestation

deformed

deformity noun
deformities

defrost verb
defrosts
defrosting
defrosted

deft adjective
defter
deftest
deftly

defuse verb
defuses
defusing
defused

defy verb
defies
defying
defied

degenerate verb
degenerates
degenerating
degenerated

degeneration

degradation

degrade verb
degrades
degrading
degraded

degree noun
degrees

dehydrated

dehydration

de-ice verb
de-ices
de-icing
de-iced

de-icer

deity noun
deities

dejected

dejection

delay verb
delays
delaying
delayed

delay noun
delays

delegate noun
delegates

delegate verb
delegates
delegating
delegated

delegation

delete verb
deletes
deleting
deleted

deletion

de

deliberate *adjective*
deliberately

deliberate *verb*
deliberates
deliberating
deliberated

deliberation

delicacy *noun*
delicacies

delicate *adjective*
delicately

delicatessen *noun*
delicatessens

delicious *adjective*
deliciously

delight *verb*
delights
delighting
delighted

delight *noun*
delights

delightful *adjective*
delightfully

delinquency

delinquent *noun*
delinquents

delirious *adjective*
deliriously

delirium *noun*

deliver *verb*
delivers
delivering
delivered

delivery *noun*
deliveries

delta *noun*
deltas

delude *verb*
deludes
deluding
deluded

deluge *noun*
deluges

deluge *verb*
deluges
deluging
deluged

delusion *noun*
delusions

de luxe

demand *verb*
demands
demanding
demanded

demand *noun*
demands

demanding

demerara

demist *verb*
demists
demisting
demisted

demo *noun*
demos

democracy *noun*
democracies

democrat *noun*
democrats

democratic *adjective*
democratically

demolish *verb*
demolishes
demolishing
demolished

demolition

demon *noun*
demons

demonstrate *verb*
demonstrates
demonstrating
demonstrated

demonstration
noun
demonstrations

demonstrator *noun*
demonstrators

demoralize *verb*
demoralizes
demoralizing
demoralized

demote *verb*
demotes
demoting
demoted

den *noun*
dens

denial *noun*
denials

denim

denominator *noun*
denominators

denote *verb*
denotes
denoting
denoted

denounce *verb*
denounces
denouncing
denounced

denunciation

dense *adjective*
denser
densest
densely

density *noun*

dent *noun*
dents

dental

dentist *noun*
dentists

dentistry

denture *noun*
dentures

63   de

deny *verb*
denies
denying
denied

deodorant *noun*
deodorants

depart *verb*
departs
departing
departed

department *noun*
departments

departure *noun*
departures

depend *verb*
depends
depending
depended

dependable

★ **dependant** *noun*
dependants

dependence

☆ **dependent** *adjective*

depict *verb*
depicts
depicting
depicted

deplorable *adjective*
deplorably

deplore *verb*
deplores
deploring
deplored

deport *verb*
deports
deporting
deported

deposit *verb*
deposits
depositing
deposited

deposit *noun*
deposits

depot *noun*
depots

depress *verb*
depresses
depressing
depressed

depression *noun*
depressions

deprivation

deprive *verb*
deprives
depriving
deprived

depth *noun*
depths

deputize *verb*
deputizes
deputizing
deputized

deputy *noun*
deputies

derail *verb*
derails
derailing
derailed

derby *noun*
derbies

derelict

deride *verb*
derides
deriding
derided

derision

derive *verb*
derives
deriving
derived

derrick *noun*
derricks

derv

○ **descant** *noun*
descants

descend *verb*
descends
descending
descended

descendant *noun*
descendants

✱ **descent**

describe *verb*
describes
describing
described

description *noun*
descriptions

descriptive *adjective*
descriptively

✳ **desert** *noun*
deserts

desert *verb*
deserts
deserting
deserted

deserter *noun*
deserters

desertion

deserve *verb*
deserves
deserving
deserved

design *verb*
designs
designing
designed

design *noun*
designs

designate *verb*
designates
designating
designated

- -
★ **Dependant** is a noun: *She has three dependants.* ! **dependent**.
☆ **Dependent** is an adjective: *She has three dependent children.* ! **dependant**.
○ **Descant** is a term in music. ! **descent**.
✱ **Descent** is a way down. ! **descant**.
✳ A **desert** is a very dry area of land. ! **dessert**.

designer noun
designers

desirable

desire verb
desires
desiring
desired

desire noun
desires

desk noun
desks

desktop

desolate

desolation

despair verb
despairs
despairing
despaired

despair noun

despatch verb
use dispatch

desperate adjective
desperately

desperation

despicable adjective
despicably

despise verb
despises
despising
despised

despite

★ **dessert** noun
desserts

dessertspoon noun
dessertspoons

destination noun
destinations

destined

destiny noun
destinies

destroy verb
destroys
destroying
destroyed

destroyer noun
destroyers

destruction

destructive

detach verb
detaches
detaching
detached

detachable

detached

detachment noun
detachments

detail noun
details

detain verb
detains
detaining
detained

detect verb
detects
detecting
detected

detection

detector

detective noun
detectives

detention noun
detentions

deter verb
deters
deterring
deterred

detergent noun
detergents

deteriorate verb
deteriorates
deteriorating
deteriorated

deterioration

determination

determine verb
determines
determining
determined

determined

deterrence

deterrent noun
deterrents

detest verb
detests
detesting
detested

detestable

detonate verb
detonates
detonating
detonated

detonation

detonator

detour noun
detours

☆ **deuce**

devastate verb
devastates
devastating
devastated

devastation

develop verb
develops
developing
developed

development noun
developments

device noun
devices

devil noun
devils

. . . .

★ A **dessert** is a sweet pudding. **!** desert.
☆ **Deuce** is a score in tennis. **!** juice.

devilish
devilment
devious adjective
  deviously
devise verb
  devises
  devising
  devised
devolution
devote verb
  devotes
  devoting
  devoted
devotee
devotion
devour verb
  devours
  devouring
  devoured
devout
★ **dew**
dewy
☆ **dhoti** noun
  dhotis
diabetes
diabetic
diabolical adjective
  diabolically
diagnose verb
  diagnoses
  diagnosing
  diagnosed
diagnosis noun
  diagnoses
diagonal adjective
  diagonally
diagonal noun
  diagonals
diagram noun
  diagrams

dial noun
  dials
dial verb
  dials
  dialling
  dialled
dialect noun
  dialects
dialogue noun
  dialogues
diameter noun
  diameters
diamond noun
  diamonds
diaphragm noun
  diaphragms
diarrhoea
diary noun
  diaries
dice noun
  dice
dictate verb
  dictates
  dictating
  dictated
dictation
dictator noun
  dictators
dictatorial adjective
  dictatorially
dictionary noun
  dictionaries
did see do
diddle verb
  diddles
  diddling
  diddled
didn't verb

die verb
  dies
  dying
  died
diesel noun
  diesels
diet noun
  diets
diet verb
  diets
  dieting
  dieted
differ verb
  differs
  differing
  differed
difference noun
  differences
different adjective
  differently
difficult
difficulty noun
  difficulties
dig verb
  digs
  digging
  dug
dig noun
  digs
digest verb
  digests
  digesting
  digested
digestible
digestion
digestive
digger
digit noun
  digits
digital adjective
  digitally

★ **Dew** is moisture on grass and plants. ! **due**.
☆ A **dhoti** is a piece of clothing worn by Hindus.

dignified
dignity
dike noun
  use **dyke**
dilemma noun
  dilemmas
dilute verb
  dilutes
  diluting
  diluted
dilution
dim adjective
  dimmer
  dimmest
  dimly
dimension noun
  dimensions
diminish verb
  diminishes
  diminishing
  diminished
dimple noun
  dimples
din noun
  dins
dine verb
  dines
  dining
  dined
★ **diner** noun
  diners
☆ **dinghy** noun
  dinghies
⊙ **dingy** adjective
  dingier
  dingiest
✳ **dinner** noun
  dinners
dinosaur noun
  dinosaurs

dioxide noun
  dioxides
dip verb
  dips
  dipping
  dipped
dip noun
  dips
diphtheria
diploma noun
  diplomas
diplomacy
diplomat
diplomatic adjective
  diplomatically
dire adjective
  direr
  direst
direct adjective
  directly
direct verb
  directs
  directing
  directed
direction noun
  directions
director noun
  directors
directory noun
  directories
dirt
dirtiness
dirty adjective
  dirtier
  dirtiest
  dirtily

dis-
dis- makes a word
with an opposite
meaning, e.g. **disobey**
means 'to refuse to
obey' and **disloyal**
means 'not loyal'.
These words are spelt
joined up.

disability noun
  disabilities
disabled
disadvantage noun
  disadvantages
disagree verb
  disagrees
  disagreeing
  disagreed
disagreeable
  adjective
  disagreeably
disagreement noun
  disagreements
disappear verb
  disappears
  disappearing
  disappeared
disappearance
noun
  disappearances
disappoint verb
  disappoints
  disappointing
  disappointed
disappointing
disappointment
noun
  disappointments
disapproval

- -

★ A **diner** is someone who eats dinner. ! **dinner**.
☆ A **dinghy** is a small sailing boat. ! **dingy**.
⊙ **Dingy** means 'dirty-looking, drab, dull-coloured'. ! **dinghy**.
✳ **Dinner** is a meal. ! **diner**.

disapprove verb
disapproves
disapproving
disapproved

disarm verb
disarms
disarming
disarmed

disarmament

disaster noun
disasters

disastrous adjective
disastrously

★ **disc** noun
discs

discard verb
discards
discarding
discarded

discharge verb
discharges
discharging
discharged

disciple noun
disciples

discipline

disc jockey noun
disc jockeys

disclose verb
discloses
disclosing
disclosed

disclosure

disco noun
discos

discomfort

disconnect verb
disconnects
disconnecting
disconnected

disconnection

discontent

discontented

discotheque noun
discotheques

discount noun
discounts

discourage verb
discourages
discouraging
discouraged

discouragement

discover verb
discovers
discovering
discovered

discovery noun
discoveries

discreet adjective
discreetly

discriminate verb
discriminates
discriminating
discriminated

discrimination

discus noun
discuses

discuss verb
discusses
discussing
discussed

discussion noun
discussions

disease noun
diseases

diseased

disgrace verb
disgraces
disgracing
disgraced

disgrace noun

disgraceful adjective
disgracefully

disguise verb
disguises
disguising
disguised

disguise noun
disguises

disgust verb
disgusts
disgusting
disgusted

disgust noun

disgusting

dish noun
dishes

dish verb
dishes
dishing
dished

dishcloth noun
dishcloths

dishevelled

dishonest adjective
dishonestly

dishonesty

dishwasher noun
dishwashers

disinfect verb
disinfects
disinfecting
disinfected

disinfectant noun
disinfectants

disintegrate verb
disintegrates
disintegrating
disintegrated

disintegration

disinterested

☆ **disk** noun
disks

. . . .

★ A **disc** is a flat round object. ! **disk.**
☆ A **disk** is what you put in a computer. ! **disc.**

dislike verb
dislikes
disliking
disliked

dislike noun
dislikes

dislocate verb
dislocates
dislocating
dislocated

dislodge verb
dislodges
dislodging
dislodged

disloyal adjective
disloyally

disloyalty

dismal adjective
dismally

dismantle verb
dismantles
dismantling
dismantled

dismay

dismayed

dismiss verb
dismisses
dismissing
dismissed

dismissal

dismount verb
dismounts
dismounting
dismounted

disobedience

disobedient

disobey verb
disobeys
disobeying
disobeyed

disorder noun
disorders

disorderly

dispatch verb
dispatches
dispatching
dispatched

dispense verb
dispenses
dispensing
dispensed

dispenser noun
dispensers

dispersal

disperse verb
disperses
dispersing
dispersed

display verb
displays
displaying
displayed

display noun
displays

displease verb
displeases
displeasing
displeased

disposable

disposal

dispose verb
disposes
disposing
disposed

disprove verb
disproves
disproving
disproved

dispute noun
disputes

disqualification

disqualify verb
disqualifies
disqualifying
disqualified

disregard verb
disregards
disregarding
disregarded

disrespect

disrespectful
adjective
disrespectfully

disrupt verb
disrupts
disrupting
disrupted

disruption

disruptive

dissatisfaction

dissatisfied

dissect verb
dissects
dissecting
dissected

dissection

dissolve verb
dissolves
dissolving
dissolved

dissuade verb
dissuades
dissuading
dissuaded

distance noun
distances

distant adjective
distantly

distil verb
distils
distilling
distilled

distillery noun
distilleries

distinct *adjective*
distinctly
distinction *noun*
distinctions
distinctive
distinguish *verb*
distinguishes
distinguishing
distinguished
distinguished
distort *verb*
distorts
distorting
distorted
distortion *noun*
distortions
distract *verb*
distracts
distracting
distracted
distraction *noun*
distractions
distress *verb*
distresses
distressing
distressed
distress *noun*
distribute *verb*
distributes
distributing
distributed
distribution
distributor
district *noun*
districts
distrust
distrustful
disturb *verb*
disturbs
disturbing
disturbed

disturbance *noun*
disturbances
disused
ditch *noun*
ditches
dither *verb*
dithers
dithering
dithered
divan *noun*
divans
dive *verb*
dives
diving
dived
diver *noun*
divers
diverse
diversify *verb*
diversifies
diversifying
diversified
diversion *noun*
diversions
diversity
divert *verb*
diverts
diverting
diverted
divide *verb*
divides
dividing
divided
dividend *noun*
dividends
dividers *plural noun*
divine *adjective*
divinely
divine *verb*
divines
divining
divined

divinity
divisible
division *noun*
divisions
divorce *verb*
divorces
divorcing
divorced
divorce *noun*
divorces
★ **Diwali**
dizziness
dizzy *adjective*
dizzier
dizziest
dizzily
do *verb*
does
doing
did
done
docile *adjective*
docilely
dock *noun*
docks
dock *verb*
docks
docking
docked
dock *noun*
docks
docker *noun*
dockers
dockyard *noun*
dockyards
doctor *noun*
doctors
doctrine *noun*
doctrines

• •
★ **Diwali** is a Hindu festival.

do

document *noun*
documents

documentary *noun*
documentaries

doddery

dodge *verb*
dodges
dodging
dodged

dodge *noun*
dodges

dodgem *noun*
dodgems

dodgy *adjective*
dodgier
dodgiest

⋆ **doe** *noun*
does

doesn't *abbreviation*

dog *noun*
dogs

dog-eared

dogged *adjective*
doggedly

doldrums *plural noun*

dole *verb*
doles
doling
doled

dole *noun*

doll *noun*
dolls

dollar *noun*
dollars

dolly *noun*
dollies

dolphin *noun*
dolphins

-dom
-dom makes nouns,
e.g. kingdom. Other
noun suffixes are
-hood, **-ment**, **-ness**,
and **-ship**.

domain *noun*
domains

dome *noun*
domes

domestic *adjective*
domestically

domesticated

dominance

dominant *adjective*
dominantly

dominate *verb*
dominates
dominating
dominated

domination

dominion *noun*
dominions

domino *noun*
dominoes

donate *verb*
donates
donating
donated

donation *noun*
donations

done see **do**

donkey *noun*
donkeys

donor *noun*
donors

don't *abbreviation*

doodle *verb*
doodles
doodling
doodled

doodle *noun*
doodles

doom *verb*
dooms
dooming
doomed

doom *noun*

door *noun*
doors

doorstep *noun*
doorsteps

doorway *noun*
doorways

dope *noun*
dopes

dopey *adjective*
dopier
dopiest

dormitory *noun*
dormitories

dose *noun*
doses

dossier *noun*
dossiers

dot *verb*
dots
dotting
dotted

dot *noun*
dots

dottiness

dotty *adjective*
dottier
dottiest
dottily

double *adjective*
doubly

double *noun*
doubles

⋆ A doe is a female deer. ! **dough**.

double verb
doubles
doubling
doubled

double-cross verb
double-crosses
double-crossing
double-crossed

double-decker noun
double-deckers

doubt verb
doubts
doubting
doubted

doubt noun
doubts

doubtful adjective
doubtfully

doubtless

★ **dough**

doughnut noun
doughnuts

doughy adjective
doughier
doughiest

dove noun
doves

dowel noun
dowels

down

downcast

downfall noun
downfalls

downhill

downpour noun
downpours

downright adjective

downs plural noun

downstairs

downstream

downward adjective
and adverb

downwards adverb

downy adjective
downier
downiest

doze verb
dozes
dozing
dozed

dozen noun
dozens

dozy adjective
dozier
doziest

drab adjective
drabber
drabbest

draft verb
drafts
drafting
drafted

draft noun
drafts

drag verb
drags
dragging
dragged

drag noun

dragon noun
dragons

dragonfly noun
dragonflies

drain verb
drains
draining
drained

drain noun
drains

drainage

drake noun
drakes

drama noun
dramas

dramatic adjective
dramatically

dramatist noun
dramatists

dramatization

dramatize verb
dramatizes
dramatizing
dramatized

drank see **drink**

drape verb
drapes
draping
draped

drastic adjective
drastically

draught noun
draughts

draughty adjective
draughtier
draughtiest

draughts noun

draughtsman noun
draughtsmen

☆ **draw** verb
draws
drawing
drew
drawn

draw noun
draws

drawback noun
drawbacks

drawbridge noun
drawbridges

○ **drawer** noun
drawers

• •

★ **Dough** is a mixture of flour and water used for baking. ! **doe.**
☆ To **draw** is to make a picture with a pencil, pen, or crayon. ! **drawer.**
○ A **drawer** is part of a cupboard. ! **draw.**

drawing noun
drawings
drawl verb
drawls
drawling
drawled
dread verb
dreads
dreading
dreaded
dread noun
dreadful adjective
dreadfully
dreadlocks
dream noun
dreams
dream verb
dreams
dreaming
dreamt or dreamed
dreamy adjective
dreamier
dreamiest
dreariness
dreary adjective
drearier
dreariest
drearily
dredge verb
dredges
dredging
dredged
dredger
drench verb
drenches
drenching
drenched
dress verb
dresses
dressing
dressed

dress noun
dresses
dresser noun
dressers
dressing noun
dressings
dressmaker noun
dressmakers
drew see draw
dribble verb
dribbles
dribbling
dribbled
dried see dry
drier noun
driers
drift verb
drifts
drifting
drifted
drift noun
drifts
driftwood
drill verb
drills
drilling
drilled
drill noun
drills
drink verb
drinks
drinking
drank
drunk
drink noun
drinks
drinker noun
drinkers
drip noun
drips

drip verb
drips
dripping
dripped
dripping
drive verb
drives
driving
drove
driven
drive noun
drives
driver noun
drivers
drizzle verb
drizzles
drizzling
drizzled
drizzle noun
drone verb
drones
droning
droned
drone noun
drones
drool verb
drools
drooling
drooled
droop verb
droops
drooping
drooped
drop verb
drops
dropping
dropped
drop noun
drops
droplet noun
droplets

drought *noun*
droughts

drove see **drive**

drown *verb*
drowns
drowning
drowned

drowsiness

drowsy *adjective*
drowsier
drowsiest
drowsily

drug *noun*
drugs

drug *verb*
drugs
drugging
drugged

Druid *noun*
Druids

drum *noun*
drums

drum *verb*
drums
drumming
drummed

drummer *noun*
drummers

drumstick *noun*
drumsticks

drunk see **drink**

drunk *adjective* and
noun
drunks

drunkard *noun*
drunkards

dry *adjective*
drier
driest
drily

dry *verb*
dries
drying
dried

dryness

★ **dual** *adjective*
dually

dub *verb*
dubs
dubbing
dubbed

duchess *noun*
duchesses

duck *noun*
ducks

duck *verb*
ducks
ducking
ducked

duckling *noun*
ducklings

duct *noun*
ducts

dud *noun*
duds

☆ **due**

◐ **duel** *noun*
duels

duet *noun*
duets

duff

duffel coat *noun*
duffel coats

dug see **dig**

dugout *noun*
dugouts

duke *noun*
dukes

dull *adjective*
duller
dullest
dully

dullness

duly

dumb *adjective*
dumber
dumbest

dumbfounded

dummy *noun*
dummies

dump *verb*
dumps
dumping
dumped

dump *noun*
dumps

dumpling *noun*
dumplings

dumpy *adjective*
dumpier
dumpiest

dune *noun*
dunes

dung

dungarees

dungeon *noun*
dungeons

duo *noun*
duos

duplicate *noun*
duplicates

duplicate *verb*
duplicates
duplicating
duplicated

duplication

durability

durable

duration

during

. . . .

★ **Dual** means 'having two parts'. ! **duel.**
☆ **Due** means 'expected'. ! **dew.**
◐ A **duel** is a fight between two people. ! **dual.**

dusk

dust

dust *verb*
dusts
dusting
dusted

dustbin *noun*
dustbins

duster *noun*
dusters

dustman *noun*
dustmen

dustpan *noun*
dustpans

dusty *adjective*
dustier
dustiest

dutiful *adjective*
dutifully

duty *noun*
duties

duvet *noun*
duvets

dwarf *noun*
dwarfs *or* dwarves

dwarf *verb*
dwarfs
dwarfing
dwarfed

dwell *verb*
dwells
dwelling
dwelt

dwelling *noun*
dwellings

dwindle *verb*
dwindles
dwindling
dwindled

★ **dye** *verb*
dyes
dyeing
dyed

dye *noun*
dyes

dying see die

dyke *noun*
dykes

dynamic *adjective*
dynamically

dynamite

dynamo *noun*
dynamos

dynasty *noun*
dynasties

dyslexia

dyslexic

dystrophy *noun*

Ee

e-
e- stands for
'electronic' and
makes words about
computers and the
Internet, e.g. email
(spelt joined up),
e-commerce and
e-shopping (spelt with
hyphens).

each

eager *adjective*
eagerly

eagerness

eagle *noun*
eagles

ear *noun*
ears

earache

eardrum *noun*
eardrums

earl *noun*
earls

early *adjective* and
adverb
earlier
earliest

earmark *verb*
earmarks
earmarking
earmarked

earn *verb*
earns
earning
earned

earnest *adjective*
earnestly

earnings *plural noun*

earphones

earring *noun*
earrings

earth *noun*
earths

earthenware

earthly

earthquake *noun*
earthquakes

earthworm *noun*
earthworms

earthy *adjective*
earthier
earthiest

earwig *noun*
earwigs

ease *verb*
eases
easing
eased

ease *noun*

· ·

★ **Dye** means 'to change the colour of something'. **! die.**

easel *noun*
easels

east *adjective* and *adverb*

★ **east** *noun*

Easter

easterly *adjective* and *noun*
easterlies

eastern

eastward *adjective* and *adverb*

eastwards *adverb*

easy *adjective* and *adverb*
easier
easiest
easily

eat *verb*
eats
eating
ate
eaten

eatable

eaves

ebb *verb*
ebbs
ebbing
ebbed

ebb

ebony

eccentric

eccentricity *noun*
eccentricities

echo *verb*
echoes
echoing
echoed

echo *noun*
echoes

éclair *noun*
éclairs

eclipse *noun*
eclipses

ecological

ecology

economic

economical *adjective*
economically

economics

economist *noun*
economists

economize *verb*
economizes
economizing
economized

economy *noun*
economies

ecstasy *noun*
ecstasies

ecstatic *adjective*
ecstatically

eczema

-ed and -t
Some verbs ending in
l, m, n, and p have
past forms and past
participles ending in
-ed and -t, e.g.
burned/burnt, leaped/
leapt. Both forms are
correct, and the -t
form is especially
common when it
comes before a noun,
e.g. *burnt cakes.*

edge *noun*
edges

edge *verb*
edges
edging
edged

edgeways

edgy *adjective*
edgier
edgiest

edible

edit *verb*
edits
editing
edited

edition *noun*
editions

editor *noun*
editors

editorial *noun*
editorials

educate *verb*
educates
educating
educated

education

educational

educator

eel *noun*
eels

eerie *adjective*
eerier
eeriest
eerily

eeriness

☆ **effect** *noun*
effects

effective *adjective*
effectively

effectiveness

effeminate

effervescence

effervescent

efficiency

efficient *adjective*
efficiently

- -

★ You use a capital E in the **East**, meaning China, Japan, etc.
☆ An **effect** is something that is caused by something else. ! affect.

effort *noun*
efforts

effortless *adjective*
effortlessly

egg *noun*
eggs

egg *verb*
eggs
egging
egged

-ei- and -ie-
The rule 'i before e
except after c' is true
when it is pronounced
-ee-, e.g. thief,
ceiling. There are a
few exceptions, of
which the most
important are seize
and protein.

★ **Eid**

eiderdown *noun*
eiderdowns

☆ **eight**

eighteen

eighteenth

○ **eighth** *adjective and
noun*
eighthly

eightieth

eighty *noun*
eighties

either

eject *verb*
ejects
ejecting
ejected

ejection

elaborate *adjective*
elaborately

elaborate *verb*
elaborates
elaborating
elaborated

elaboration

elastic

elated

elation

elbow *noun*
elbows

elbow *verb*
elbows
elbowing
elbowed

elder *adjective and
noun*
elders

elderberry *noun*
elderberries

elderly

eldest

elect *verb*
elects
electing
elected

election *noun*
elections

electorate

electric

electrical *adjective*
electrically

electrician *noun*
electricians

electricity

electrification

electrify *verb*
electrifies
electrifying
electrified

electrocute *verb*
electrocutes

electrocuting
electrocuted

electrocution

electromagnet
noun
electromagnets

electron *noun*
electrons

electronic *adjective*
electronically

electronics

elegance

elegant *adjective*
elegantly

element *noun*
elements

elementary

elephant *noun*
elephants

elevate *verb*
elevates
elevating
elevated

elevation *noun*
elevations

eleven

eleventh

elf *noun*
elves

eligibility

eligible

eliminate *verb*
eliminates
eliminating
eliminated

elimination

élite *noun*
élites

elk *noun*
elk *or* elks

★ **Eid** is a Muslim festival.
☆ **Eight** is the number. ! ate.
○ Note that there are two h's in **eighth**.

ellipse noun
ellipses

elliptical adjective
elliptically

elm noun
elms

elocution

eloquence

eloquent

else

elsewhere

elude verb
eludes
eluding
eluded

elusive adjective
elusively

elves see elf

★ **email** noun
emails

email verb
emails
emailing
emailed

emancipate verb
emancipates
emancipating
emancipated

emancipation

embankment noun
embankments

embark verb
embarks
embarking
embarked

embarkation

☆ **embarrass** verb
embarrasses
embarrassing
embarrassed

embarrassment

embassy noun
embassies

embedded

embers plural noun

emblem noun
emblems

embrace verb
embraces
embracing
embraced

embroider verb
embroiders
embroidering
embroidered

embroidery noun
embroideries

embryo noun
embryos

emerald noun
emeralds

emerge verb
emerges
emerging
emerged

emergence

emergency noun
emergencies

emery paper

emigrant noun
emigrants

emigrate verb
emigrates
emigrating
emigrated

emigration

eminence

eminent

✿ **emission** noun
emissions

emit verb
emits
emitting
emitted

emotion noun
emotions

emotional adjective
emotionally

emperor noun
emperors

emphasis noun
emphases

emphasize verb
emphasizes
emphasizing
emphasized

emphatic adjective
emphatically

empire noun
empires

employ verb
employs
employing
employed

employee noun
employees

employer noun
employers

employment

empress noun
empresses

empties plural noun

emptiness

empty adjective
emptier
emptiest

empty verb
empties
emptying
emptied

emu noun
emus

• •

★ **Email** is short for **electronic mail.**
☆ Note that there are two **r**s in **embarrass** and **embarrassment.**
✿ An **emission** is something that escapes, like fumes. **! omission.**

emulsion *noun*
emulsions

enable *verb*
enables
enabling
enabled

enamel *noun*
enamels

encampment *noun*
encampments

-ence
See the note at -ance.

enchant *verb*
enchants
enchanting
enchanted

enchantment

encircle *verb*
encircles
encircling
encircled

enclose *verb*
encloses
enclosing
enclosed

enclosure

encore *noun*
encores

encounter *verb*
encounters
encountering
encountered

encourage *verb*
encourages
encouraging
encouraged

encouragement

encyclopedia *noun*
encyclopedias

encyclopedic

end *verb*
ends
ending
ended

end *noun*
ends

endanger *verb*
endangers
endangering
endangered

endeavour *verb*
endeavours
endeavouring
endeavoured

ending *noun*
endings

endless *adjective*
endlessly

endurance

endure *verb*
endures
enduring
endured

enemy *noun*
enemies

energetic *adjective*
energetically

energy *noun*
energies

enforce *verb*
enforces
enforcing
enforced

enforceable

enforcement

engage *verb*
engages
engaging
engaged

engagement *noun*
engagements

engine *noun*
engines

engineer *noun*
engineers

engineering

engrave *verb*
engraves
engraving
engraved

engraver

engrossed

engulf *verb*
engulfs
engulfing
engulfed

enhance *verb*
enhances
enhancing
enhanced

enhancement

enjoy *verb*
enjoys
enjoying
enjoyed

enjoyable

enjoyment

enlarge *verb*
enlarges
enlarging
enlarged

enlargement *noun*
enlargements

enlist *verb*
enlists
enlisting
enlisted

enmity *noun*
enmities

★ **enormity** *noun*
enormities

★ An **enormity** is a wicked act. If you mean 'large size', use **enormousness**.

enormous *adjective*
enormously

enormousness

enough

enquire *verb*
enquires
enquiring
enquired

★ **enquiry** *noun*
enquiries

enrage *verb*
enrages
enraging
enraged

enrich *verb*
enriches
enriching
enriched

enrichment

enrol *verb*
enrols
enrolling
enrolled

enrolment

ensemble *noun*
ensembles

ensue *verb*
ensues
ensuing
ensued

ensure *verb*
ensures
ensuring
ensured

-ent
See the note at -ant.

entangle *verb*
entangles
entangling
entangled

entanglement

enter *verb*
enters
entering
entered

enterprise *noun*
enterprises

enterprising

entertain *verb*
entertains
entertaining
entertained

entertainer *noun*
entertainers

entertainment
noun
entertainments

enthusiasm *noun*
enthusiasms

enthusiast *noun*
enthusiasts

enthusiastic
adjective
enthusiastically

entire *adjective*
entirely

entirety

entitle *verb*
entitles
entitling
entitled

entrance *noun*
entrances

entrance *verb*
entrances
entrancing
entranced

entrant *noun*
entrants

entreat *verb*
entreats
entreating
entreated

entreaty *noun*
entreaties

entrust *verb*
entrusts
entrusting
entrusted

entry *noun*
entries

envelop *verb*
envelops
enveloping
enveloped

envelope *noun*
envelopes

envious *adjective*
enviously

environment *noun*
environments

environmental

environmentalist
noun
environmentalists

envy *verb*
envies
envying
envied

envy *noun*

enzyme *noun*
enzymes

epic *noun*
epics

epidemic *noun*
epidemics

epilepsy

epileptic *adjective*
and *noun*
epileptics

epilogue *noun*
epilogues

★ An **enquiry** is a question. ! inquiry.

episode noun
episodes

epistle noun
epistles

epitaph noun
epitaphs

epoch noun
epochs

equal adjective
equally

equal verb
equals
equalling
equalled

equal noun
equals

equality

equalize verb
equalizes
equalizing
equalized

equalizer noun
equalizers

equation noun
equations

equator

equatorial

equestrian

equilateral

equilibrium noun
equilibria

equinox noun
equinoxes

equip verb
equips
equipping
equipped

equipment

equivalence

equivalent

-er and -est

-er and -est make adjectives and adverbs meaning 'more' or 'most', e.g. **faster, slowest**. You can do this when the word has one syllable, and when a consonant comes at the end of the word after a single vowel you double it, e.g. **fatter, bigger**. You can use -er and -est with some two-syllable adjectives, e.g. **commoner, pleasantest**, and words ending in y, which change to -ier and -iest, e.g. **angrier, happiest**.

-er and -or

-er makes nouns meaning 'a person or thing that does something', e.g. a **helper** is a person who helps and an **opener** is a tool that opens things. You can make new words this way, e.g. **complainer, repairer**. Some words end in -or, e.g. **actor, visitor**, but you can't use -or to make new words.

---

era noun
eras

erase verb
erases
erasing
erased

eraser

erect adjective

erect verb
erects
erecting
erected

erection noun
erections

ermine noun
ermine

erode verb
erodes
eroding
eroded

erosion

errand noun
errands

erratic adjective
erratically

erroneous adjective
erroneously

error noun
errors

erupt verb
erupts
erupting
erupted

eruption

escalate verb
escalates
escalating
escalated

escalation

escalator noun
escalators

escape verb
escapes
escaping
escaped

escape *noun*
escapes

escort *verb*
escorts
escorting
escorted

escort *noun*
escorts

Eskimo *noun*
Eskimos *or* Eskimo

especially

espionage

esplanade *noun*
esplanades

-ess
makes nouns for
female people and
animals, e.g.
manageress, lioness.

essay *noun*
essays

essence *noun*
essences

essential *adjective*
essentially

essential *noun*
essentials

establish *verb*
establishes
establishing
established

establishment *noun*
establishments

estate *noun*
estates

esteem *verb*
esteems
esteeming
esteemed

estimate *noun*
estimates

estimate *verb*
estimates
estimating
estimated

estuary *noun*
estuaries

etch *verb*
etches
etching
etched

etching *noun*
etchings

eternal *adjective*
eternally

eternity

ether

ethnic

etymology *noun*
etymologies

eucalyptus *noun*
eucalyptuses

euphemism *noun*
euphemisms

euphemistic
adjective
euphemistically

Eurasian

European *adjective*
and *noun*
Europeans

euthanasia

evacuate *verb*
evacuates
evacuating
evacuated

evacuation

evacuee

evade *verb*
evades
evading
evaded

evaluate *verb*
evaluates
evaluating
evaluated

evaluation

evangelical

evangelism

evangelist *noun*
evangelists

evaporate *verb*
evaporates
evaporating
evaporated

evaporation

evasion *noun*
evasions

evasive

eve *noun*
eves

even *adjective*
evenly

even *adverb*

even *verb*
evens
evening
evened

evening *noun*
evenings

evenness

event *noun*
events

eventful *adjective*
eventfully

eventual *adjective*
eventually

ever

evergreen *adjective*
and *noun*
evergreens

everlasting

every
everybody
everyday
everyone
everything
everywhere

evict verb
evicts
evicting
evicted

eviction

evidence

evident adjective
evidently

evil adjective
evilly

evil noun
evils

evolution

evolutionary

evolve verb
evolves
evolving
evolved

★ **ewe** noun
ewes

ex-
ex- makes nouns with
the meaning 'former'
or 'who used to be',
e.g. ex-president,
ex-wife. You use a
hyphen to make these
words.

exact adjective
exactly

exactness

exaggerate verb
exaggerates
exaggerating
exaggerated

exaggeration

exalt verb
exalts
exalting
exalted

exam noun
exams

examination noun
examinations

examine verb
examines
examining
examined

examiner noun
examiners

example noun
examples

exasperate verb
exasperates
exasperating
exasperated

exasperation

excavate verb
excavates
excavating
excavated

excavation noun
excavations

excavator noun
excavators

exceed verb
exceeds
exceeding
exceeded

exceedingly

excel verb
excels
excelling
excelled

excellence

excellent adjective
excellently

☆ **except**

exception noun
exceptions

exceptional
adjective
exceptionally

excerpt noun
excerpts

excess noun
excesses

excessive adjective
excessively

exchange verb
exchanges
exchanging
exchanged

exchange noun
exchanges

excitable adjective
excitably

excite verb
excites
exciting
excited

excitedly

excitement noun
excitements

exclaim verb
exclaims
exclaiming
exclaimed

exclamation noun
exclamations

★ A ewe is a female sheep. ! yew, you.
☆ You use except in e.g. *everyone except me.* ! accept.

exclude verb
  excludes
  excluding
  excluded
exclusion
exclusive adjective
  exclusively
excrement
excrete verb
  excretes
  excreting
  excreted
excretion
excursion noun
  excursions
excusable
excuse verb
  excuses
  excusing
  excused
excuse noun
  excuses
execute verb
  executes
  executing
  executed
execution noun
  executions
executioner noun
  executioners
executive noun
  executives
exempt adjective
exemption noun
exercise noun
  exercises
★ **exercise** verb
  exercises
  exercising
  exercised

exert verb
  exerts
  exerting
  exerted
exertion noun
  exertions
exhale verb
  exhales
  exhaling
  exhaled
exhalation
exhaust verb
  exhausts
  exhausting
  exhausted
exhaust noun
  exhausts
exhaustion
exhibit verb
  exhibits
  exhibiting
  exhibited
exhibit noun
  exhibits
exhibition noun
  exhibitions
exhibitor noun
  exhibitors
exile verb
  exiles
  exiling
  exiled
exile noun
  exiles
exist verb
  exists
  existing
  existed
existence noun
  existences
exit verb
  exits

  exiting
  exited
exit noun
  exits
exorcism
exorcist
☆ **exorcize** verb
  exorcizes
  exorcizing
  exorcized
exotic adjective
  exotically
expand verb
  expands
  expanding
  expanded
expanse noun
  expanses
expansion
expect verb
  expects
  expecting
  expected
expectant adjective
  expectantly
expectation noun
  expectations
expedition noun
  expeditions
expel verb
  expels
  expelling
  expelled
expenditure
expense noun
  expenses
expensive
experience verb
  experiences
  experiencing
  experienced

. . . .

★ To **exercise** is to keep your body fit. ! **exorcise**.
☆ To **exorcise** is to get rid of evil spirits. ! **exercise**.

experience *noun*
experiences
experienced
experiment *verb*
experiments
experimenting
experimented
experiment *noun*
experiments
experimental
adjective
experimentally
experimentation
expert *adjective* and
noun
experts
expertise
expire *verb*
expires
expiring
expired
expiry
explain *verb*
explains
explaining
explained
explanation *noun*
explanations
explanatory
explode *verb*
explodes
exploding
exploded
exploit *noun*
exploits
exploit *verb*
exploits
exploiting
exploited
exploitation
exploration *noun*
explorations

exploratory
explore *verb*
explores
exploring
explored
explorer *noun*
explorers
explosion *noun*
explosions
explosive *adjective*
and *noun*
explosives
export *verb*
exports
exporting
exported
export *noun*
exports
exporter *noun*
exporters
expose *verb*
exposes
exposing
exposed
exposure *noun*
exposures
express *adjective* and
noun
expresses
express *verb*
expresses
expressing
expressed
expression *noun*
expressions
expressive *adjective*
expressively
expulsion *noun*
expulsions
exquisite *adjective*
exquisitely

extend *verb*
extends
extending
extended
extension *noun*
extensions
extensive *adjective*
extensively
extent *noun*
extents
exterior *noun*
exteriors
exterminate *verb*
exterminates
exterminating
exterminated
extermination
external *adjective*
externally
extinct
extinction
extinguish *verb*
extinguishes
extinguishing
extinguished
extinguisher *noun*
extinguishers
extra *adjective* and
noun
extras
extract *verb*
extracts
extracting
extracted
extract *noun*
extracts
extraction *noun*
extractions
extraordinary
adjective
extraordinarily

extrasensory

extraterrestrial
adjective and *noun*
extraterrestrials

extravagance

extravagant
adjective
extravagantly

extreme *adjective*
extremely

extreme *noun*
extremes

extremity *noun*
extremities

exuberance

exuberant *adjective*
exuberantly

exult *verb*
exults
exulting
exulted

exultant

exultation

eye *noun*
eyes

eye *verb*
eyes
eyeing
eyed

eyeball *noun*
eyeballs

eyebrow *noun*
eyebrows

eyelash *noun*
eyelashes

eyelid *noun*
eyelids

eyepiece *noun*
eyepieces

eyesight

eyesore *noun*
eyesores

eyewitness *noun*
eyewitnesses

Ff

-f
Most nouns ending in
-f have plurals ending
in -ves, e.g. **shelf -
shelves**, but some
have plurals ending in
-fs, e.g. **chiefs**. Nouns
ending in -ff have
plurals ending in -ffs,
e.g. **cuffs**.

fable *noun*
fables

fabric *noun*
fabrics

fabricate *verb*
fabricates
fabricating
fabricated

fabulous *adjective*
fabulously

face *noun*
faces

face *verb*
faces
facing
faced

facet *noun*
facets

facetious *adjective*
facetiously

facial *adjective*
facially

facilitate *verb*
facilitates
facilitating
facilitated

facility *noun*
facilities

fact *noun*
facts

factor *noun*
factors

factory *noun*
factories

factual *adjective*
factually

fad *noun*
fads

fade *verb*
fades
fading
faded

faeces

fag *noun*
fags

fagged

faggot *noun*
faggots

Fahrenheit

fail *verb*
fails
failing
failed

fail *noun*
fails

failing *noun*
failings

failure *noun*
failures

faint *adjective*
fainter
faintest
faintly

faint *verb*
faints
fainting
fainted

faint-hearted

faintness

fair *adjective*
fairer
fairest

★ **fair** *noun*
fairs

fairground *noun*
fairgrounds

fairly

fairness

fairy *noun*
fairies

fairyland

faith *noun*
faiths

faithful *adjective*
faithfully

faithfulness

fake *noun*
fakes

fake *verb*
fakes
faking
faked

faker

falcon *noun*
falcons

falconry

fall *verb*
falls
falling
fell
fallen

fall *noun*
falls

fallacious *adjective*
fallaciously

fallacy *noun*
fallacies

fallen see **fall**

fallout

fallow

falls *plural noun*

false *adjective*
falser
falsest
falsely

falsehood *noun*
falsehoods

falseness

falter *verb*
falters
faltering
faltered

fame

famed

familiar *adjective*
familiarly

familiarity

family *noun*
families

famine *noun*
famines

famished

famous *adjective*
famously

fan *verb*
fans
fanning
fanned

fan *noun*
fans

fanatic *noun*
fanatics

fanatical *adjective*
fanatically

fanciful *adjective*
fancifully

fancy *adjective*
fancier
fanciest

fancy *verb*
fancies
fancying
fancied

fancy *noun*
fancies

fanfare *noun*
fanfares

fang *noun*
fangs

fantastic *adjective*
fantastically

fantasy *noun*
fantasies

far *adjective* and *adverb*
farther
farthest

far-away

farce *noun*
farces

farcical *adjective*
farcically

fare *verb*
fares
faring
fared

☆ **fare** *noun*
fares

farewell

far-fetched

- -

★ A **fair** is a group of outdoor entertainments or an exhibition. ! **fare**.
☆ A **fare** is money you pay, for example on a bus. ! **fair**.

farm noun
farms

farm verb
farms
farming
farmed

farmer noun
farmers

farmhouse noun
farmhouses

farmyard noun
farmyards

★ **farther**

☆ **farthest**

farthing noun
farthings

fascinate verb
fascinates
fascinating
fascinated

fascination

fascism

fascist noun
fascists

fashion noun
fashions

fashion verb
fashions
fashioning
fashioned

fashionable

fast adjective and
adverb
faster
fastest

fast verb
fasts
fasting
fasted

fasten verb
fastens
fastening
fastened

fastener

fastening

fat adjective
fatter
fattest

fat noun
fats

fatal adjective
fatally

fatality noun
fatalities

○ **fate** noun
fates

father noun
fathers

father-in-law noun
fathers-in-law

fathom noun
fathoms

fathom verb
fathoms
fathoming
fathomed

fatigue

fatigued

fatten verb
fattens
fattening
fattened

fattening

fatty adjective
fattier
fattiest

fault noun
faults

fault verb
faults

faulting
faulted

faultless adjective
faultlessly

faulty adjective
faultier
faultiest

fauna

favour noun
favours

favour verb
favours
favouring
favoured

favourable adjective
favourably

favourite adjective
and noun
favourites

favouritism

fawn noun
fawns

fax noun
faxes

fax verb
faxes
faxing
faxed

-fe
Most nouns ending
in -fe have plurals
ending in -ves,
e.g. **life - lives.**

fear noun
fears

fear verb
fears
fearing
feared

fearful adjective
fearfully

....

★ You can use **farther** or **further** in e.g. *farther up the road.* See **further.**
☆ You can use **farthest** or **furthest** in e.g. *the place farthest from here.* See
   furthest.
○ **Fate** is a power that is thought to make things happen. ! **fête.**

fearless adjective
fearlessly
fearsome
feasible
feast noun
feasts
feast verb
feasts
feasting
feasted
★ **feat** noun
feats
feather noun
feathers
feathery
feature noun
features
feature verb
features
featuring
featured
☆ **February** noun
Februaries
fed see feed
federal
federation
fee noun
fees
feeble adjective
feebler
feeblest
feebly
feed verb
feeds
feeding
fed
feed noun
feeds
feedback

feel verb
feels
feeling
felt
feel noun
feeler noun
feelers
feeling noun
feelings
◉ **feet** see foot
feline
fell see fall
fell verb
fells
felling
felled
fell noun
fells
fellow noun
fellows
fellowship noun
fellowships
felt see feel
felt noun
felt-tip pen or
felt-tipped pen
noun
felt-tip pens or
felt-tipped pens
female adjective and
noun
females
feminine
femininity
feminism
feminist noun
feminists
fen noun
fens

fence noun
fences
fence verb
fences
fencing
fenced
fencer adjective
fencers
fencing
fend verb
fends
fending
fended
fender noun
fenders
ferment verb
ferments
fermenting
fermented
fermentation
ferment
fern noun
ferns
ferocious adjective
ferociously
ferocity
ferret noun
ferrets
ferret verb
ferrets
ferreting
ferreted
ferry noun
ferries
ferry verb
ferries
ferrying
ferried
fertile
fertility
fertilization

. . . .

★ A feat is an achievement. ! feet.
☆ Note that **February** has two rs.
◉ Feet is the plural of foot. ! feat.

fertilize verb
fertilizes
fertilizing
fertilized

fertilizer noun
fertilizers

fervent adjective
fervently

fervour

festival noun
festivals

festive

festivity

festoon verb
festoons
festooning
festooned

fetal

fetch verb
fetches
fetching
fetched

★ **fête** noun
fêtes

fetlock noun
fetlocks

fetters plural noun

☆ **fetus** noun
fetuses

feud noun
feuds

feudal

feudalism

fever noun
fevers

fevered

feverish adjective
feverishly

few adjective
fewer
fewest

fez noun
fezzes

○ **fiancé** noun
fiancés

✳ **fiancée** noun
fiancées

fiasco noun
fiascos

fib noun
fibs

fibber noun
fibbers

fibre noun
fibres

fibreglass

fibrous

fickle

fiction noun
fictions

fictional adjective
fictionally

fictitious adjective
fictitiously

fiddle verb
fiddles
fiddling
fiddled

fiddle noun
fiddles

fiddler noun
fiddlers

fiddling

fiddly

fidelity

fidget verb
fidgets
fidgeting
fidgeted

fidgety

field noun
fields

field verb
fields
fielding
fielded

fielder noun
fielders

field Marshal noun
field Marshals

fieldwork

fiend noun
fiends

fiendish adjective
fiendishly

fierce adjective
fiercer
fiercest
fiercely

fierceness

fiery adjective
fierier
fieriest

fife noun
fifes

fifteen

fifteenth

fifth

fifthly

fiftieth

fifty noun
fifties

fig noun
figs

fight verb
fights
fighting
fought

fight noun
fights

★ A fête is an outdoor entertainment with stalls. ! fate.
☆ You will also see this word spelt foetus.
○ A woman's fiancé is the man who is going to marry her.
✳ A man's fiancée is the woman who is going to marry him.

fighter noun
fighters

figurative adjective
figuratively

figure noun
figures

figure verb
figures
figuring
figured

filament noun
filaments

file verb
files
filing
filed

file noun
files

filings plural noun

fill verb
fills
filling
filled

fill noun
fills

filler noun
fillers

fillet noun
fillets

filling noun
fillings

filly noun
fillies

film noun
films

film verb
films
filming
filmed

filter noun
filters

filter verb
filters
filtering
filtered

filth

filthy adjective
filthier
filthiest

fin noun
fins

final adjective
finally

final noun
finals

finale noun
finales

finalist noun
finalists

finality

finance

finance verb
finances
financing
financed

finances plural noun

financial adjective
financially

financier noun
financiers

finch noun
finches

find verb
finds
finding
found

finder noun
finders

findings plural noun

fine adjective
finer
finest
finely

fine noun
fines

fine verb
fines
fining
fined

finger noun
fingers

finger verb
fingers
fingering
fingered

fingernail noun
fingernails

fingerprint noun
fingerprints

finicky

finish verb
finishes
finishing
finished

finish noun
finishes

★ **fir** noun
firs

fire noun
fires

fire verb
fires
firing
fired

firearm noun
firearms

firefighter noun
firefighters

fireman noun
firemen

fireplace noun
fireplaces

fireproof

★ A **fir** is a tree. ! **fur**.

fireside *noun*
f100 firesides

firewood

firework *noun*
fireworks

firm *adjective*
firmer
firmest
firmly

firm *noun*
firms

firmness

first *adjective* and
adverb
firstly

first-class

first floor *noun*
first floors

first-hand *adjective*

first-rate

fish *noun*
fish *or* fishes

fish *verb*
fishes
fishing
fished

fisherman *noun*
fishermen

fishmonger *noun*
fishmongers

fishy *adjective*
fishier
fishiest

fission

fist *noun*
fists

fit *adjective*
fitter
fittest

fit *verb*
fits
fitting
fitted

fit *noun*
fits

fitness

fitter *noun*
fitters

fitting *adjective*

fitting *noun*
fittings

five

fiver *noun*
fivers

fix *verb*
fixes
fixing
fixed

fix *noun*
fixes

fixture *noun*
fixtures

fizz *verb*
fizzes
fizzing
fizzed

fizzy *adjective*
fizzier
fizziest

fizzle *verb*
fizzles
fizzling
fizzled

fjord *noun*
fjords

flabbergasted

flabby *adjective*
flabbier
flabbiest

flag *noun*
flags

flag *verb*
flags
flagging
flagged

flagpole *noun*
flagpoles

flagship *noun*
flagships

flagstaff *noun*
flagstaffs

flagstone *noun*
flagstones

★ **flair** *noun*

flake *noun*
flakes

flake *verb*
flakes
flaking
flaked

flaky *adjective*
flakier
flakiest

flame *noun*
flames

flame *verb*
flames
flaming
flamed

flamingo *noun*
flamingos

flan *noun*
flans

flank *noun*
flanks

flannel *noun*
flannels

flap *noun*
flaps

- -

★ **Flair** is a special talent. **!** flare.

flap verb
flaps
flapping
flapped

flapjack noun
flapjacks

★ **flare** noun
flares

flare verb
flares
flaring
flared

flash noun
flashes

flash verb
flashes
flashing
flashed

flashback noun
flashbacks

flashy adjective
flashier
flashiest

flask noun
flasks

flat adjective
flatter
flattest
flatly

flat noun
flats

flatness

flatten verb
flattens
flattening
flattened

flatter verb
flatters
flattering
flattered

flatterer noun
flatterers

flattery

flaunt verb
flaunts
flaunting
flaunted

flavour noun
flavours

flavour verb
flavours
flavouring
flavoured

flavouring

flaw noun
flaws

flawed

flawless adjective
flawlessly

flax

☆ **flea** noun
fleas

fleck noun
flecks

○ **flee** verb
flees
fleeing
fled

fleece noun
fleeces

fleece verb
fleeces
fleecing
fleeced

fleecy adjective
fleecier
fleeciest

fleet noun
fleets

fleeting

flesh

fleshy adjective
fleshier
fleshiest

✳ **flew** see fly

flex noun
flexes

flex verb
flexes
flexing
flexed

flexibility

flexible adjective
flexibly

flick verb
flicks
flicking
flicked

flick noun
flicks

flicker verb
flickers
flickering
flickered

flight noun
flights

flimsy adjective
flimsier
flimsiest

flinch verb
flinches
flinching
flinched

fling verb
flings
flinging
flung

flint noun
flints

flinty adjective
flintier
flintiest

- -

★ A flare is a bright light. ! flair.
☆ A flea is an insect. ! flee.
○ To flee is to run away. ! flea.
✳ Flew is the past of fly. ! flu, flue.

flip verb
  flips
  flipping
  flipped

flippancy

flippant adjective
  flippantly

flipper noun
  flippers

flirt verb
  flirts
  flirting
  flirted

flirtation

flit verb
  flits
  flitting
  flitted

float verb
  floats
  floating
  floated

float noun
  floats

flock verb
  flocks
  flocking
  flocked

flock noun
  flocks

flog verb
  flogs
  flogging
  flogged

flood verb
  floods
  flooding
  flooded

flood noun
  floods

floodlight noun
  floodlights

floodlit

floor noun
  floors

floor verb
  floors
  flooring
  floored

floorboard noun
  floorboards

flop verb
  flops
  flopping
  flopped

flop noun
  flops

floppy adjective
  floppier
  floppiest

floppy disk noun
  floppy disks

flora

floral

florist noun
  florists

floss

flounder verb
  flounders
  floundering
  floundered

★ **flour**

flourish verb
  flourishes
  flourishing
  flourished

floury adjective
  flourier
  flouriest

flow verb
  flows
  flowing
  flowed

flow noun
  flows

☆ **flower** noun
  flowers

flower verb
  flowers
  flowering
  flowered

flowerpot noun
  flowerpots

flowery

flown

○ **flu**

fluctuate verb
  fluctuates
  fluctuating
  fluctuated

fluctuation

✽ **flue** noun
  flues

fluency

fluent adjective
  fluently

fluff

fluffy adjective
  fluffier
  fluffiest

fluid noun
  fluids

fluke noun
  flukes

flung see **fling**

fluorescent

fluoridation

fluoride

flurry noun
  flurries

flush verb
  flushes
  flushing
  flushed

. . . .

★ **Flour** is powder used in making bread. ! **flower.**
☆ A **flower** is a part of a plant. ! **flour.**
○ **Flu** is an illness. ! **flew, flue.**
✽ A **flue** is a pipe for smoke and fumes. ! **flew, flu.**

flush noun
flushes

flush adjective

flustered

flute noun
flutes

flutter verb
flutters
fluttering
fluttered

flutter noun
flutters

fly verb
flies
flying
flew
flown

fly noun
flies

flyleaf noun
flyleaves

flyover noun
flyovers

flywheel noun
flywheels

foal noun
foals

foam noun

foam verb
foams
foaming
foamed

foamy adjective
foamier
foamiest

focal

focus verb
focuses
focusing
focused

focus noun
focuses or foci

fodder

foe noun
foes

foetus noun use fetus

fog noun
fogs

★ **foggy** adjective
foggier
foggiest

foghorn noun
foghorns

☆ **fogy** noun
fogies

foil verb
foils
foiling
foiled

foil noun
foils

fold verb
folds
folding
folded

fold noun
folds

folder noun
folders

foliage

folk

folklore

follow verb
follows
following
followed

follower noun
followers

fond adjective
fonder
fondest
fondly

fondness

font noun
fonts

food noun
foods

fool noun
fools

fool verb
fools
fooling
fooled

foolhardiness

foolhardy
adjective
foolhardier
foolhardiest

foolish adjective
foolishly

foolishness

foolproof

✪ **foot** noun
feet

football noun
footballs

footballer noun
footballers

foothill noun
foothills

foothold noun
footholds

footing

footlights

footnote noun
footnotes

footpath noun
footpaths

footprint noun
footprints

footstep noun
footsteps

· ·

★ **Foggy** means 'covered in fog'. ! **fogy**.
☆ A **fogy** is someone with old-fashioned ideas. ! **foggy**.
✪ The plural is **foot** in e.g. *a six-foot pole*.

★ **for** *preposition* and *conjunction*

forbid *verb*
forbids
forbidding
forbade
forbidden

force *verb*
forces
forcing
forced

force *noun*
forces

forceful *adjective*
forcefully

forceps *plural noun*

forcible *adjective*
forcibly

ford *verb*
fords
fording
forded

ford *noun*
fords

☆ **fore** *adjective* and *noun*

forecast *verb*
forecasts
forecasting
forecast
forecasted

forecast *noun*
forecasts

forecourt *noun*
forecourts

forefathers *plural noun*

forefinger *noun*
forefingers

○ **foregone** *adjective*

foreground *noun*
foregrounds

forehead *noun*
foreheads

foreign

foreigner *noun*
foreigners

foreman *noun*
foremen

foremost

forename *noun*
forenames

foresee *verb*
foresees
foreseeing
foresaw
foreseen

foreseeable

foresight

forest *noun*
forests

forester *noun*
foresters

forestry

foretell *verb*
foretells
foretelling
foretold

＊ **forever** *adverb*

forfeit *verb*
forfeits
forfeiting
forfeited

forfeit *noun*
forfeits

forgave see **forgive**

forge *verb*
forges
forging
forged

forge *noun*
forges

forgery *noun*
forgeries

forget *verb*
forgets
forgetting
forgot
forgotten

forgetful

forgetfulness

forget-me-not *noun*
forget-me-nots

forgive *verb*
forgives
forgiving
forgave
forgiven

forgiveness

fork *noun*
forks

fork *verb*
forks
forking
forked

fork-lift truck *noun*
fork-lift trucks

forlorn

form *verb*
forms
forming
formed

form *noun*
forms

formal *adjective*
formally

formality *noun*
formalities

format *noun*
formats

formation *noun*
formations

· ·

★ You use **for** in phrases like *a present for you*. ! **fore**.
☆ You use **fore** in phrases like *come to the fore*. ! **for**.
○ You can use **foregone** in *a foregone conclusion*.
＊ You use **forever** in e.g. *They are forever complaining*. You can also use **for ever** in e.g. *The rain seemed to go on for ever*.

former adjective
- formerly

formidable adjective
formidably

formula noun
formulas or
formulae

formulate verb
formulates
formulating
formulated

forsake verb
forsakes
forsaking
forsook
forsaken

fort noun
forts

★ **forth**

fortieth

fortification noun
fortifications

fortify verb
fortifies
fortifying
fortified

fortnight noun
fortnights

fortnightly

fortress noun
fortresses

fortunate adjective
fortunately

fortune noun
fortunes

fortune-teller noun
fortune-tellers

forty noun
forties

forward adjective
and adverb

forward noun
forwards

forwards adverb

fossil noun
fossils

fossilized

foster verb
fosters
fostering
fostered

foster child noun
foster children

foster parent noun
foster parents

fought see fight

☆ **foul** adjective
fouler
foulest
foully

◐ **foul** verb
fouls
fouling
fouled

✳ **foul** noun
fouls

foulness

found verb
founds
founding
founded

found see find

foundation noun
foundations

founder noun
founders

founder verb
founders
foundering
foundered

foundry noun
foundries

fountain noun
fountains

four noun
fours

fourteen noun
fourteens

fourteenth

✳ **fourth**

fourthly

✳ **fowl** noun
fowl or fowls

fox noun
foxes

fox verb
foxes
foxing
foxed

foxglove noun
foxgloves

foxy adjective
foxier
foxiest

foyer noun
foyers

fraction noun
fractions

fractionally

fracture verb
fractures
fracturing
fractured

fracture noun
fractures

fragile adjective
fragilely

fragility

fragment noun
fragments

fragmentary

fragmentation

- -

★ You use **forth** in e.g. *to go forth*. ! **fourth**.
☆ **Foul** means 'dirty' or 'disgusting'. ! **fowl**.
◐ To **foul** is to break a rule in a game. ! **fowl**.
✳ A **foul** is breaking a rule in a game. ! **fowl**.
✳ You use **fourth** in e.g. *for the fourth time*. ! **forth**.
✳ A **fowl** is a kind of bird. ! **foul**.

fragrance noun
fragrances
fragrant
frail adjective
frailer
frailest
frailly
frailty noun
frailties
frame verb
frames
framing
framed
frame noun
frames
framework noun
frameworks
★ **franc** noun
francs
franchise noun
franchises
☆ **frank** adjective
franker
frankest
frankly
○ **frank** verb
franks
franking
franked
frankness
frantic adjective
frantically
fraud noun
frauds
fraudulent adjective
fraudulently
fraught
frayed
freak noun
freaks

freakish
freckle noun
freckles
freckled
free adjective
freer
freest
freely
free verb
frees
freeing
freed
freedom noun
freedoms
freehand adjective
freewheel verb
freewheels
freewheeling
freewheeled
✳ **freeze** verb
freezes
freezing
froze
frozen
freezer noun
freezers
freight
freighter noun
freighters
frenzied
frenzy noun
frenzies
frequency noun
frequencies
frequent adjective
frequently
frequent verb
frequents
frequenting
frequented

fresh adjective
fresher
freshest
freshly
freshness
freshen verb
freshens
freshening
freshened
freshwater
fret verb
frets
fretting
fretted
fretful adjective
fretfully
fretsaw noun
fretsaws
fretwork
friar noun
friars
friary noun
friaries
friction
Friday noun
Fridays
fridge noun
fridges
friend noun
friends
friendless
friendliness
friendly adjective
friendlier
friendliest
friendship noun
friendships
✴ **frieze** noun
friezes
frigate noun
frigates

. . . .

★ A **franc** is a French unit of money. ! **frank**.
☆ **Frank** means 'speaking honestly'. ! **franc**.
○ To **frank** is to mark a letter with a postmark. ! **franc**.
✳ To **freeze** is to be very cold. ! **frieze**.
✴ A **frieze** is a strip of designs along a wall. ! **freeze**.

fr - fu   Try also words beginning with ph-

fright noun
frights

frighten verb
frightens
frightening
frightened

frightful adjective
frightfully

frill noun
frills

frilled

frilly adjective
frillier
frilliest

fringe noun
fringes

fringed

frisk verb
frisks
frisking
frisked

friskiness

frisky adjective
friskier
friskiest
friskily

fritter verb
fritters
frittering
frittered

fritter noun
fritters

frivolous adjective
frivolously

frivolity noun
frivolities

frizzy adjective
frizzier
frizziest

★ **fro**

frock noun
frocks

frog noun
frogs

frogman noun
frogmen

frolic noun
frolics

frolicsome

frolic verb
frolics
frolicking
frolicked

front noun
fronts

frontier noun
frontiers

frost
noun
frosts

frost verb
frosts
frosting
frosted

frostbite

frostbitten

frosty adjective
frostier
frostiest

froth noun

froth verb
froths
frothing
frothed

frothy adjective
frothier
frothiest

froth verb
froths
frothing
frothed

frown verb
frowns
frowning
frowned

frown noun
frowns

froze see **freeze**

frozen see **freeze**

frugal adjective
frugally

frugality

fruit noun
fruit or fruits

fruitful adjective
fruitfully

fruitless adjective
fruitlessly

fruity adjective
fruitier
fruitiest

frustrate verb
frustrates
frustrating
frustrated

frustration noun
frustrations

fry verb
fries
frying
fried

fudge

fuel noun
fuels

fuel verb
fuels
fuelling
fuelled

fug noun
fugs

fuggy adjective
fuggier
fuggiest

★ You use **fro** in *to and fro*.

fugitive noun
  fugitives

-ful
-ful makes nouns for amounts, e.g. **handful, spoonful**. The plural of these words ends in -fuls, e.g. **handfuls**. -ful also makes adjectives, e.g. **graceful**, and when the adjective ends in -y following a consonant, you change the y to i, e.g. **beauty - beautiful**.

fulcrum noun
  fulcra or fulcrums

fulfil verb
  fulfils
  fulfilling
  fulfilled

fulfilment

full adjective
  fully

fullness

fumble verb
  fumbles
  fumbling
  fumbled

fume verb
  fumes
  fuming
  fumed

fumes plural noun

fun

function verb
  functions
  functioning
  functioned

function noun
  functions

functional adjective
  functionally

fund noun
  funds

fundamental adjective
  fundamentally

funeral noun
  funerals

fungus noun
  fungi

funk verb
  funks
  funking
  funked

funnel noun
  funnels

funny adjective
  funnier
  funniest
  funnily

★ **fur** noun
  furs

furious adjective
  furiously

furl verb
  furls
  furling
  furled

furlong noun
  furlongs

furnace noun
  furnaces

furnish verb
  furnishes
  furnishing
  furnished

furniture

furrow noun
  furrows

furry adjective
  furrier
  furriest

☆ **further** adjective

◐ **further** verb
  furthers
  furthering
  furthered

furthermore

✳ **furthest**

furtive adjective
  furtively

fury noun
  furies

fuse verb
  fuses
  fusing
  fused

fuse noun
  fuses

fuselage noun
  fuselages

fusion noun
  fusions

fuss verb
  fusses
  fussing
  fussed

fuss noun
  fusses

fussiness

fussy adjective
  fussier
  fussiest
  fussily

futile adjective
  futilely

futility

futon noun
  futons

★ **Fur** is the hair of animals. ! **fir**.
☆ You use **further** in e.g. *We need further information.* See **farther**.
◐ To **further** something is to make it progress.
✳ You use **furthest** in e.g. *Who has read the furthest?* See **farthest**.

future
fuzz
fuzziness noun
fuzzy adjective
  fuzzier
  fuzziest
  fuzzily

Gg

gabardine noun
  gabardines
gabble verb
  gabbles
  gabbling
  gabbled
gable noun
  gables
gabled
gadget noun
  gadgets
Gaelic
gag verb
  gags
  gagging
  gagged
gag noun
  gags
gaiety
gaily
gain verb
  gains
  gaining
  gained
gain noun
  gains
gala noun
  galas

galactic
galaxy noun
  galaxies
gale noun
  gales
gallant adjective
  gallantly
gallantry
★ **galleon** noun
  galleons
gallery noun
  galleries
galley noun
  galleys
☆ **gallon** noun
  gallons
gallop verb
  gallops
  galloping
  galloped
gallop noun
  gallops
gallows
galore
galvanize verb
  galvanizes
  galvanizing
  galvanized
gamble verb
  gambles
  gambling
  gambled
gamble noun
  gambles
gambler noun
  gamblers
game noun
  games
gamekeeper noun
  gamekeepers
gammon

gander noun
  ganders
gang noun
  gangs
gang verb
  gangs
  ganging
  ganged
gangplank noun
  gangplanks
gangster noun
  gangsters
gangway noun
  gangways
gaol noun
  use jail
gaoler noun
  use jailer
gap noun
  gaps
gape verb
  gapes
  gaping
  gaped
garage noun
  garages
garbage
garden noun
  gardens
gardener noun
  gardeners
gardening
gargle verb
  gargles
  gargling
  gargled
gargoyle noun
  gargoyles
garland noun
  garlands
garlic

- -

★ A galleon is a type of ship. **!** **gallon**.
☆ A gallon is a measurement of liquid. **!** **galleon**.

garment noun
  garments
garnish verb
  garnishes
  garnishing
  garnished
garrison noun
  garrisons
garter noun
  garters
gas noun
  gases
gas verb
  gasses
  gassing
  gassed
gaseous
gash noun
  gashes
gasket noun
  gaskets
gasoline
gasometer noun
  gasometers
gasp verb
  gasps
  gasping
  gasped
gasp noun
  gasps
gastric
gate noun
  gates
★ **gateau** noun
  gateaux
gateway noun
  gateways
gather verb
  gathers
  gathering
  gathered

gathering noun
  gatherings
gaudy adjective
  gaudier
  gaudiest
gauge verb
  gauges
  gauging
  gauged
gauge noun
  gauges
gaunt
gauntlet noun
  gauntlets
gauze
gave see **give**
gay adjective
  gayer
  gayest
gaze verb
  gazes
  gazing
  gazed
gaze noun
  gazes
gazetteer noun
  gazetteers
gear noun
  gears
geese see **goose**
Geiger counter noun
  Geiger counters
gel noun
  gels
gelatine
gelding noun
  geldings
gem noun
  gems

gender noun
  genders
gene noun
  genes
genealogy noun
  genealogies
general adjective
  generally
general noun
  generals
generalization noun
  generalizations
generalize verb
  generalizes
  generalizing
  generalized
generate verb
  generates
  generating
  generated
generation noun
  generations
generator noun
  generators
generosity
generous adjective
  generously
genetic adjective
  genetically
genetics plural noun
genial adjective
  genially
genie noun
  genies
genitals plural noun
genius noun
  geniuses
gent noun
  gents

★ **Gateau** is a French word used in English. It means 'a rich cream cake'.

gentle *adjective*
gentler
gentlest
gently
gentleman *noun*
gentlemen
gentlemanly
gentleness
genuine *adjective*
genuinely
genus *noun*
genera

geo-
geo- means 'earth',
e.g. geography (= the
study of the earth).

geographer
geographical *adjective*
geographically
geography
geological *adjective*
geologically
geologist
geology
geometric *adjective*
geometrically
geometrical *adjective*
geometrically
geometry
geranium *noun*
geraniums
gerbil *noun*
gerbils
germ *noun*
germs
germinate *verb*
germinates
germinating

germinated
germination
gesticulate *verb*
gesticulates
gesticulating
gesticulated
gesture *noun*
gestures
get *verb*
gets
getting
got
getaway *noun*
getaways
geyser *noun*
geysers
ghastly *adjective*
ghastlier
ghastliest
ghetto *noun*
ghettos
ghost *noun*
ghosts
ghostly *adjective*
ghostlier
ghostliest
ghoulish *adjective*
ghoulishly
giant *noun*
giants
giddiness
giddy *adjective*
giddier
giddiest
giddily
gift *noun*
gifts
gifted
gigantic *adjective*
gigantically

giggle *verb*
giggles
giggling
giggled
giggle *noun*
giggles
★ **gild** *verb*
gilds
gilding
gilded
gills *plural noun*
gimmick *noun*
gimmicks
gin
ginger
gingerbread
gingerly
gingery
gipsy *noun* use gypsy
giraffe *noun*
giraffes
girder *noun*
girders
girdle *noun*
girdles
girl *noun*
girls
girlfriend *noun*
girlfriends
girlhood
girlish
☆ **giro** *noun*
giros
girth *noun*
girths
gist
give *verb*
gives
giving
gave
given

★ To **gild** something is to cover it with gold. ! **guild**.
☆ A **giro** is a system of paying money. ! **gyro**.

given see give
giver noun
  givers
glacial
glacier noun
  glaciers
glad adjective
  gladder
  gladdest
  gladly
gladden verb
  gladdens
  gladdening
  gladdened
gladiator noun
  gladiators
gladness
glamorize verb
  glamorizes
  glamorizing
  glamorized
glamorous adjective
  glamorously
glamour
glance verb
  glances
  glancing
  glanced
glance noun
  glances
gland noun
  glands
glandular
glare verb
  glares
  glaring
  glared
glare noun
  glares
glass noun
  glasses

glassful noun
  glassfuls
glassy adjective
  glassier
  glassiest
glaze verb
  glazes
  glazing
  glazed
glaze noun
  glazes
glazier noun
  glaziers
gleam noun
  gleams
gleam verb
  gleams
  gleaming
  gleamed
glee
gleeful adjective
  gleefully
glen noun
  glens
glide verb
  glides
  gliding
  glided
glider noun
  gliders
glimmer verb
  glimmers
  glimmering
  glimmered
glimmer noun
  glimmers
glimpse verb
  glimpses
  glimpsing
  glimpsed

glimpse noun
  glimpses
glint verb
  glints
  glinting
  glinted
glint noun
  glints
glisten verb
  glistens
  glistening
  glistened
glitter verb
  glitters
  glittering
  glittered
gloat verb
  gloats
  gloating
  gloated
global adjective
  globally
globe noun
  globes
gloom
gloominess
gloomy adjective
  gloomier
  gloomiest
  gloomily
glorification
glorify verb
  glorifies
  glorifying
  glorified
glorious adjective
  gloriously
glory noun
  glories
gloss noun
  glosses

glossary noun
glossaries

glossy adjective
glossier
glossiest

glove noun
gloves

glow verb
glows
glowing
glowed

glow noun
glows

glower verb
glowers
glowering
glowered

glow-worm noun
glow-worms

glucose

glue noun
glues

glue verb
glues
gluing
glued

gluey adjective
gluier
gluiest

glum adjective
glummer
glummest
glumly

glutton noun
gluttons

gluttonous

gluttony

★ **gnarled**

★ **gnash** verb
gnashes
gnashing
gnashed

★ **gnat** noun
gnats

★ **gnaw** verb
gnaws
gnawing
gnawed

★ **gnome** noun
gnomes

go verb
goes
going
went
gone

go noun
goes

goal noun
goals

goalie noun
goalies

goalkeeper noun
goalkeepers

goalpost noun
goalposts

goat noun
goats

gobble verb
gobbles
gobbling
gobbled

gobbledegook

goblet noun
goblets

goblin noun
goblins

☆ **God**

◉ **god** noun
gods

godchild noun
godchildren

goddess noun
goddesses

godparent noun
godparents

goggles plural noun

gold

golden

goldfinch noun
goldfinches

goldfish noun
goldfish

golf

golfer noun
golfers

golfing

gondola noun
gondolas

gondolier noun
gondoliers

gone see go

gong noun
gongs

good adjective
better
best

goodbye interjection

Good Friday

good-looking

good-natured

goodness

goods plural noun

goodwill

gooey adjective
gooier
gooiest

goose noun
geese

gooseberry noun
gooseberries

★ In these words beginning with gn- the 'g' is silent.
☆ You use a capital G when you mean the Christian, Jewish, and Muslim creator.
◉ You use a small g when you mean any male divine being.

gore verb
gores
goring
gored

gorge noun
gorges

gorgeous adjective
gorgeously

★ **gorilla** noun
gorillas

gorse

gory adjective
gorier
goriest

gosling noun
goslings

gospel noun
gospels

gossip verb
gossips
gossiping
gossiped

gossip noun
gossips

got see get

gouge verb
gouges
gouging
gouged

gourd noun
gourds

govern verb
governs
governing
governed

government noun
governments

governor noun
governors

gown noun
gowns

grab verb
grabs
grabbing
grabbed

grace noun
graces

graceful adjective
gracefully

gracefulness

gracious adjective
graciously

grade noun
grades

grade verb
grades
grading
graded

gradient noun
gradients

gradual adjective
gradually

graduate noun
graduates

graduate verb
graduates
graduating
graduated

graduation

graffiti plural noun

grain noun
grains

grainy adjective
grainier
grainiest

gram noun
grams

grammar noun
grammars

grammatical
adjective
grammatically

gramophone noun
gramophones

grand adjective
grander
grandest
grandly

grandad noun
grandads

grandchild noun
grandchildren

grandeur

grandfather noun
grandfathers

grandma noun
grandmas

grandmother noun
grandmothers

grandpa noun
grandpas

grandparent noun
grandparents

grandstand noun
grandstands

granite

granny noun
grannies

grant verb
grants
granting
granted

grant noun
grants

granulated

grape noun
grapes

grapefruit noun
grapefruit

grapevine noun
grapevines

graph noun
graphs

★ A **gorilla** is a large ape. **! guerrilla.**

graphic *adjective*
  graphically
graphics *plural noun*
graphite

> **-graphy**
> *-graphy* makes words
> for subjects of study,
> e.g. **geography** (= the
> study of the earth). A
> **bibliography** is a list
> of books on a subject,
> and the plural is
> **bibliographies**.

grapple *verb*
  grapples
  grappling
  grappled
grasp *verb*
  grasps
  grasping
  grasped
grasp *noun*
  grasps
grass *noun*
  grasses
grasshopper *noun*
  grasshoppers
grassy *adjective*
  grassier
  grassiest
★ **grate** *verb*
  grates
  grating
  grated
☆ **grate** *noun*
  grates
grateful *adjective*
  gratefully
grating *noun*
  gratings

gratitude
grave *noun*
  graves
grave *adjective*
  graver
  gravest
  gravely
gravel
gravelled
gravestone *noun*
  gravestones
graveyard *noun*
  graveyards
gravitation
gravitational
gravity
gravy
graze *verb*
  grazes
  grazing
  grazed
graze *noun*
  grazes
grease
greasy *adjective*
  greasier
  greasiest
great *adjective*
  greater
  greatest
  greatly
greatness
greed
greediness
greedy *adjective*
  greedier
  greediest
  greedily

green *adjective* and *noun*
  greener
  greenest
greenery
greengage *noun*
  greengages
greengrocer *noun*
  greengrocers
greengrocery *noun*
  greengroceries
greenhouse *noun*
  greenhouses
greens *plural noun*
greet *verb*
  greets
  greeting
  greeted
greeting *noun*
  greetings
grenade *noun*
  grenades
grew see **grow**
grey *adjective* and *noun*
  greyer
  greyest
greyhound *noun*
  greyhounds
grid *noun*
  grids
grief
grievance *noun*
  grievances
grieve *verb*
  grieves
  grieving
  grieved
◐ **grievous** *adjective*
  grievously

★ To grate something is to shred it. **!** great.
☆ A grate is a fireplace. **!** great.
◐ Note that this word does not end *-ious*.

grill *verb*
grills
grilling
grilled

grill *noun*
grills

grim *adjective*
grimmer
grimmest
grimly

grimace *noun*
grimaces

grime

grimness

grimy *adjective*
grimier
grimiest

grin *noun*
grins

grin *verb*
grins
grinning
grinned

grind *verb*
grinds
grinding
ground

grinder *noun*
grinders

grindstone *noun*
grindstones

grip *verb*
grips
gripping
gripped

grip *noun*
grips

★ **grisly** *adjective*
grislier
grisliest

gristle

gristly *adjective*
gristlier
gristliest

grit *verb*
grits
gritting
gritted

grit *noun*

gritty *adjective*
grittlier
grittliest

☆ **grizzly** *adjective*

groan *verb*
groans
groaning
groaned

groan *noun*
groans

grocer *noun*
grocers

grocery *noun*
groceries

groggy *adjective*
groggier
groggiest

groin *noun*
groins

groom *verb*
grooms
grooming
groomed

groom *noun*
grooms

groove *noun*
grooves

grope *verb*
gropes
groping
groped

gross *adjective*
grosser
grossest

grossly

gross *noun*
gross

grossness

○ **grotesque** *adjective*
grotesquely

grotty *adjective*
grottier
grottiest

ground *noun*
grounds

ground see **grind**
grounded

grounds *plural noun*

groundsheet *noun*
groundsheets

groundsman *noun*
groundsmen

group *noun*
groups

group *verb*
groups
grouping
grouped

grouse *verb*
grouses
grousing
groused

grouse *noun*
grouse

grove *noun*
groves

grovel *verb*
grovels
grovelling
grovelled

grow *verb*
grows
growing
grew
grown

· ·

★ **Grisly** means 'revolting' or 'horrible'. **! grizzly.**
☆ You use **grizzly** in *grizzly bear*. **! grisly.**
○ **Grotesque** means 'strange' and 'ugly'. It sounds like 'grotesk'.

grower noun
  growers
growl verb
  growls
  growling
  growled
growl noun
  growls
grown-up noun
  grown-ups
growth noun
  growths
grub noun
  grubs
grubby adjective
  grubbier
  grubbiest
grudge verb
  grudges
  grudging
  grudged
grudge noun
  grudges
grudgingly
gruelling
gruesome
gruff adjective
  gruffer
  gruffest
  gruffly
grumble verb
  grumbles
  grumbling
  grumbled
grumbler noun
  grumblers
grumpiness
grumpy adjective
  grumpier
  grumpiest
  grumpily

grunt verb
  grunts
  grunting
  grunted
grunt noun
  grunts
guarantee noun
  guarantees
guarantee verb
  guarantees
  guaranteeing
  guaranteed
guard verb
  guards
  guarding
  guarded
guard noun
  guards
guardian noun
  guardians
guardianship
★ **guerrilla** noun
  guerrillas
guess verb
  guesses
  guessing
  guessed
guess noun
  guesses
guesswork
guest noun
  guests
guidance
guide verb
  guides
  guiding
  guided
guide noun
  guides
guidelines plural
  noun

☆ **guild** noun
  guilds
guillotine noun
  guillotines
guilt
guilty adjective
  guiltier
  guiltiest
guinea noun
  guineas
guinea pig noun
  guinea pigs
guitar noun
  guitars
guitarist
gulf noun
  gulfs
gull noun
  gulls
gullet noun
  gullets
gullible
gully noun
  gullies
gulp verb
  gulps
  gulping
  gulped
gulp noun
  gulps
gum noun
  gums
gum verb
  gums
  gumming
  gummed
gummy adjective
  gummier
  gummiest
gun noun
  guns

★ A **guerrilla** is a member of a small army. ! **gorilla**.
☆ A **guild** is an organization of people. ! **gild**.

gun verb
 guns
 gunning
 gunned

gunboat noun
 gunboats

gunfire

gunman noun
 gunmen

gunner noun
 gunners

gunnery

gunpowder

gunshot noun
 gunshots

★ **gurdwara** noun
 gurdwaras

gurgle verb
 gurgles
 gurgling
 gurgled

guru noun
 gurus

☆ **Guru Granth Sahib**

gush verb
 gushes
 gushing
 gushed

gust noun
 gusts

gusty adjective
 gustier
 gustiest

gut noun
 guts

gut verb
 guts
 gutting
 gutted

gutter noun
 gutters

guy noun
 guys

guzzle verb
 guzzles
 guzzling
 guzzled

gym noun
 gyms

gymkhana noun
 gymkhanas

gymnasium noun
 gymnasiums

gymnast noun
 gymnasts

gymnastics plural noun

gypsy noun
 gypsies

✪ **gyro** noun
 gyros

gyroscope noun
 gyroscopes

Hh

habit noun
 habits

habitat noun
 habitats

habitual adjective
 habitually

hack verb
 hacks
 hacking
 hacked

hacker noun
 hackers

hacksaw noun
 hacksaws

had see **has**

haddock noun
 haddock

hadn't verb

hag noun
 hags

haggard

haggis noun
 haggises

haggle verb
 haggles
 haggling
 haggled

✳ **haiku** noun
 haiku

hail verb
 hails
 hailing
 hailed

hail

hailstone noun
 hailstones

✱ **hair** noun
 hairs

hairbrush noun
 hairbrushes

haircut noun
 haircuts

hairdresser noun
 hairdressers

hairpin noun
 hairpins

hair-raising

hairstyle noun
 hairstyles

★ A Sikh place of worship.
☆ The holy book of Sikhs.
✪ A **gyro** is type of compass. ! **giro**.
✳ A Japanese poem.
✱ **Hair** is the covering on the head. ! **hare**.

hairy adjective
hairier
hairiest

hake noun
hake

halal

half adjective and noun
halves

half-baked

half-hearted adjective
half-heartedly

half-life noun
half-lives

half-mast

★ **halfpenny** noun
halfpennies or halfpence

half-term noun
half-terms

half-time noun
half-times

halfway

halibut noun
halibut

☆ **hall** noun
halls

hallo

◐ **Halloween**

hallucination noun
hallucinations

halo noun
haloes

halt verb
halts
halting
halted

halt noun
halts

halter noun
halters

halting adjective
haltingly

halve verb
halves
halving
halved

halves see half

ham noun
hams

hamburger noun
hamburgers

hammer noun
hammers

hammer verb
hammers
hammering
hammered

hammock noun
hammocks

hamper verb
hampers
hampering
hampered

hamper noun
hampers

hamster noun
hamsters

hand noun
hands

hand verb
hands
handing
handed

handbag noun
handbags

handbook noun
handbooks

handcuffs plural noun

handful noun
handfuls

handicap noun
handicaps

handicapped

handicraft noun
handicrafts

handiwork

handkerchief noun
handkerchiefs

handle noun
handles

handle verb
handles
handling
handled

handlebars plural noun

handrail noun
handrails

handsome adjective
handsomer
handsomest
handsomely

hands-on

handstand noun
handstands

handwriting

handwritten

handy adjective
handier
handiest

handyman noun
handymen

hang verb
hangs
hanging
hung

- -

★ You use **halfpennies** when you mean several coins and **halfpence** for a sum of money.

☆ A **hall** is a large space in a building. ! **haul**.

◐ You will also see this word spelt *Hallowe'en*.

★ **hangar** noun
  hangars

☆ **hanger** noun
  hangers

hang-glider noun
  hang-gliders

hang-gliding

hangman noun
  hangmen

hangover noun
  hangovers

hank noun
  hanks

hanker verb
  hankers
  hankering
  hankered

hanky noun
  hankies

✿ **Hanukkah**

haphazard adjective
  haphazardly

happen verb
  happens
  happening
  happened

happening noun
  happenings

happiness

happy adjective
  happier
  happiest
  happily

happy-go-lucky

✳ **harass** verb
  harasses
  harassing
  harassed

harassment

harbour noun
  harbours

harbour verb
  harbours
  harbouring
  harboured

hard adjective
  harder
  hardest

hard adverb
  harder
  hardest

hardboard

hard-boiled

hard disk noun
  hard disks

harden verb
  hardens
  hardening
  hardened

hardly

hardness

hardship noun
  hardships

hardware

hardwood noun
  hardwoods

hardy adjective
  hardier
  hardiest

✱ **hare** noun
  hares

hark verb
  harks
  harking
  harked

harm verb
  harms
  harming
  harmed

harm noun

harmful adjective
  harmfully

harmless adjective
  harmlessly

harmonic

harmonica noun
  harmonicas

harmonious
  adjective
  harmoniously

harmonization

harmonize verb
  harmonizes
  harmonizing
  harmonized

harmony noun
  harmonies

harness verb
  harnesses
  harnessing
  harnessed

harness noun
  harnesses

harp noun
  harps

harp verb
  harps
  harping
  harped

harpist noun
  harpists

harpoon noun
  harpoons

harpsichord noun
  harpsichords

harrow noun
  harrows

harsh adjective
  harsher
  harshest
  harshly

. . . .

★ A **hangar** is a shed for aircraft. ! **hanger**.
☆ A **hanger** is a thing for hanging clothes on. ! **hangar**.
✿ A Jewish festival.
✳ Note that there is only one r in **harass** and **harassment**.
✱ A **hare** is an animal like a large rabbit. ! **hair**.

harshness
harvest noun
 harvests
harvest verb
 harvests
 harvesting
 harvested
hash noun
 hashes
hasn't verb
hassle noun
 hassles
haste
hasten verb
 hastens
 hastening
 hastened
hastiness
hasty adjective
 hastier
 hastiest
 hastily
hatch verb
 hatches
 hatching
 hatched
hatch noun
 hatches
hatchback noun
 hatchbacks
hatchet noun
 hatchets
hate verb
 hates
 hating
 hated
hate noun
 hates
hateful adjective
 hatefully
hatred

hat trick noun
 hat tricks
haughtiness
haughty adjective
 haughtier
 haughtiest
 haughtily
★ **haul** verb
 hauls
 hauling
 hauled
haul noun
 hauls
haunt verb
 haunts
 haunting
 haunted
have verb
 has
 having
 had
haven noun
 havens
haven't verb
haversack noun
 haversacks
hawk noun
 hawks
hawk verb
 hawks
 hawking
 hawked
hawker noun
 hawkers
hawthorn noun
 hawthorns
hay fever
haymaking
haystack noun
 haystacks

hazard noun
 hazards
hazardous
haze noun
 hazes
hazel noun
 hazels
haziness
hazy adjective
 hazier
 haziest
 hazily
H-bomb noun
 H-bombs
head noun
 heads
head verb
 heads
 heading
 headed
headache noun
 headaches
headdress noun
 headdresses
header noun
 headers
heading noun
 headings
headland noun
 headlands
headlight noun
 headlights
headline noun
 headlines
headlong
headmaster noun
 headmasters
headmistress noun
 headmistresses
head-on
headphones

★ To **haul** is to pull something heavy. ! **hall**.

113

headquarters noun
headquarters
headteacher noun
headteachers
headway
heal verb
heals
healing
healed
healer noun
healers
health
healthiness
healthy adjective
healthier
healthiest
healthily
heap verb
heaps
heaping
heaped
heap noun
heaps
★ **hear** verb
hears
hearing
heard
hearing noun
hearings
hearse noun
hearses
heart noun
hearts
hearth noun
hearths
heartiness
heartless
hearty adjective
heartier
heartiest
heartily

heat verb
heats
heating
heated
heat noun
heats
heater noun
heaters
heath noun
heaths
heathen noun
heathens
heather
heatwave noun
heatwaves
☆ **heave** verb
heaves
heaving
heaved or hove
heaven
heavenly
heaviness
heavy adjective
heavier
heaviest
heavily
heavyweight noun
heavyweights
Hebrew
hectare noun
hectares
hectic adjective
hectically
he'd verb
hedge noun
hedges
hedge verb
hedges
hedging
hedged

hedgehog noun
hedgehogs
hedgerow noun
hedgerows
heed verb
heeds
heeding
heeded
heed noun
heedless
heel noun
heels
heel verb
heels
heeling
heeled
hefty adjective
heftier
heftiest
heifer noun
heifers
height noun
heights
heighten verb
heightens
heightening
heightened
○ **heir** noun
heirs
heiress noun
heiresses
held see **hold**
helicopter noun
helicopters
helium
helix noun
helices
hell
he'll verb
hellish adjective
hellishly

★ You use **hear** in e.g. *I can't hear you.* ! **here**.
☆ You use **hove** in e.g. *the ship hove to.*
○ You do not pronounce the 'h' in **heir** (sounds like *air*).

hello

helm noun
helms

helmsman noun
helmsmen

helmet noun
helmets

helmeted

help verb
helps
helping
helped

help noun
helps

helper noun
helpers

helpful adjective
helpfully

helping noun
helpings

helpless adjective
helplessly

helter-skelter noun
helter-skelters

hem noun
hems

hem verb
hems
hemming
hemmed

hemisphere noun
hemispheres

hemp

hence

henceforth

herald noun
heralds

herald verb
heralds
heralding
heralded

heraldic

heraldry

herb noun
herbs

herbal

herbivore noun
herbivores

herd noun
herds

★ **herd** verb
herds
herding
herded

☆ **here**

hereditary

heredity

heritage noun
heritages

hermit noun
hermits

hermitage

hero noun
heroes

heroic adjective
heroically

○ **heroin** noun

✳ **heroine** noun
heroines

heroism

heron noun
herons

herring noun
herring
herrings

✱ **hers**

herself

he's verb

hesitant adjective
hesitantly

hesitate verb
hesitates
hesitating
hesitated

hesitation

hexagon noun
hexagons

hexagonal

hibernate verb
hibernates
hibernating
hibernated

hibernation

hiccup noun
hiccups

hide verb
hides
hiding
hidden
hid
hidden

hide-and-seek

hideous adjective
hideously

hideout noun
hideouts

hiding noun
hidings

hieroglyphics plural noun

hi-fi noun
hi-fis

higgledy-piggledy

high adjective
higher
highest

highland adjective

highlands plural noun

- -

★ A **herd** is a group of sheep. ! **heard**.
☆ You use **here** in e.g. *come here*. ! **hear**.
○ **Heroin** is a drug. ! **heroine**.
✳ A **heroine** is a woman or girl in a story. ! **heroin**.
✱ You use **hers** in e.g. *the book is hers*. Note that there is no apostrophe in this word.

highlander noun
highlanders
highlight noun
highlights
highlighter noun
highlighters
highly
Highness noun
Highnesses
high-rise
highway noun
highways
highwayman noun
highwaymen
hijack verb
hijacks
hijacking
hijacked
hijacker noun
hijackers
hike verb
hikes
hiking
hiked
hike noun
hikes
hiker noun
hikers
hilarious adjective
hilariously
hilarity
hill noun
hills
hillside noun
hillsides
hilly adjective
hillier
hilliest
hilt noun
hilts
himself

hind adjective
hind noun
hinds
hinder verb
hinders
hindering
hindered
Hindi
hindrance noun
hindrances
Hindu noun
Hindus
hinge noun
hinges
hinge verb
hinges
hinging
hinged
hint noun
hints
hint verb
hints
hinting
hinted
hip noun
hips
hippo noun
hippos
hippopotamus noun
hippopotamuses
hire verb
hires
hiring
hired
hiss verb
hisses
hissing
hissed
histogram noun
histograms

historian noun
historians
historic
historical adjective
historically
history noun
histories
hit verb
hits
hitting
hit
hit noun
hits
hitch verb
hitches
hitching
hitched
hitch noun
hitches
hitch-hike verb
hitch-hikes
hitch-hiking
hitch-hiked
hitch-hiker noun
hitch-hikers
hi-tech
hither
hitherto
hive noun
hives
hoard verb
hoards
hoarding
hoarded
★ **hoard** noun
hoards
hoarder noun
hoarders
hoarding noun
hoardings
hoar frost

★ A **hoard** is a secret store. ! horde.

* **hoarse** adjective
  hoarser
  hoarsest

hoax verb
  hoaxes
  hoaxing
  hoaxed

hoax noun
  hoaxes

hobble verb
  hobbles
  hobbling
  hobbled

hobby noun
  hobbies

hockey

hoe noun
  hoes

hoe verb
  hoes
  hoeing
  hoed

hog noun
  hogs

hog verb
  hogs
  hogging
  hogged

Hogmanay

hoist verb
  hoists
  hoisting
  hoisted

hold verb
  holds
  holding
  held

hold noun
  holds

holdall noun
  holdalls

holder noun
  holders

hold-up noun
  hold-ups

☆ **hole** noun
  holes

○ **holey** adjective

✳ **Holi**

holiday noun
  holidays

holiness

hollow adjective and
  adverb

hollow verb
  hollows
  hollowing
  hollowed

hollow noun
  hollows

holly

holocaust noun
  holocausts

hologram noun
  holograms

holster noun
  holsters

● **holy** adjective
  holier
  holiest

home noun
  homes

home verb
  homes
  homing
  homed

homeless

homely

home-made

homesick

homesickness

homestead noun
  homesteads

homeward adjective

homewards
  adjective and adverb

homework

homing

homosexual
  adjective and noun
  homosexuals

honest adjective
  honestly

honesty

honey noun
  honeys

honeycomb noun
  honeycombs

honeymoon noun
  honeymoons

honeysuckle

honk verb
  honks
  honking
  honked

honk noun
  honks

honour verb
  honours
  honouring
  honoured

honour noun
  honours

honourable adjective
  honourably

hood noun
  hoods

-hood
-hood makes nouns,
e.g. **childhood**. Other
noun suffixes are
-dom, -ment, -ness,
and **-ship.**

---

* A **hoarse** voice is rough or croaking. ! **horse.**
☆ A **hole** is a gap or opening. ! **whole.**
○ **Holey** means 'full of holes'. ! **holy.**
✳ A Hindu festival.
● You use **holy** in e.g. *a holy man.* ! **holey.**

hooded

hoof *noun*
hoofs

hook *noun*
hooks

hook *verb*
hooks
hooking
hooked

hooligan *noun*
hooligans

hoop *noun*
hoops

hoopla

hooray

hoot *verb*
hoots
hooting
hooted

hoot *noun*
hoots

hooter *noun*
hooters

hop *verb*
hops
hopping
hopped

hop *noun*
hops

hope *verb*
hopes
hoping
hoped

hope *noun*
hopes

hopeful *adjective*
hopefully

hopeless *adjective*
hopelessly

hopscotch

★ **horde** *noun*
hordes

horizon *noun*
horizons

horizontal *adjective*
horizontally

hormone *noun*
hormones

horn *noun*
horns

hornet *noun*
hornets

horoscope *noun*
horoscopes

horrible *adjective*
horribly

horrid

horrific *adjective*
horrifically

horrify *verb*
horrifies
horrifying
horrified

horror *noun*
horrors

horse *noun*
horses

horseback

horseman *noun*
horsemen

horsemanship

horsepower *noun*
horsepower

horseshoe *noun*
horseshoes

horsewoman *noun*
horsewomen

horticulture

hose *noun*
hoses

hospitable *adjective*
hospitably

hospital *noun*
hospitals

hospitality

host *noun*
hosts

hostage *noun*
hostages

hostel *noun*
hostels

hostess *noun*
hostesses

hostile

hostility *noun*
hostilities

hot *adjective*
hotter
hottest
hotly

hot *verb*
hots
hotting
hotted

hotel *noun*
hotels

hothouse *noun*
hothouses

hotpot *noun*
hotpots

hound *noun*
hounds

hound *verb*
hounds
hounding
hounded

☆ **hour** *noun*
hours

hourglass *noun*
hourglasses

· ·

★ A **horde** is a large crowd. **! hoard.**
☆ An **hour** is a measure of time. **! our.**

hourly adjective and
  adverb
house noun
  houses
house verb
  houses
  housing
  housed
houseboat noun
  houseboats
household noun
  households
householder noun
  householders
housekeeper noun
  housekeepers
housekeeping
housewife noun
  housewives
housework
housing noun
  housings
hove see heave
hover verb
  hovers
  hovering
  hovered
hovercraft noun
  hovercraft
however
howl verb
  howls
  howling
  howled
howl noun
  howls
howler noun
  howlers
hub noun
  hubs

huddle verb
  huddles
  huddling
  huddled
hue noun
  hues
huff
hug verb
  hugs
  hugging
  hugged
hug noun
  hugs
huge adjective
  huger
  hugest
  hugely
hugeness
hulk noun
  hulks
hulking
hull noun
  hulls
hullabaloo noun
  hullabaloos
hullo
hum verb
  hums
  humming
  hummed
hum noun
  hums
human adjective and
  noun
  humans
humane adjective
  humanely
humanitarian
humanity noun
  humanities

humble adjective
  humbler
  humblest
  humbly
humid
humidity
humiliate verb
  humiliates
  humiliating
  humiliated
humiliation
humility
hummingbird noun
  hummingbirds
humorous adjective
  humorously
humour noun
humour verb
  humours
  humouring
  humoured
hump noun
  humps
hump verb
  humps
  humping
  humped
humpback
humus
hunch verb
  hunches
  hunching
  hunched
hunch noun
  hunches
hunchback noun
  hunchbacks
hunchbacked
hundred noun
  hundreds
hundredth

hundredweight noun
hundredweights

hung see **hang**

hunger

hungry adjective
hungrier
hungriest
hungrily

hunk noun
hunks

hunt verb
hunts
hunting
hunted

hunt noun
hunts

hunter noun
hunters

hurdle noun
hurdles

hurdler noun
hurdlers

hurdling

hurl verb
hurls
hurling
hurled

hurrah or **hurray**

hurricane noun
hurricanes

hurriedly

hurry verb
hurries
hurrying
hurried

hurry noun
hurries

hurt verb
hurts
hurting
hurt

hurt noun

hurtle verb
hurtles
hurtling
hurtled

husband noun
husbands

hush verb
hushes
hushing
hushed

hush noun

husk noun
husks

huskiness

husky adjective
huskier
huskiest
huskily

husky noun
huskies

hustle verb
hustles
hustling
hustled

hutch noun
hutches

hyacinth noun
hyacinths

hybrid noun
hybrids

hydrangea noun
hydrangeas

hydrant noun
hydrants

hydraulic adjective
hydraulically

hydroelectric

hydrofoil noun
hydrofoils

hydrogen

hydrophobia

hyena noun
hyenas

hygiene

hygienic adjective
hygienically

hymn noun
hymns

hyperactive

hypermarket noun
hypermarkets

hyphen noun
hyphens

hyphenated

hypnosis

hypnotism

hypnotist

hypnotize verb
hypnotizes
hypnotizing
hypnotized

hypocrisy

hypocrite noun
hypocrites

hypocritical
adjective
hypocritically

hypodermic

hypotenuse noun
hypotenuses

hypothermia

hypothesis noun
hypotheses

hypothetical
adjective
hypothetically

hysteria

hysterical adjective
hysterically

hysterics plural noun

Ii

-i
Most nouns ending in
-i, e.g. **ski**, **taxi**, have
plurals ending in -is,
e.g. **skis**, **taxis**.

-ible
See the note at -able.

-ic and -ically
Most adjectives
ending in -ic have
adverbs ending in
-ically, e.g. **heroic** -
heroically, **scientific** -
scientifically. An
exception is **public**,
which has an adverb -
publicly.

ice noun
 ices
ice verb
 ices
 icing
 iced
iceberg noun
 icebergs
ice cream noun
 ice creams
icicle noun
 icicles
icing
icon noun
 icons
icy adjective
 icier
 iciest
 icily

I'd verb
idea noun
 ideas
ideal adjective
 ideally
ideal noun
 ideals
identical adjective
 identically
identification
identify verb
 identifies
 identifying
 identified
identity noun
 identities
idiocy noun
 idiocies
idiom noun
 idioms
idiomatic
idiot noun
 idiots
idiotic adjective
 idiotically
★ **idle** adjective
 idler
 idlest
 idly
idle verb
 idles
 idling
 idled
☆ **idol** noun
 idols
idolatry
idolize verb
 idolizes
 idolizing
 idolized

-ie-
See the note at -ei-.

igloo noun
 igloos
igneous
ignite verb
 ignites
 igniting
 ignited
ignition
ignorance
ignorant
ignore verb
 ignores
 ignoring
 ignored
I'll verb
ill
illegal adjective
 illegally
illegible adjective
 illegibly
illegitimate
illiteracy
illiterate
illness noun
 illnesses
illogical adjective
 illogically
illuminate verb
 illuminates
 illuminating
 illuminated
illumination noun
 illuminations
illusion noun
 illusions

. . . .

★ **Idle** means 'lazy'. **! idol**.
☆ An **idol** is someone people admire. **! idle**.

illustrate *verb*
illustrates
illustrating
illustrated

illustration *noun*
illustrations

illustrious

I'm *verb*

image *noun*
images

imagery

imaginable

imaginary

imagination *noun*
imaginations

imaginative
adjective
imaginatively

imagine *verb*
imagines
imagining
imagined

★ **imam** *noun*
imams

imbecile *noun*
imbeciles

imitate *verb*
imitates
imitating
imitated

imitation *noun*
imitations

imitator *noun*
imitators

immature

immaturity

immediate *adjective*
immediately

immense *adjective*
immensely

immensity

immerse *verb*
immerses
immersing
immersed

immersion

immigrant *noun*
immigrants

immigrate *verb*
immigrates
immigrating
immigrated

immigration

immobile

immobility

immobilize *verb*
immobilizes
immobilizing
immobilized

immoral *adjective*
immorally

immorality

immortal

immortality

immune

immunity *noun*
immunities

immunization

immunize *verb*
immunizes
immunizing
immunized

imp *noun*
imps

impish

impact *noun*
impacts

impair *verb*
impairs
impairing
impaired

impale *verb*
impales
impaling
impaled

impartial *adjective*
impartially

impartiality

impassable

impatience

impatient *adjective*
impatiently

impede *verb*
impedes
impeding
impeded

imperative

imperceptible
adjective
imperceptibly

imperfect *adjective*
imperfectly

imperfection *noun*
imperfections

imperial

impersonal *adjective*
impersonally

impersonate *verb*
impersonates
impersonating
impersonated

impersonation
noun
impersonations

impersonator *noun*
impersonators

impertinence

impertinent
adjective
impertinently

. . . .

★ A Muslim religious leader.

implement *verb*
implements
implementing
implemented

implement *noun*
implements

implication *noun*
implications

implore *verb*
implores
imploring
implored

imply *verb*
implies
implying
implied

impolite *adjective*
impolitely

import *verb*
imports
importing
imported

import *noun*
imports

importance

important *adjective*
importantly

importer *noun*
importers

impose *verb*
imposes
imposing
imposed

imposition *noun*
impositions

impossibility

impossible *adjective*
impossibly

impostor *noun*
impostors

impracticable

impractical

impress *verb*
impresses
impressing
impressed

impression *noun*
impressions

impressive *adjective*
impressively

imprison *verb*
imprisons
imprisoning
imprisoned

imprisonment

improbability

improbable *adjective*
improbably

impromptu

improper *adjective*
improperly

impropriety *noun*
improprieties

improve *verb*
improves
improving
improved

improvement *noun*
improvements

improvisation *noun*
improvisations

improvise *verb*
improvises
improvising
improvised

impudence

impudent *adjective*
impudently

impulse *noun*
impulses

impulsive *adjective*
impulsively

impure

impurity *adjective*
impurities

in-
in- makes words with the meaning 'not', e.g. **inedible, infertile.** There is a fixed number of these, and you cannot freely add *in-* as you can with *un-. in-* changes to *il-* or *im-* before certain sounds, e.g. **illogical, impossible.**

inability

inaccessible

inaccuracy *noun*
inaccuracies

inaccurate *adjective*
inaccurately

inaction

inactive

inactivity

inadequacy

inadequate *adjective*
inadequately

inanimate

inappropriate *adjective*
inappropriately

inattention

inattentive

inaudible *adjective*
inaudibly

incapable

incapacity

incendiary

incense *noun*

incense verb
incenses
incensing
incensed
incentive noun
incentives
incessant adjective
incessantly
inch noun
inches
incident noun
incidents
incidental adjective
incidentally
incinerator noun
incinerators
inclination noun
inclinations
incline verb
inclines
inclining
inclined
incline noun
inclines
include verb
includes
including
included
inclusion
inclusive
income noun
incomes
incompatible
incompetence
incompetent
adjective
incompetently
incomplete adjective
incompletely
incomprehensible
adjective
incomprehensibly

incongruity
incongruous
adjective
incongruously
inconsiderate
adjective
inconsiderately
inconsistency noun
inconsistencies
inconsistent
adjective
inconsistently
inconspicuous
adjective
inconspicuously
inconvenience
inconvenient
adjective
inconveniently
incorporate verb
incorporates
incorporating
incorporated
incorporation
incorrect adjective
incorrectly
increase verb
increases
increasing
increased
increase noun
increases
increasingly
incredible adjective
incredibly
incredulity
incredulous
incubate verb
incubates
incubating
incubated

incubation
incubator noun
incubators
indebted
indecency
indecent adjective
indecently
indeed
indefinite adjective
indefinitely
indelible adjective
indelibly
indent verb
indents
indenting
indented
indentation
independence
independent
adjective
independently
index noun
indexes
Indian adjective and
noun
Indians
indicate verb
indicates
indicating
indicated
indication noun
indications
indicative
indicator noun
indicators
indifference
indifferent adjective
indifferently
indigestible
indigestion

indignant *adjective*
indignantly

indignation

indigo

indirect *adjective*
indirectly

indispensable
adjective
indispensably

indistinct *adjective*
indistinctly

indistinguishable

individual *adjective*
individually

individual *noun*
individuals

individuality

indoctrinate *verb*
indoctrinates
indoctrinating
indoctrinated

indoctrination

indoor *adjective*

indoors *adverb*

induce *verb*
induces
inducing
induced

inducement *noun*
inducements

indulge *verb*
indulges
indulging
indulged

indulgence *noun*
indulgences

indulgent

industrial

industrialist *noun*
industrialists

industrialization

industrialize *verb*
industrializes
industrializing
industrialized

industrious *adjective*
industriously

industry *noun*
industries

ineffective *adjective*
ineffectively

ineffectual *adjective*
ineffectually

inefficiency *noun*
inefficiencies

inefficient *adjective*
inefficiently

inequality *noun*
inequalities

inert

inertia

inevitability

inevitable *adjective*
inevitably

inexhaustible

inexpensive *adjective*
inexpensively

inexperience

inexperienced

inexplicable *adjective*
inexplicably

infallibility

infallible *adjective*
infallibly

infamous *adjective*
infamously

infamy

infancy

infant *noun*
infants

infantile

infantry

infect *verb*
infects
infecting
infected

infection *noun*
infections

infectious *adjective*
infectiously

infer *verb*
infers
inferring
inferred

inference *noun*
inferences

inferior *adjective* and
noun
inferiors

inferiority

infernal *adjective*
infernally

inferno *noun*
infernos

infested

infiltrate *verb*
infiltrates
infiltrating
infiltrated

infiltration

infinite *adjective*
infinitely

infinitive *noun*
infinitives

infinity

infirm

infirmary *noun*
infirmaries

infirmity

inflame verb
inflames
inflaming
inflamed

inflammable

inflammation noun
inflammations

inflammatory

inflatable

inflate verb
inflates
inflating
inflated

inflation

inflect verb
inflects
inflecting
inflected

inflection noun
inflections

inflexibility

inflexible adjective
inflexibly

inflict verb
inflicts
inflicting
inflicted

influence verb
influences
influencing
influenced

influence noun
influences

influential adjective
influentially

influenza

inform verb
informs
informing
informed

informal adjective
informally

informality

informant noun
informants

information

informative

informed

informer noun
informers

infrequency

infrequent adjective
infrequently

infuriate verb
infuriates
infuriating
infuriated

-ing
-ing makes present
participles and nouns,
e.g. **hunt - hunting.**
You normally drop an
e at the end, e.g.
change - changing,
smoke - smoking. An
exception is **ageing.**
Words ending in a
consonant following a
single vowel double
the consonant, e.g.
run - running.

ingenious adjective
ingeniously

ingenuity

ingot noun
ingots

ingrained

ingredient noun
ingredients

inhabit verb
inhabits
inhabiting
inhabited

inhabitant noun
inhabitants

inhale verb
inhales
inhaling
inhaled

inhaler noun
inhalers

inherent adjective
inherently

inherit verb
inherits
inheriting
inherited

inheritance

inhibited

inhospitable adjective
inhospitably

inhuman

inhumanity

initial adjective
initially

initial noun
initials

initiate verb
initiates
initiating
initiated

initiation

initiative noun
initiatives

inject verb
injects
injecting
injected

injection noun
injections

injure verb
injures
injuring
injured

injurious *adjective*
injuriously

injury *noun*
injuries

injustice *noun*
injustices

ink *noun*
inks

inkling *noun*
inklings

inky *adjective*
inkier
inkiest

inland

inlet *noun*
inlets

inn *noun*
inns

innkeeper *noun*
innkeepers

inner

innermost

innings *noun*
innings

innocence

innocent *adjective*
innocently

innocuous *adjective*
innocuously

innovation *noun*
innovations

innovative

innovator *noun*
innovators

innumerable

inoculate *verb*
inoculates
inoculating
inoculated

inoculation

input *verb*
inputs
inputting
input

input *noun*
inputs

inquest *noun*
inquests

inquire *verb*
inquires
inquiring
inquired

★ **inquiry** *noun*
inquiries

inquisitive *adjective*
inquisitively

insane *adjective*
insanely

insanitary

insanity

inscribe *verb*
inscribes
inscribing
inscribed

inscription *noun*
inscriptions

insect *noun*
insects

insecticide *noun*
insecticides

insecure *adjective*
insecurely

insecurity

insensitive *adjective*
insensitively

insensitivity

inseparable
adjective
inseparably

insert *verb*
inserts
inserting
inserted

insertion *noun*
insertions

inshore *adjective* and
adverb

inside *noun*
insides

inside *adverb,
adjective, and
preposition*

insight *noun*
insights

insignificance

insignificant
adjective
insignificantly

insincere *adjective*
insincerely

insincerity

insist *verb*
insists
insisting
insisted

insistence

insistent *adjective*
insistently

insolence

insolent *adjective*
insolently

insolubility

insoluble *adjective*
insolubly

insomnia

inspect *verb*
inspects
inspecting
inspected

- -

★ An **inquiry** is an official investigation. ! **enquiry**.

inspection noun
inspections
inspector noun
inspectors
inspiration
inspire verb
inspires
inspiring
inspired
install verb
installs
installing
installed
installation noun
installations
instalment noun
instalments
instance noun
instances
instant adjective
instantly
instant noun
instants
instantaneous
adjective
instantaneously
instead
instep noun
insteps
instinct noun
instincts
instinctive adjective
instinctively
institute verb
institutes
instituting
instituted
institute noun
institutes
institution noun
institutions

instruct verb
instructs
instructing
instructed
instruction noun
instructions
instrument noun
instruments
instrumental
insufficient adjective
insufficiently
insulate verb
insulates
insulating
insulated
insulation
insulin
insult verb
insults
insulting
insulted
insult noun
insults
insurance
insure verb
insures
insuring
insured
intact
intake noun
intakes
integer noun
integers
integral adjective
integrally
integrate verb
integrates
integrating
integrated
integration
integrity

intellect noun
intellects
intellectual adjective
intellectually
intellectual noun
intellectuals
intelligence
intelligent adjective
intelligently
intelligibility
intelligible adjective
intelligibly
intend verb
intends
intending
intended
intense adjective
intensely
intensification
intensify verb
intensifies
intensifying
intensified
intensity noun
intensities
intensive adjective
intensively
intent adjective
intently
intent noun
intents
intention noun
intentions
intentional adjective
intentionally
interact verb
interacts
interacting
interacted
interaction

interactive

intercept *verb*
intercepts
intercepting
intercepted

interception

interchange *noun*
interchanges

interchangeable
adjective
interchangeably

intercom *noun*
intercoms

intercourse

interest *verb*
interests
interesting
interested

interest *noun*
interests

interface *noun*
interfaces

interfere *verb*
interferes
interfering
interfered

interference

interior *noun*
interiors

interjection *noun*
interjections

interlock *verb*
interlocks
interlocking
interlocked

interlude *noun*
interludes

intermediate

interminable
adjective
interminably

intermission *noun*
intermissions

intermittent
adjective
intermittently

intern *verb*
interns
interning
interned

internal *adjective*
internally

international
adjective
internationally

internee

internment

internet

interplanetary

interpret *verb*
interprets
interpreting
interpreted

interpretation *noun*
interpretations

interpreter *noun*
interpreters

interrogate *verb*
interrogates
interrogating
interrogated

interrogation

interrogative

interrogator *noun*
interrogators

interrupt *verb*
interrupts
interrupting
interrupted

interruption *noun*
interruptions

intersect *verb*
intersects
intersecting
intersected

intersection *noun*
intersections

interval *noun*
intervals

intervene *verb*
intervenes
intervening
intervened

intervention *noun*
interventions

interview *noun*
interviews

interview *verb*
interviews
interviewing
interviewed

interviewer *noun*
interviewers

intestinal

intestine

intimacy

intimate *adjective*
intimately

intimate *verb*
intimates
intimating
intimated

intimation *noun*
intimations

intimidate *verb*
intimidates
intimidating
intimidated

intimidation

into *preposition*

intolerable *adjective*
intolerably

intolerance
intolerant *adjective*
  intolerantly
intonation *noun*
  intonations
intoxicate *verb*
  intoxicates
  intoxicating
  intoxicated
intoxication
intransitive
intrepid *adjective*
  intrepidly
intricacy *noun*
  intricacies
intricate *adjective*
  intricately
intrigue *verb*
  intrigues
  intriguing
  intrigued
introduce *verb*
  introduces
  introducing
  introduced
introduction *noun*
  introductions
introductory
intrude *verb*
  intrudes
  intruding
  intruded
intruder *noun*
  intruders
intrusion *noun*
  intrusions
intrusive *adjective*
  intrusively
intuition
intuitive *adjective*
  intuitively

Inuit *noun*
  Inuit *or* Inuits
inundate *verb*
  inundates
  inundating
  inundated
inundation *noun*
  inundations
invade *verb*
  invades
  invading
  invaded
invader *noun*
  invaders
invalid *noun*
  invalids
invalid *adjective*
  invalidly
invaluable
invariable *adjective*
  invariably
invasion *noun*
  invasions
invent *verb*
  invents
  inventing
  invented
invention *noun*
  inventions
inventive *adjective*
  inventively
inventor *noun*
  inventors
inverse *noun* and
  adjective
  inversely
inversion *noun*
  inversions
invert *verb*
  inverts
  inverting
  inverted

invertebrate *noun*
  invertebrates
invest *verb*
  invests
  investing
  invested
investigate *verb*
  investigates
  investigating
  investigated
investigation *noun*
  investigations
investigator *noun*
  investigators
investiture *noun*
  investitures
investment *noun*
  investments
investor *noun*
  investors
invigilate *verb*
  invigilates
  invigilating
  invigilated
invigilation
invigilator *noun*
  invigilators
invigorate *verb*
  invigorates
  invigorating
  invigorated
invincible
invisibility
invisible *adjective*
  invisibly
invitation *noun*
  invitations
invite *verb*
  invites
  inviting
  invited

invoice noun
invoices

involuntary

involve verb
involves
involving
involved

involvement

inward adjective
inwardly

inwards adverb

iodine

ion noun
ions

iris noun
irises

iron noun
irons

iron verb
irons
ironing
ironed

ironic adjective
ironically

ironmonger noun
ironmongers

ironmongery

irony noun
ironies

irrational adjective
irrationally

irregular adjective
irregularly

irregularity noun
irregularities

irrelevance

irrelevant adjective
irrelevantly

irresistible adjective
irresistibly

irresponsible
adjective
irresponsibly

irresponsibility

irreverence

irreverent adjective
irreverently

irrigate verb
irrigates
irrigating
irrigated

irrigation

irritability

irritable adjective
irritably

irritant

irritate verb
irritates
irritating
irritated

irritation noun
irritations

-ish
-ish makes words
meaning 'rather' or
'fairly', e.g. soft -
softish. You normally
drop an e at the end,
e.g. blue - bluish.
Words ending in a
consonant following a
single vowel double
the consonant, e.g.
fat - fattish.

Islam

Islamic

island noun
islands

islander noun
islanders

★ **isle** noun
isles

isn't verb

isobar noun
isobars

isolate verb
isolates
isolating
isolated

isolation

isosceles adjective

isotope noun
isotopes

issue verb
issues
issuing
issued

issue noun
issues

isthmus noun
isthmuses

italics

itch verb
itches
itching
itched

itch noun
itches

itchy adjective
itchier
itchiest

item noun
items

itinerary noun
itineraries

it'll verb

☆ **its**

✪ **it's** verb

itself

★ An isle is a small island. ! aisle.
☆ You use its in e.g. the cat licked its paw. ! it's.
✪ You use it's in it's (= it is) raining and it's (= it has) been raining. ! its.

I've *verb*

ivory *adjective* and
noun
 ivories

ivy

-ize and -ise
You can use *-ize* or
-ise at the end of
many verbs, e.g.
realize or **realise,**
privatize or **privatise.**
This book prefers
-ize, but some words
have to be spelt *-ise,*
e.g. **advertise,**
exercise, supervise.
Check each spelling if
you are not sure.

Jj

jab *verb*
 jabs
 jabbing
 jabbed

jab *noun*
 jabs

jabber *verb*
 jabbers
 jabbering
 jabbered

jack *noun*
 jacks

jack *verb*
 jacks
 jacking
 jacked

jackal *noun*
 jackals

jackass *noun*
 jackasses

jackdaw *noun*
 jackdaws

jacket *noun*
 jackets

jack-in-the-box
 noun
 jack-in-the-boxes

jackknife *verb*
 jackknifes
 jackknifing
 jackknifed

jackpot *noun*
 jackpots

jacuzzi *noun*
 jacuzzis

jade

jaded

jagged

jaguar *noun*
 jaguars

jail *noun*
 jails

jail *verb*
 jails
 jailing
 jailed

jailer *noun*
 jailers

★ **Jain** *noun*
 Jains

jam *noun*
 jams

jam *verb*
 jams
 jamming
 jammed

jamboree *noun*
 jamborees

jammy *adjective*
 jammier
 jammiest

jangle *verb*
 jangles
 jangling
 jangled

January *noun*
 Januaries

jar *noun*
 jars

jar *verb*
 jars
 jarring
 jarred

jaundice

jaunt *noun*
 jaunts

jauntiness

jaunty *adjective*
 jauntier
 jauntiest
 jauntily

javelin *noun*
 javelins

jaw *noun*
 jaws

jay *noun*
 jays

jazz

jazzy *adjective*
 jazzier
 jazziest

jealous *adjective*
 jealously

jealousy

jeans

Jeep *noun*
 Jeeps

. . . .

★ A member of an Indian religion.

jeer verb
jeers
jeering
jeered

jellied

jelly noun
jellies

jellyfish noun
jellyfish

jerk verb
jerks
jerking
jerked

jerk noun
jerks

jerky adjective
jerkier
jerkiest
jerkily

jersey noun
jerseys

jest verb
jests
jesting
jested

jest noun
jests

jester noun
jesters

jet noun
jets

jet verb
jets
jetting
jetted

jet-propelled

jetty noun
jetties

Jew noun
Jews

jewel noun
jewels

jewelled

jeweller noun
jewellers

jewellery

Jewish

jib noun
jibs

jiffy noun
jiffies

jig noun
jigs

jig verb
jigs
jigging
jigged

jigsaw noun
jigsaws

jingle verb
jingles
jingling
jingled

jingle noun
jingles

job noun
jobs

jobcentre noun
jobcentres

jockey noun
jockeys

jodhpurs plural noun

jog verb
jogs
jogging
jogged

jogger noun
joggers

jogtrot noun
jogtrots

join verb
joins
joining
joined

join noun
joins

joiner noun
joiners

joinery

joint noun
joints

joint adjective
jointly

joist noun
joists

jojoba

joke verb
jokes
joking
joked

joke noun
jokes

joker noun
jokers

jollity

jolly adjective
jollier
jolliest

jolly adverb

jolly verb
jollies
jollying
jollied

jolt verb
jolts
jolting
jolted

jolt noun
jolts

jostle verb
jostles
jostling
jostled

jot verb
jots
jotting
jotted

jot noun
jots

jotter noun
jotters

joule noun
joules

journal noun
journals

journalism

journalist noun
journalists

journey noun
journeys

journey verb
journeys
journeying
journeyed

joust verb
jousts
jousting
jousted

jovial adjective
jovially

joviality

joy noun
joys

joyful adjective
joyfully

joyous adjective
joyously

joyride noun
joyrides

joystick noun
joysticks

jubilant adjective
jubilantly

jubilation

jubilee noun
jubilees

Judaism

judge verb
judges
judging
judged

judge noun
judges

judgement noun
judgements

judicial adjective
judicially

judicious adjective
judiciously

judo

jug noun
jugs

juggernaut noun
juggernauts

juggle verb
juggles
juggling
juggled

juggler noun
jugglers

★ **juice** noun
juices

juicy adjective
juicier
juiciest

jukebox noun
jukeboxes

July noun
Julys

jumble verb
jumbles
jumbling
jumbled

jumble noun

jumbo jet noun
jumbo jets

jump verb
jumps
jumping
jumped

jump noun
jumps

jumper noun
jumpers

jumpy adjective
jumpier
jumpiest

junction noun
junctions

June noun
Junes

jungle noun
jungles

jungly adjective
junglier
jungliest

junior adjective and noun
juniors

junk noun
junks

junket noun
junkets

juror noun
jurors

jury noun
juries

just adjective
justly

★ **Juice** is the liquid from fruit. **! deuce.**

just adverb
justice noun
  justices
justifiable adjective
  justifiably
justification
justify verb
  justifies
  justifying
  justified
jut verb
  juts
  jutting
  jutted
juvenile

Kk

kaleidoscope noun
  kaleidoscopes
kangaroo noun
  kangaroos
karaoke
karate
kayak noun
  kayaks
kebab noun
  kebabs
keel noun
  keels
keel verb
  keels
  keeling
  keeled
keen adjective
  keener
  keenest
  keenly

keenness
keep verb
  keeps
  keeping
  kept
keep noun
  keeps
keeper noun
  keepers
keg noun
  kegs
kennel noun
  kennels
kept see **keep**
★ **kerb** noun
  kerbs
kerbstone noun
  kerbstones
☆ **kernel** noun
  kernels
kestrel noun
  kestrels
ketchup
kettle noun
  kettles
kettledrum noun
  kettledrums
◉ **key** noun
  keys
keyboard noun
  keyboards
keyhole noun
  keyholes
keynote noun
  keynotes
khaki
kibbutz noun
  kibbutzim

kick verb
  kicks
  kicking
  kicked
kick noun
  kicks
kick-off noun
  kick-offs
kid noun
  kids
kid verb
  kids
  kidding
  kidded
kidnap verb
  kidnaps
  kidnapping
  kidnapped
kidnapper noun
  kidnappers
kidney noun
  kidneys
kill verb
  kills
  killing
  killed
killer noun
  killers
kiln noun
  kilns
kilo noun
  kilos
kilogram noun
  kilograms
kilometre noun
  kilometres
kilowatt noun
  kilowatts
kilt noun
  kilts
kin

★ A **kerb** is the edge of a pavement. ! **curb.**
☆ **Kernel** is part of a nut. ! **colonel.**
◉ A **key** is a device for opening a lock. ! **quay.**

kind adjective
kinder
kindest
kindly

kind noun
kinds

kindergarten noun
kindergartens

kind-hearted

kindle verb
kindles
kindling
kindled

kindliness

kindling

kindly adjective
kindlier
kindliest

kindness

kinetic

king noun
kings

kingdom noun
kingdoms

kingfisher noun
kingfishers

kingly

kink noun
kinks

kinky adjective
kinkier
kinkiest

kiosk noun
kiosks

kipper noun
kippers

kiss verb
kisses
kissing
kissed

kiss noun
kisses

kit noun
kits

kitchen noun
kitchens

kite noun
kites

kitten noun
kittens

kitty noun
kitties

kiwi noun
kiwis

knack

knapsack noun
knapsacks

knave noun
knaves

★ **knead** verb
kneads
kneading
kneaded

knee noun
knees

kneecap noun
kneecaps

kneel verb
kneels
kneeling
knelt

☆ **knew** see **know**

knickers plural noun

knife noun
knives

knife verb
knifes
knifing
knifed

○ **knight** noun
knights

knight verb
knights
knighting
knighted

knighthood noun
knighthoods

knit verb
knits
knitting
knitted

knives see **knife**

knob noun
knobs

knobbly adjective
knobblier
knobbliest

knock verb
knocks
knocking
knocked

knock noun
knocks

knocker noun
knockers

knockout noun
knockouts

knot noun
knots

knot verb
knots
knotting
knotted

knotty adjective
knottier
knottiest

know verb
knows
knowing
knew
known

★ To **knead** is to work a mixture into a dough. ! **need.**
☆ **Knew** is the past tense of know. ! **new.**
○ A **knight** is a soldier in old times. ! **night.**

know-all noun
  know-alls
know-how
knowing adjective
  knowingly
knowledge
knowledgeable
  adjective
  knowledgeably
knuckle noun
  knuckles
koala noun
  koalas
kookaburra noun
  kookaburras
Koran
kosher
kung fu

Ll

label noun
  labels
label verb
  labels
  labelling
  labelled
laboratory noun
  laboratories
laborious adjective
  laboriously
labour noun
  labours
labourer noun
  labourers
Labrador noun
  Labradors

laburnum noun
  laburnums
labyrinth noun
  labyrinths
lace noun
  laces
lace verb
  laces
  lacing
  laced
lack verb
  lacks
  lacking
  lacked
lack noun
lacquer
lacrosse
lad noun
  lads
ladder noun
  ladders
laden
ladle noun
  ladles
lady noun
  ladies
ladybird noun
  ladybirds
ladylike
ladyship noun
  ladyships
lag verb
  lags
  lagging
  lagged
lager noun
  lagers
lagoon noun
  lagoons
laid see lay

lain see lie
lair noun
  lairs
lake noun
  lakes
lama noun
  lamas
lamb noun
  lambs
lame adjective
  lamer
  lamest
  lamely
lameness
lament verb
  laments
  lamenting
  lamented
lament noun
  laments
lamentation noun
  lamentations
laminated
lamp noun
  lamps
lamp-post noun
  lamp-posts
lampshade noun
  lampshades
lance noun
  lances
lance corporal
  noun
  lance corporals
land noun
  lands
land verb
  lands
  landing
  landed

landing noun
  landings
landlady noun
  landladies
landlord noun
  landlords
landmark noun
  landmarks
landowner noun
  landowners
landscape noun
  landscapes
landslide noun
  landslides
lane noun
  lanes
language noun
  languages
lankiness
lanky adjective
  lankier
  lankiest
lantern noun
  lanterns
lap verb
  laps
  lapping
  lapped
lap noun
  laps
lapel noun
  lapels
lapse verb
  lapses
  lapsing
  lapsed
lapse noun
  lapses
laptop noun
  laptops

lapwing noun
  lapwings
larch noun
  larches
lard
larder noun
  larders
large adjective
  larger
  largest
  largely
largeness
lark noun
  larks
lark verb
  larks
  larking
  larked
larva noun
  larvae
lasagne noun
  lasagnes
laser noun
  lasers
lash verb
  lashes
  lashing
  lashed
lash noun
  lashes
lass noun
  lasses
lasso noun
  lassos
lasso verb
  lassoes
  lassoing
  lassoed
last adjective and
  adverb
  lastly

last verb
  lasts
  lasting
  lasted
last noun
latch noun
  latches
late adjective and
  adverb
  later
  latest
lately
lateness
latent
lateral adjective
  laterally
lathe noun
  lathes
lather noun
  lathers
Latin
latitude noun
  latitudes
latter adjective
  latterly
lattice noun
  lattices
laugh verb
  laughs
  laughing
  laughed
laugh noun
  laughs
laughable adjective
  laughably
laughter
launch verb
  launches
  launching
  launched

launch noun
launches

launder verb
launders
laundering
laundered

launderette noun
launderettes

laundry noun
laundries

laurel noun
laurels

lava

lavatory noun
lavatories

lavender

lavish adjective
lavishly

law noun
laws

lawcourt noun
lawcourts

lawful adjective
lawfully

lawless adjective
lawlessly

lawn noun
lawns

lawnmower noun
lawnmowers

lawsuit noun
lawsuits

lawyer noun
lawyers

lax adjective
laxly

laxative noun
laxatives

lay verb
lays
laying
laid

lay see lie

layabout noun
layabouts

layer noun
layers

layman noun
laymen

layout noun
layouts

laze verb
lazes
lazing
lazed

laziness

lazy adjective
lazier
laziest
lazily

lead verb
leads
leading
led

★ **lead** noun
leads

leader noun
leaders

leadership

leaf noun
leaves

leaflet noun
leaflets

leafy adjective
leafier
leafiest

league noun
leagues

leak verb
leaks
leaking
leaked

☆ **leak** noun
leaks

leakage noun
leakages

leaky adjective
leakier
leakiest

lean verb
leans
leaning
leaned or leant

lean adjective
leaner
leanest

leap verb
leaps
leaping
leapt
leaped

leap noun
leaps

leapfrog

leap year noun
leap years

learn verb
learns
learning
learnt or learned

◐ **learned** adjective

learner noun
learners

lease noun
leases

leash noun
leashes

least adjective and noun

leather noun
leathers

- -

★ A **lead** (pronounced *leed*) is a cord for leading a dog. **Lead** (pronounced *led*) is a metal.

☆ A **leak** is a hole or crack that liquid or gas can get through. ! **leek**.

◐ Pronounced *ler-nid*.

leathery
leave *verb*
  leaves
  leaving
  left
leave *noun*
leaves *see* leaf
lectern *noun*
  lecterns
lecture *verb*
  lectures
  lecturing
  lectured
lecture *noun*
  lectures
lecturer *noun*
  lecturers
led *see* lead
ledge *noun*
  ledges
lee
★ leek *noun*
  leeks
leer *verb*
  leers
  leering
  leered
leeward
left *adjective* and
  noun
left *see* leave
left-handed
leftovers *plural noun*
leg *noun*
  legs
legacy *noun*
  legacies

legal *adjective*
  legally
legality
legalize *verb*
  legalizes
  legalizing
  legalized
legend *noun*
  legends
legendary
legibility
legible *adjective*
  legibly
legion *noun*
  legions
legislate *verb*
  legislates
  legislating
  legislated
legislation
legislator *noun*
  legislators
legitimacy
legitimate *adjective*
  legitimately
leisure
leisurely
lemon *noun*
  lemons
lemonade *noun*
  lemonades
lend *verb*
  lends
  lending
  lent
length *noun*
  lengths

lengthen *verb*
  lengthens
  lengthening
  lengthened
lengthways *adverb*
lengthwise *adverb*
lengthy *adjective*
  lengthier
  lengthiest
  lengthily
lenience
lenient *adjective*
  leniently
lens *noun*
  lenses
☆ Lent
lent *see* lend
lentil *noun*
  lentils
leopard *noun*
  leopards
leotard *noun*
  leotards
leper *noun*
  lepers
leprosy
less
○ lessen *verb*
  lessens
  lessening
  lessened
lesser
✳ lesson *noun*
  lessons
lest *conjunction*
let *verb*
  lets
  letting
  let

· ·

★ A leek is a vegetable. ! leak.
☆ Lent is the Christian time of fasting. ! lent.
○ To lessen something is to make it less. lesson.
✳ A lesson is a period of learning. ! lessen.

-let
-let makes nouns meaning 'a small version of', e.g. **booklet, piglet**. It also makes words for pieces of jewellery, e.g. **anklet** (worn on the ankle), **bracelet** (from a French word *bras* meaning 'arm')

lethal adjective
lethally

let's verb

letter noun
letters

letter box noun
letter boxes

lettering

lettuce noun
lettuces

leukaemia

level verb
levels
levelling
levelled

level adjective and noun
levels

lever noun
levers

leverage

liability noun
liabilities

liable

liar noun
liars

liberal adjective
liberally

liberate verb
liberates
liberating
liberated

liberation

liberty noun
liberties

librarian noun
librarians

librarianship

library noun
libraries

licence noun
licences

license verb
licenses
licensing
licensed

lichen noun
lichens

lick verb
licks
licking
licked

lick noun
licks

lid noun
lids

★ **lie** verb
lies
lying
lay
lain

☆ **lie** verb
lies
lying
lied

lie noun
lies

lieutenant noun
lieutenants

life noun
lives

lifebelt noun
lifebelts

lifeboat noun
lifeboats

life cycle noun
life cycles

lifeguard noun
lifeguards

lifeless adjective
lifelessly

lifelike

lifelong

lifestyle noun
lifestyles

lifetime noun
lifetimes

lift verb
lifts
lifting
lifted

lift noun
lifts

lift-off noun
lift-offs

light adjective
lighter
lightest
lightly

light verb
lights
lighting
lit or lighted

light noun
lights

lighten verb
lightens
lightening
lightened

★ As in *to lie on the bed*.
☆ Meaning 'to say something untrue'.

lighter noun
lighters

lighthouse noun
lighthouses

lighting

lightning

lightweight

like verb
likes
liking
liked

like preposition

likeable

likely adjective
likelier
likeliest

liken verb
likens
likening
likened

likeness noun
likenesses

likewise

liking noun
likings

lilac noun
lilacs

lily noun
lilies

limb noun
limbs

limber verb
limbers
limbering
limbered

lime noun
limes

limelight

limerick noun
limericks

limestone

limit noun
limits

limit verb
limits
limiting
limited

limitation noun
limitations

limited

limitless

limp adjective
limper
limpest
limply

limp verb
limps
limping
limped

limp noun
limps

limpet noun
limpets

line noun
lines

line verb
lines
lining
lined

linen

liner noun
liners

linesman noun
linesmen

-ling
-ling makes words for
small things, e.g.
duckling.

linger verb
lingers
lingering
lingered

lingerie

linguist noun
linguists

linguistic

linguistics

lining noun
linings

link verb
links
linking
linked

link noun
links

lino

linoleum

lint

lion noun
lions

lioness noun
lionesses

lip noun
lips

lip-read verb
lip-reads
lip-reading
lip-read

lipstick noun
lipsticks

liquid adjective and
noun
liquids

liquidizer noun
liquidizers

liquor noun
liquors

liquorice

lisp noun
lisps

lisp verb
lisps
lisping
lisped

list noun
lists

list verb
lists
listing
listed

listen verb
listens
listening
listened

listener noun
listeners

listless adjective
listlessly

lit see light

literacy

literal adjective
literally

literary

literate

literature

litmus

litre noun
litres

litter noun
litters

litter verb
litters
littering
littered

★ **little** adjective and
adverb
less
least

live verb
lives
living
lived

live adjective

livelihood noun
livelihoods

liveliness

lively adjective
livelier
liveliest

liver noun
livers

livery noun
liveries

lives see life

livestock

livid

living noun
livings

lizard noun
lizards

llama noun
llamas

load verb
loads
loading
loaded

load noun
loads

loaf noun
loaves

loaf verb
loafs
loafing
loafed

loafer noun
loafers

loam

loamy adjective
loamier
loamiest

☆ **loan** noun
loans

loan verb
loans
loaning
loaned

◐ **loath** adjective

✳ **loathe** verb
loathes
loathing
loathed

loathsome

loaves see loaf

lob verb
lobs
lobbing
lobbed

lobby noun
lobbies

lobby verb
lobbies
lobbying
lobbied

lobe noun
lobes

lobster noun
lobsters

local adjective
locally

local noun
locals

locality noun
localities

locate verb
locates
locating
located

. . . .

★ You can also use **littler** and **littlest** when you are talking about size.

☆ A **loan** is a thing that is lent to someone. ! **lone**.

◐ **Loath** means 'unwilling'. ! **loathe**.

✳ To **loathe** is to dislike very much. ! **loath**.

location noun
locations

★ **loch** noun
lochs

☆ **lock** noun
locks

lock verb
locks
locking
locked

locker noun
lockers

locket noun
lockets

locomotive noun
locomotives

locust noun
locusts

lodge noun
lodges

lodge verb
lodges
lodging
lodged

lodger noun
lodgers

lodgings plural noun

loft noun
lofts

lofty adjective
loftier
loftiest
loftily

log noun
logs

log verb
logs
logging
logged

logarithm noun
logarithms

logbook noun
logbooks

logic

logical adjective
logically

logo noun
logos

-logy
-logy makes words for
subjects of study, e.g.
archaeology (= the
study of ancient
remains). Most of
these words end in
-ology, but an
important exception
is genealogy. Some
words have plurals,
e.g. **genealogies**.

loiter verb
loiters
loitering
loitered

loiterer noun
loiterers

loll verb
lolls
lolling
lolled

lollipop noun
lollipops

lolly noun
lollies

○ **lone**

loneliness

lonely adjective
lonelier
loneliest

long adjective and
adverb
longer
longest

long verb
longs
longing
longed

longitude noun
longitudes

longitudinal
adjective
longitudinally

loo noun
loos

look verb
looks
looking
looked

look noun
looks

lookout noun
lookouts

loom noun
looms

loom verb
looms
looming
loomed

loop noun
loops

loop verb
loops
looping
looped

loophole noun
loopholes

loose adjective
looser
loosest
loosely

loose verb
looses
loosing
loosed

★ A **loch** is a lake in Scotland. ! **lock**.
☆ A **lock** is a mechanism for keeping something closed. ! **loch**.
○ **Lone** means 'alone'. ! **loan**.

lo - lu

loosen verb
loosens
loosening
loosened
looseness
loot verb
loots
looting
looted
loot noun
looter noun
looters
lopsided
lord noun
lords
lordly
lordship
lorry noun
lorries
lose verb
loses
losing
lost
loser noun
losers
loss noun
losses
lot noun
lots
lotion noun
lotions
lottery noun
lotteries
lotto
loud adjective
louder
loudest
loudly

loudness
loudspeaker noun
loudspeakers
lounge noun
lounges
lounge verb
lounges
lounging
lounged
louse noun
lice
lousy adjective
lousier
lousiest
lousily
lout noun
louts
lovable adjective
lovably
love verb
loves
loving
loved
love noun
loves
loveliness
lovely adjective
lovelier
loveliest
lover noun
lovers
loving adjective
lovingly
low adjective
lower
lowest
low verb
lows
lowing
lowed

lower verb
lowers
lowering
lowered
lowland adjective
lowlands plural
nouns
lowlander noun
lowlanders
lowliness
lowly adjective
lowlier
lowliest
lowness
loyal adjective
loyally
loyalty noun
loyalties
lozenge noun
lozenges
lubricant noun
lubricants
lubricate verb
lubricates
lubricating
lubricated
lubrication
lucid adjective
lucidly
lucidity
luck
lucky adjective
luckier
luckiest
luckily
ludicrous adjective
ludicrously
ludo

lug verb
lugs
lugging
lugged

luggage

lukewarm

lull verb
lulls
lulling
lulled

lull noun
lulls

lullaby noun
lullabies

lumber verb
lumbers
lumbering
lumbered

lumber noun

lumberjack noun
lumberjacks

luminosity

luminous

lump noun
lumps

lump verb
lumps
lumping
lumped

lumpy adjective
lumpier
lumpiest

lunacy noun
lunacies

lunar

lunatic noun
lunatics

lunch noun
lunches

lung noun
lungs

lunge verb
lunges
lunging or lungeing
lunged

lupin noun
lupins

lurch verb
lurches
lurching
lurched

lurch noun
lurches

lure verb
lures
luring
lured

lurk verb
lurks
lurking
lurked

luscious adjective
lusciously

lush adjective
lusher
lushest
lushly

lushness

lust noun
lusts

lustful adjective
lustfully

lustre noun
lustres

lustrous

lute noun
lutes

luxury noun
luxuries

luxurious adjective
luxuriously

Lycra

-ly
-ly makes adverbs from adjectives, e.g. **slow - slowly**. When the adjective ends in -y following a consonant, you change the y to i, e.g. **happy - happily**. -ly is also used to make some adjectives, e.g. **lovely**, and some words that are adjectives and adverbs, e.g. **kindly, hourly**.

lying see **lie**

lynch verb
lynches
lynching
lynched

lyre noun
lyres

lyric noun
lyrics

lyrical adjective
lyrically

lyrics plural noun

Mm

ma noun
mas

mac noun
macs

macabre

macaroni

machine noun
machines

machinery

mackerel *noun*
mackerel

mackintosh *noun*
mackintoshes

mad *adjective*
madder
maddest
madly

madam

madden *verb*
maddens
maddening
maddened

★ **made** see **make**

madman *noun*
madmen

madness

magazine *noun*
magazines

maggot *noun*
maggots

magic *noun* and
adjective

magical *adjective*
magically

magician *noun*
magicians

magistrate *noun*
magistrates

magma

magnesium

magnet *noun*
magnets

magnetism

magnetic *adjective*
magnetically

magnetize *verb*
magnetizes
magnetizing
magnetized

magnificent
adjective
magnificently

magnificence

magnification

magnifier

magnify *verb*
magnifies
magnifying
magnified

magnitude *noun*
magnitudes

magnolia *noun*
magnolias

magpie *noun*
magpies

mahogany

☆ **maid** *noun*
maids

maiden *noun*
maidens

◦ **mail** *noun*

mail *verb*
mails
mailing
mailed

maim *verb*
maims
maiming
maimed

✳ **main** *adjective*
mainly

mainland

mainly

mains *plural noun*

maintain *verb*
maintains
maintaining
maintained

maintenance

maisonette *noun*
maisonettes

maize

majestic *adjective*
majestically

majesty *noun*
majesties

major *adjective*

major *noun*
majors

majority *noun*
majorities

make *verb*
makes
making
made

make *noun*
makes

make-believe

maker *noun*
makers

make-up

maladjusted

malaria

✱ **male** *adjective* and
noun
males

malevolence

malevolent *adjective*
malevolently

malice

malicious *adjective*
maliciously

mallet *noun*
mallets

malnourished

malnutrition

malt

malted

. . . .

★ You use **made** in e.g. *I made a cake*. ! **maid**.
☆ A **maid** is a female servant. ! **made**.
◦ **Mail** is letters and parcels sent by post. ! **male**.
✳ **Main** means 'most important'. ! **mane**.
✱ A **male** is a man or an animal of the same gender as a man. ! **mail**.

mammal noun
mammals

mammoth adjective
and noun
mammoths

man noun
men

man verb
mans
manning
manned

manage verb
manages
managing
managed

manageable

management

manager noun
managers

manageress noun
manageresses

★ **mane** noun
manes

manger noun
mangers

mangle verb
mangles
mangling
mangled

mango noun
mangoes

manhandle verb
manhandles
manhandling
manhandled

manhole noun
manholes

mania noun
manias

maniac noun
maniacs

manic adjective
manically

manifesto noun
manifestos

manipulate verb
manipulates
manipulating
manipulated

manipulation

manipulator

mankind

manliness

manly adjective
manlier
manliest

☆ **manner** noun
manners

manoeuvrable

manoeuvre verb
manoeuvres
manoeuvring
manoeuvred

manoeuvre noun
manoeuvres

man-of-war noun
men-of-war

⊙ **manor** noun
manors

mansion noun
mansions

manslaughter

mantelpiece noun
mantelpieces

mantle noun
mantles

manual adjective
manually

manual noun
manuals

manufacture verb
manufactures
manufacturing
manufactured

manufacture noun

manufacturer noun
manufacturers

manure

manuscript noun
manuscripts

Manx

many adjective and
noun
more
most

Maori noun
Maoris

map noun
maps

map verb
maps
mapping
mapped

maple noun
maples

mar verb
mars
marring
marred

marathon noun
marathons

marauder noun
marauders

marauding

marble noun
marbles

March noun
Marches

. . . .

★ A mane is the long piece of hair on a horse or lion. ! main.
☆ You use manner in e.g. *a friendly manner*. ! manor.
⊙ A manor is a big house in the country. ! manner.

march *verb*
marches
marching
marched

march *noun*
marches

marcher *noun*
marchers

★ **mare** *noun*
mares

margarine

margin *noun*
margins

marginal *adjective*
marginally

marigold *noun*
marigolds

marijuana

marina *noun*
marinas

marine *adjective* and *noun*
marines

mariner *noun*
mariners

marionette *noun*
marionettes

mark *verb*
marks
marking
marked

mark *noun*
marks

market *noun*
markets

market *verb*
markets
marketing
marketed

marksman *noun*
marksmen

marksmanship

marmalade

maroon *verb*
maroons
marooning
marooned

maroon *adjective* and *noun*

marquee *noun*
marquees

marriage *noun*
marriages

marrow *noun*
marrows

marry *verb*
marries
marrying
married

marsh *noun*
marshes

marshal *noun*
marshals

marshmallow *noun*
marshmallows

marshy *adjective*
marshier
marshiest

marsupial *noun*
marsupials

martial

Martian *noun*
Martians

martin *noun*
martins

martyr *noun*
martyrs

martyrdom

marvel *verb*
marvels
marvelling
marvelled

marvel *noun*
marvels

marvellous *adjective*
marvellously

Marxism

Marxist

marzipan

mascot *noun*
mascots

masculine

masculinity

mash *verb*
mashes
mashing
mashed

mash *noun*

mask *noun*
masks

mask *verb*
masks
masking
masked

☆ **Mason** *noun*
Masons

○ **mason** *noun*
masons

masonry

✳ **Mass** *noun*
Masses

mass *noun*
masses

mass *verb*
masses
massing
massed

massacre *verb*
massacres
massacring
massacred

• •

★ A mare is a female horse. ! mayor.
☆ You use a capital M when you mean a member of the Freemasons.
○ Use a small m when you mean someone who builds with stone.
✳ Use a capital M when you mean the Roman Catholic service.

massacre noun
massacres

massage verb
massages
massaging
massaged

massage noun

massive adjective
massively

mast noun
masts

master noun
masters

master verb
masters
mastering
mastered

masterly

mastermind noun
masterminds

masterpiece noun
masterpieces

mastery

★ **mat** noun
mats

matador noun
matadors

match verb
matches
matching
matched

match noun
matches

mate noun
mates

mate verb
mates
mating
mated

material noun
materials

materialistic

maternal adjective
maternally

maternity

mathematical
adjective
mathematically

mathematician
noun
mathematicians

mathematics

maths

matinée noun
matinées

matrimonial

matrimony

matrix noun
matrices

matron noun
matrons

☆ **matt**

matted

matter verb
matters
mattering
mattered

matter noun
matters

matting

mattress noun
mattresses

mature

maturity

mauve

maximum adjective
and noun
maxima or
maximums

May noun
Mays

may verb
might

may

maybe

May Day

✪ **mayday** noun
maydays

mayonnaise

✽ **mayor** noun
mayors

mayoress noun
mayoresses

maypole noun
maypoles

maze noun
mazes

meadow noun
meadows

meagre

meal noun
meals

mean adjective
meaner
meanest
meanly

mean verb
means
meaning
meant

meander verb
meanders
meandering
meandered

meaning noun
meanings

meaningful adjective
meaningfully

meaningless
adjective
meaninglessly

. . . .

★ A **mat** is a covering for a floor. ! matt.
☆ **Matt** means 'not shiny'. ! mat.
✪ An international radio signal.
✽ You use **mayor** in e.g. the Mayor of London. ! mare.

me

means *plural noun*
meantime
meanwhile
measles *plural noun*
measly *adjective*
  measlier
  measliest
measure *verb*
  measures
  measuring
  measured
measure *noun*
  measures
measurement *noun*
  measurements
★ meat *noun*
  meats
meaty *adjective*
  meatier
  meatiest
mechanic *noun*
  mechanics
mechanical
  adjective
  mechanically
mechanics
mechanism *noun*
  mechanisms
medal *noun*
  medals
medallist *noun*
  medallists
meddle *verb*
  meddles
  meddling
  meddled
meddler *noun*
  meddlers
meddlesome

media *plural noun*
median *noun*
  medians
medical *adjective*
  medically
medicine *noun*
  medicines
medicinal
medieval
mediocre
mediocrity
meditate *verb*
  meditates
  meditating
  meditated
meditation
Mediterranean
medium *adjective*
medium *noun*
  media *or* mediums
meek *adjective*
  meeker
  meekest
  meekly
meekness
☆ meet *verb*
  meets
  meeting
  met
meeting *noun*
  meetings
megaphone *noun*
  megaphones
melancholy
mellow *adjective*
  mellower
  mellowest
melodious *adjective*
  melodiously

melodrama *noun*
  melodramas
melodramatic
  adjective
  melodramatically
melody *noun*
  melodies
melodic
melon *noun*
  melons
melt *verb*
  melts
  melting
  melted
member *noun*
  members
membership
Member of
Parliament *noun*
  Members of
Parliament
membrane *noun*
  membranes
memoirs *plural noun*
memorable
  adjective
  memorably
memorial *noun*
  memorials
memorize *verb*
  memorizes
  memorizing
  memorized
memory *noun*
  memories
men *see* man
menace *verb*
  menaces
  menacing
  menaced

★ Meat is the flesh of an animal. ! meet.
☆ People meet when they come together. ! meat.

menace *noun*
menaces

menagerie *noun*
menageries

mend *verb*
mends
mending
mended

mender *noun*
menders

menstrual

menstruation

-ment
-ment makes nouns
from adjectives e.g.
contentment. There
is a fixed number of
these, and you cannot
freely add *-ment* as
you can with *-ness*.
When the adjective
ends in *-y* following a
consonant, you
change the *y* to *i*, e.g.
merry - merriment.

mental *adjective*
mentally

mention *verb*
mentions
mentioning
mentioned

mention *noun*
mentions

menu *noun*
menus

mercenary *adjective*
and *noun*
mercenaries

merchandise

merchant *noun*
merchants

merciful *adjective*
mercifully

merciless *adjective*
mercilessly

mercury

mercy *noun*
mercies

mere *adjective*

mere *noun*
meres

merely *adverb*

merge *verb*
merges
merging
merged

merger *noun*
mergers

meridian *noun*
meridians

meringue *noun*
meringues

merit *noun*
merits

merit *verb*
merits
meriting
merited

mermaid *noun*
mermaids

merriment

merry *adjective*
merrier
merriest
merrily

merry-go-round
noun
merry-go-rounds

mesh *noun*
meshes

mess *noun*
messes

mess *verb*
messes
messing
messed

message *noun*
messages

messenger *noun*
messengers

Messiah

messiness

messy *adjective*
messier
messiest
messily

met see **meet**

★ **metal** *noun*
metals

metallic

metallurgical

metallurgist

metallurgy

metamorphosis
noun
metamorphoses

metaphor *noun*
metaphors

metaphorical
adjective
metaphorically

meteor *noun*
meteors

meteoric

meteorite *noun*
meteorites

meteorological

meteorologist

meteorology

☆ **meter** *noun*
meters

methane

★ **Metal** is a hard substance used to make things. **! mettle.**
☆ A **meter** is a device that shows how much of something has been used. **! metre.**

method noun
methods

methodical adjective
methodically

Methodist noun
Methodists

meths

methylated spirit

meticulous adjective
meticulously

★ **metre** noun
metres

metric adjective

metrical adjective
metrically

metronome noun
metronomes

☆ **mettle**

mew verb
mews
mewing
mewed

miaow verb
miaows
miaowing
miaowed

mice see mouse

micro-
micro- makes words
meaning 'small', e.g.
microwave. When the
word begins with a
vowel you add a
hyphen, e.g.
micro-organism.

microbe noun
microbes

microchip noun
microchips

microcomputer
noun
microcomputers

microfilm noun
microfilms

microphone noun
microphones

microprocessor
noun
microprocessors

microscope noun
microscopes

microscopic
adjective
microscopically

microwave noun
microwaves

microwave verb
microwaves
microwaving
microwaved

○ **mid**

midday

middle noun
middles

Middle Ages

Middle East

midge noun
midges

midget noun
midgets

midland adjective

midnight

midst

midsummer

midway

midwife noun
midwives

midwifery

✳ **might** noun

might see may

mightiness

mighty adjective
mightier
mightiest
mightily

migraine noun
migraines

migrant noun
migrants

migrate verb
migrates
migrating
migrated

migration noun
migrations

migratory

mike noun
mikes

mild adjective
milder
mildest
mildly

mildness

mile noun
miles

mileage noun
mileages

milestone noun
milestones

militancy

militant

militarism

militaristic

military

milk noun

milk verb
milks
milking
milked

- -

★ A metre is a unit of length. ! meter.
☆ As in to be on your mettle. ! metal.
○ You use a hyphen, e.g. mid-August.
✳ **Might** means 'force' or 'strength'. ! mite.

milkman *noun*
milkmen

milky *adjective*
milkier
milkiest

Milky Way

mill *noun*
mills

mill *verb*
mills
milling
milled

millennium *noun*
millenniums

miller *noun*
millers

millet

milligram *noun*
milligrams

millilitre *noun*
millilitres

millimetre *noun*
millimetres

million *noun*
millions

millionth

millionaire *noun*
millionaires

millstone *noun*
millstones

milometer *noun*
milometers

mime *verb*
mimes
miming
mimed

mime *noun*
mimes

mimic *verb*
mimics
mimicking
mimicked

mimic *noun*
mimics

mimicry

minaret *noun*
minarets

mince *verb*
minces
mincing
minced

mince *noun*

mincemeat

mincer *noun*
mincers

mind *noun*
minds

mind *verb*
minds
minding
minded

mindless *adjective*
mindlessly

mine *adjective*

mine *verb*
mines
mining
mined

mine *noun*
mines

minefield *noun*
minefields

miner *noun*
miners

mineral *noun*
minerals

mingle *verb*
mingles
mingling
mingled

mini-
mini- makes words
meaning 'small', e.g.
miniskirt. You do not
normally need a
hyphen.

mingy *adjective*
mingier
mingiest

miniature *adjective*
and *noun*
miniatures

minibus *noun*
minibuses

minim *noun*
minims

minimal *adjective*
minimally

minimize *verb*
minimizes
minimizing
minimized

minimum *adjective*
and *noun*
minima *or* minimums

minister *noun*
ministers

ministry *noun*
ministries

mink *noun*
minks

minnow *noun*
minnows

minor *adjective* and
noun
minors

minority *noun*
minorities

minstrel *noun*
minstrels

mint noun
mints

mint verb
mints
minting
minted

minus preposition

minute adjective
minutely

minute noun
minutes

miracle noun
miracles

miraculous adjective
miraculously

mirage noun
mirages

mirror noun
mirrors

mirth

misbehave verb
misbehaves
misbehaving
misbehaved

misbehaviour

miscarriage noun
miscarriages

miscellaneous

miscellany noun
miscellanies

mischief

mischievous
adjective
mischievously

miser noun
misers

miserable adjective
miserably

miserly

misery noun
miseries

misfire verb
misfires
misfiring
misfired

misfit noun
misfits

misfortune noun
misfortunes

mishap noun
mishaps

misjudge verb
misjudges
misjudging
misjudged

mislay verb
mislays
mislaying
mislaid

mislead verb
misleads
misleading
misled

misprint noun
misprints

miss verb
misses
missing
missed

miss noun
misses

missile noun
missiles

missing

mission noun
missions

missionary noun
missionaries

misspell verb
misspells
misspelling
misspelt or
misspelled

★ **mist** noun
mists

mistake noun
mistakes

mistake verb
mistakes
mistaking
mistook
mistaken

mister

mistiness

mistletoe

mistreat verb
mistreats
mistreating
mistreated

mistreatment

mistress noun
mistresses

mistrust verb
mistrusts
mistrusting
mistrusted

misty adjective
mistier
mistiest
mistily

misunderstand verb
misunderstands
misunderstanding
misunderstood

misunderstanding
noun
misunderstandings

misuse verb
misuses
misusing
misused

misuse noun
misuses

★ **Mist** is damp air that is difficult to see through. **! missed.**

★ **mite** noun
  mites
mitre noun
  mitres
mitten noun
  mittens
mix verb
  mixes
  mixing
  mixed
mixer noun
  mixers
mixture noun
  mixtures
mix-up noun
  mix-ups
moan verb
  moans
  moaning
  moaned
moan noun
  moans
moat noun
  moats
mob noun
  mobs
mob verb
  mobs
  mobbing
  mobbed
mobile adjective and
  noun
  mobiles
mobility
mobilization
mobilize verb
  mobilizes
  mobilizing
  mobilized
moccasin noun
  moccasins
mock adjective

mock verb
  mocks
  mocking
  mocked
mockery noun
  mockeries
mock-up noun
  mock-ups
mode noun
  modes
model noun
  models
model verb
  models
  modelling
  modelled
modem noun
  modems
moderate adjective
  moderately
moderate verb
  moderates
  moderating
  moderated
moderation
modern
modernity
modernization
modernize verb
  modernizes
  modernizing
  modernized
modest adjective
  modestly
modesty
modification noun
  modifications
modify verb
  modifies
  modifying
  modified

module noun
  modules
moist adjective
  moister
  moistest
moisture
moisten verb
  moistens
  moistening
  moistened
molar noun
  molars
mole noun
  moles
molecular
molecule noun
  molecules
molehill noun
  molehills
molest verb
  molests
  molesting
  molested
mollusc noun
  molluscs
molten
moment noun
  moments
momentary
  adjective
  momentarily
momentous
  adjective
  momentously
momentum
monarch noun
  monarchs
monarchy noun
  monarchies

· ·

★ A mite is a tiny insect. ! might.

monastery noun
monasteries

monastic

Monday noun
Mondays

money

mongoose noun
mongooses

mongrel noun
mongrels

monitor verb
monitors
monitoring
monitored

monitor noun
monitors

monk noun
monks

monkey noun
monkeys

monogram noun
monograms

monologue noun
monologues

monopolize verb
monopolizes
monopolizing
monopolized

monopoly noun
monopolies

monorail noun
monorails

monotonous
adjective
monotonously

monotony

monsoon noun
monsoons

monster noun
monsters

monstrosity noun
monstrosities

monstrous adjective
monstrously

month noun
months

monthly adjective
and adverb

monument noun
monuments

monumental
adjective
monumentally

moo verb
moos
mooing
mooed

mood noun
moods

moodiness

moody adjective
moodier
moodiest
moodily

moon noun
moons

moonlight

moonlit

★ **moor** verb
moors
mooring
moored

☆ **moor** noun
moors

moorhen noun
moorhens

mooring noun
moorings

◉ **moose** noun
moose

mop noun
mops

mop verb
mops
mopping
mopped

mope verb
mopes
moping
moped

moped noun
mopeds

moraine noun
moraines

moral adjective
morally

moral noun
morals

morale

morality

morals plural noun

morbid adjective
morbidly

✷ **more** adjective,
adverb, and noun

moreover

Mormon noun
Mormons

morning noun
mornings

moron noun
morons

moronic adjective
moronically

morose adjective
morosely

morphine

morris dance noun
morris dances

Morse code

. . . .

★ To **moor** a boat is to tie it up. ! **more.**
☆ A **moor** is an area of rough land. ! **more.**
◉ A **moose** is an American elk. ! **mouse, mousse.**
✷ You use **more** in e.g. I'd like **more** to eat. ! **moor.**

morsel *noun*
morsels
mortal *adjective*
mortally
mortality
mortar
mortgage *noun*
mortgages
mortuary *noun*
mortuaries
mosaic *noun*
mosaics
mosque *noun*
mosques
mosquito *noun*
mosquitoes
moss *noun*
mosses
mossy *adjective*
mossier
mossiest
most *adjective,*
adverb, and noun
mostly *adverb*
motel *noun*
motels
moth *noun*
moths
mother *noun*
mothers
motherhood
mother-in-law *noun*
mothers-in-law
motherly
motion *noun*
motions
motionless
motivate *verb*
motivates
motivating
motivated

motive *noun*
motives
motor *noun*
motors
motorbike *noun*
motorbikes
motor boat *noun*
motor boats
motor car *noun*
motor cars
motorcycle *noun*
motorcycles
motorcyclist *noun*
motorcyclists
motorist *noun*
motorists
motorway *noun*
motorways
mottled
motto *noun*
mottoes
mould *verb*
moulds
moulding
moulded
mould *noun*
moulds
mouldy *adjective*
mouldier
mouldiest
moult *verb*
moults
moulting
moulted
mound *noun*
mounds
mount *verb*
mounts
mounting
mounted

mount *noun*
mounts
mountain *noun*
mountains
mountaineer *noun*
mountaineers
mountaineering
mountainous
mourn *verb*
mourns
mourning
mourned
mourner *noun*
mourners
mournful *adjective*
mournfully
★ **mouse** *noun*
mice
mousetrap *noun*
mousetraps
☆ **mousse** *noun*
mousses
moustache *noun*
moustaches
mousy *adjective*
mousier
mousiest
mouth *noun*
mouths
mouthful *noun*
mouthfuls
mouthpiece *noun*
mouthpieces
movable
move *verb*
moves
moving
moved
move *noun*
moves

- -

★ A mouse is a small animal. ! moose, mousse.
☆ A mousse is a creamy pudding. ! moose, mouse.

mo - mu

movement noun
movements
movie noun
movies
mow verb
mows
mowing
mowed
mown
mower noun
mowers
much adjective,
adverb, and noun
muck noun
muck verb
mucks
mucking
mucked
mucky adjective
muckier
muckiest
mud
muddle verb
muddles
muddling
muddled
muddle noun
muddles
muddler noun
muddlers
muddy adjective
muddier
muddiest
mudguard noun
mudguards
muesli
★ **muezzin** noun
muezzins
muffle verb
muffles
muffling
muffled

mug noun
mugs
mug verb
mugs
mugging
mugged
mugger noun
muggers
muggy adjective
muggier
muggiest
mule noun
mules

multi-
multi- makes words
with the meaning
'many', e.g.
multicultural. You do
not normally need a
hyphen.

multiple adjective
and noun
multiples
multiplication
multiply verb
multiplies
multiplying
multiplied
multiracial
multitude noun
multitudes
mumble verb
mumbles
mumbling
mumbled
mummify verb
mummifies
mummifying
mummified

mummy noun
mummies
mumps
munch verb
munches
munching
munched
mundane
municipal
mural noun
murals
murder verb
murders
murdering
murdered
murder noun
murders
murderer noun
murderers
murderous adjective
murderously
murky adjective
murkier
murkiest
murmur verb
murmurs
murmuring
murmured
murmur noun
murmurs
☆ **muscle** noun
muscles
muscle verb
muscles
muscling
muscled
muscular
museum noun
museums
mushroom noun
mushrooms

★ A man who calls Muslims to prayer.
☆ A muscle is a part of the body. ! mussel.

mushroom verb
  mushrooms
  mushrooming
  mushroomed
music
musical adjective
  musically
musical noun
  musicals
musician noun
  musicians
musket noun
  muskets
musketeer noun
  musketeers
Muslim noun
  Muslims
muslin
★ **mussel** noun
  mussels
must
mustard
muster verb
  musters
  mustering
  mustered
mustiness
musty adjective
  mustier
  mustiest
mutation noun
  mutations
mute adjective
  mutely
mute noun
  mutes
muted
mutilate verb
  mutilates
  mutilating
  mutilated

mutilation
mutineer noun
  mutineers
mutiny noun
  mutinies
mutinous adjective
  mutinously
mutiny verb
  mutinies
  mutinying
  mutinied
mutter verb
  mutters
  muttering
  muttered
mutton
mutual adjective
  mutually
muzzle verb
  muzzles
  muzzling
  muzzled
muzzle noun
  muzzles
myself
mysterious adjective
  mysteriously
mystery noun
  mysteries
mystification
mystify verb
  mystifies
  mystifying
  mystified
myth noun
  myths
mythical
mythological
  adjective
mythology

Nn

nab verb
  nabs
  nabbing
  nabbed
nag verb
  nags
  nagging
  nagged
nag noun
  nags
nail noun
  nails
nail verb
  nails
  nailing
  nailed
naive adjective
  naively
naivety
naked
nakedness
name noun
  names
name verb
  names
  naming
  named
nameless
namely
nanny noun
  nannies
nap noun
  naps
napkin noun
  napkins

. . . .
★ A mussel is a shellfish. ! **muscle**.

nappy noun
nappies

narcissus noun
narcissi

narcotic noun
narcotics

narrate verb
narrates
narrating
narrated

narration noun
narrations

narrative noun
narratives

narrator noun
narrators

narrow adjective
narrower
narrowest
narrowly

nasal adjective
nasally

nastiness

nasturtium noun
nasturtiums

nasty adjective
nastier
nastiest
nastily

nation noun
nations

national adjective
nationally

nationalism

nationalist

nationality noun
nationalities

nationalization

nationalize verb
nationalizes
nationalizing
nationalized

nationwide adjective

native adjective and
noun
natives

Native American
noun
Native Americans

nativity noun
nativities

natural adjective
naturally

natural noun
naturals

naturalist noun
naturalists

naturalization

naturalize verb
naturalizes
naturalizing
naturalized

nature noun
natures

naughtiness

naughty adjective
naughtier
naughtiest
naughtily

nausea

nautical

★ **naval** adjective

nave noun
naves

☆ **navel** noun
navels

navigable

navigate verb
navigates
navigating
navigated

navigation

navigator noun
navigators

navy noun
navies

Nazi noun
Nazis

Nazism

near adjective and
adverb
nearer
nearest

near preposition

near verb
nears
nearing
neared

nearby

nearly

neat adjective
neater
neatest
neatly

neatness

necessarily

necessary

necessity noun
necessities

neck noun
necks

neckerchief noun
neckerchiefs

necklace noun
necklaces

nectar

nectarine noun
nectarines

need verb
needs
needing
needed

· ·

★ **Naval** means 'to do with a navy'. ! navel.
☆ A **navel** is a small hollow in your stomach. ! naval.

★ **need** noun
needs

needle noun
needles

needless adjective
needlessly

needlework

needy adjective
needier
neediest

negative adjective
negatively

negative noun
negatives

neglect verb
neglects
neglecting
neglected

neglect noun

neglectful adjective
neglectfully

negligence

negligent adjective
negligently

negligible adjective
negligibly

negotiate verb
negotiates
negotiating
negotiated

negotiation noun
negotiations

negotiator noun
negotiators

neigh verb
neighs
neighing
neighed

neigh noun
neighs

neighbour noun
neighbours

neighbouring

neighbourhood
noun
neighbourhoods

neighbourly

neither adjective and
conjunction

neon

nephew noun
nephews

nerve noun
nerves

nerve-racking

nervous adjective
nervously

nervousness

-ness
-ness makes nouns
from adjectives, e.g.
soft - softness. When
the adjective ends in
-y following a
consonant, you
change the y to i, e.g.
lively - liveliness.

nest noun
nests

nest verb
nests
nesting
nested

nestle verb
nestles
nestling
nestled

nestling noun
nestlings

net noun
nets

net adjective

netball

nettle noun
nettles

network noun
networks

neuter adjective

neuter verb
neuters
neutering
neutered

neutral adjective
neutrally

neutrality

neutralize verb
neutralizes
neutralizing
neutralized

neutron noun
neutrons

never

nevertheless
conjunction

☆ **new** adjective
newer
newest
newly

newcomer noun
newcomers

newness

news

newsagent noun
newsagents

newsletter noun
newsletters

newspaper noun
newspapers

. . . .

★ To need is to require something. ! knead.
☆ You use new in e.g She has a new bike. ! knew.

newt *noun*
newts

New Testament

newton *noun*
newtons

next *adjective* and
adverb

next door

nib *noun*
nibs

nibble *verb*
nibbles
nibbling
nibbled

nice *adjective*
nicer
nicest
nicely

niceness

nicety *noun*
niceties

nick *verb*
nicks
nicking
nicked

nick *noun*
nicks

nickel *noun*
nickels

nickname *noun*
nicknames

nicotine

niece *noun*
nieces

★ night *noun*
nights

nightclub *noun*
nightclubs

nightdress *noun*
nightdresses

nightfall

nightingale *noun*
nightingales

nightly

nightmare *noun*
nightmares

nightmarish

nil

nimble *adjective*
nimbler
nimblest
nimbly

nine *noun*
nines

nineteen *noun*
nineteens

nineteenth

ninetieth

ninety *noun*
nineties

ninth *adjective*
ninthly

nip *verb*
nips
nipping
nipped

nip *noun*
nips

nipple *noun*
nipples

nippy *adjective*
nippier
nippiest

nit *noun*
nits

nitrate *noun*
nitrates

nitric acid

nitrogen

nitty-gritty

nitwit *noun*
nitwits

nobility

noble *adjective*
nobler
noblest
nobly

noble *noun*
nobles

nobleman *noun*
noblemen

noblewoman *noun*
noblewomen

nobody *noun*
nobodies

nocturnal *adjective*
nocturnally

nod *verb*
nods
nodding
nodded

noise *noun*
noises

noiseless *adjective*
noiselessly

noisiness

noisy *adjective*
noisier
noisiest
noisily

nomad *noun*
nomads

nomadic

no man's land

nominate *verb*
nominates
nominating
nominated

nomination *noun*
nominations

★ **Night** is the opposite of day. ! **knight**.

-nomy
-nomy makes words for subjects of study, e.g. **astronomy** (= the study of the stars). Most of these words end in -onomy.

★ **none**

non-
non- makes words meaning 'not', e.g. **non-existent**, **non-smoker**. You use a hyphen to make these words. When an un- word has a special meaning, e.g. **unprofessional**, you can use non- to make a word without the special meaning, e.g. **non-professional**.

non-existent

non-fiction

non-flammable

nonsense

nonsensical adjective
nonsensically

non-stop

noodle

noon

no one

noose noun
nooses

normal adjective
normally

normality

north adjective and
adverb

☆ **north** noun

north-east noun and
adjective

northerly adjective
and noun
northerlies

northern

northerner noun
northerners

northward adjective
and adverb

northwards adverb

north-west

nose noun
noses

nose verb
noses
nosing
nosed

nosedive verb
nosedives
nosediving
nosedived

nosedive noun
nosedives

nosiness

nostalgia

nostalgic adjective
nostalgically

nostril noun
nostrils

nosy adjective
nosier
nosiest
nosily

notable adjective
notably

notch noun
notches

note noun
notes

note verb
notes
noting
noted

notebook noun
notebooks

notepaper

nothing

notice verb
notices
noticing
noticed

notice noun
notices

noticeable adjective
noticeably

noticeboard noun
noticeboards

notion noun
notions

notoriety

notorious adjective
notoriously

nougat

nought noun
noughts

noun noun
nouns

nourish verb
nourishes
nourishing
nourished

nourishment

novel adjective

novel noun
novels

novelist noun
novelists

novelty noun
novelties

. . . .

★ You use **none** in e.g. none of us went. ! **nun**.

☆ You use a capital N in **the North**, when you mean a particular region.

November noun
  Novembers

novice noun
  novices

nowadays

nowhere

nozzle noun
  nozzles

nuclear

nucleus noun
  nuclei

nude adjective and
  noun
  nudes

nudge verb
  nudges
  nudging
  nudged

nudist noun
  nudists

nudity

nugget noun
  nuggets

nuisance noun
  nuisances

numb adjective
  numbly

number noun
  numbers

number verb
  numbers
  numbering
  numbered

numbness

numeracy

numeral noun
  numerals

numerate

numerator noun
  numerators

numerical adjective
  numerically

numerous

★ **nun** noun
  nuns

nunnery noun
  nunneries

nurse noun
  nurses

nurse verb
  nurses
  nursing
  nursed

nursery noun
  nurseries

nurture verb
  nurtures
  nurturing
  nurtured

nut noun
  nuts

nutcrackers plural
  noun

nutmeg noun
  nutmegs

nutrient noun
  nutrients

nutrition

nutritional adjective
  nutritionally

nutritious

nutshell noun
  nutshells

nutty adjective
  nuttier
  nuttiest

nuzzle verb
  nuzzles
  nuzzling
  nuzzled

nylon adjective and
  noun
  nylons

nymph noun
  nymphs

Oo

-o
Most nouns ending in
-o, e.g. **hero**, **potato**,
have plurals ending in
-oes, e.g. **heroes**,
potatoes, but a few
end in -os. The most
important are **kilos**,
photos, **pianos**,
radios, **ratios**, **solos**,
videos, **zeros**. Verbs
ending in -o usually
have the forms -oes
and -oed, e.g. **video** -
videoes - **videoed**.

oak noun
  oaks

☆ **oar** noun
  oars

oarsman noun
  oarsmen

oarswoman noun
  oarswomen

oasis noun
  oases

oath noun
  oaths

oatmeal

oats plural noun

★ A nun is a member of a convent. **! none.**
☆ An oar is used for rowing a boat. **! or, ore.**

obedience
obedient *adjective*
  obediently
obey *verb*
  obeys
  obeying
  obeyed
obituary *noun*
  obituaries
object *noun*
  objects
object *verb*
  objects
  objecting
  objected
objection *noun*
  objections
objectionable
objective *adjective*
  objectively
objective *noun*
  objectives
objector *noun*
  objectors
obligation *noun*
  obligations
obligatory
oblige *verb*
  obliges
  obliging
  obliged
oblique *adjective*
  obliquely
oblong *adjective* and
noun
  oblongs
oboe *noun*
  oboes
oboist *noun*
  oboists

obscene *adjective*
  obscenely
obscenity *noun*
  obscenities
obscure *adjective*
  obscurer
  obscurest
  obscurely
obscurity
observance *noun*
  observances
observant *adjective*
  observantly
observation *noun*
  observations
observatory *noun*
  observatories
observe *verb*
  observes
  observing
  observed
observer *noun*
  observers
obsessed
obsession *noun*
  obsessions
obsolete
obstacle *noun*
  obstacles
obstinacy
obstinate *adjective*
  obstinately
obstruct *verb*
  obstructs
  obstructing
  obstructed
obstruction *noun*
  obstructions
obstructive *adjective*
  obstructively

obtain *verb*
  obtains
  obtaining
  obtained
obtainable
obtuse *adjective*
  obtuser
  obtusest
  obtusely
obvious *adjective*
  obviously
occasion *noun*
  occasions
occasional *adjective*
  occasionally
occupant *noun*
  occupants
occupation *noun*
  occupations
occupy *verb*
  occupies
  occupying
  occupied
occur *verb*
  occurs
  occurring
  occurred
occurrence *noun*
  occurrences
ocean *noun*
  oceans
o'clock
octagon *noun*
  octagons
octagonal *adjective*
  octagonally
octave *noun*
  octaves
October *noun*
  Octobers

octopus noun
octopuses

odd adjective
odder
oddest
oddly

oddity noun
oddities

oddments plural noun

oddness

odds plural noun

odour noun
odours

odorous

oesophagus noun
oesophagi or
oesophaguses

★ **of**

☆ **off**

offence noun
offences

offend verb
offends
offending
offended

offender noun
offenders

offensive adjective
offensively

offer verb
offers
offering
offered

offer noun
offers

offhand

office noun
offices

officer noun
officers

official adjective
officially

official noun
officials

officious adjective
officiously

off-licence noun
off-licences

offset verb
offsets
offsetting
offset

offshore adjective
and adverb

offside

offspring noun
offspring

often

ogre noun
ogres

ohm noun
ohms

oil noun
oils

oil verb
oils
oiling
oiled

oilfield noun
oilfields

oilskin noun
oilskins

oil well noun
oil wells

oily adjective
oilier
oiliest

ointment noun
ointments

old adjective
older
oldest

Old Testament

olive noun
olives

Olympic Games plural noun

Olympics plural noun

ombudsman noun
ombudsmen

omelette noun
omelettes

omen noun
omens

ominous adjective
ominously

◒ **omission** noun
omissions

omit verb
omits
omitting
omitted

omnivorous

once

✳ **one** adjective and noun
ones

oneself

one-sided

one-way

ongoing

onion noun
onions

onlooker noun
onlookers

only

onshore adjective
and adverb

★ You use of in e.g. a box of matches. ! off.
☆ You use off in e.g. turn off the light. ! of.
◒ An omission is something left out. ! emission.
✳ You use one in e.g. one more time. ! won.

onto preposition
onward adjective and adverb
onwards adverb
ooze verb
oozes
oozing
oozed
opaque
open adjective
openly
open verb
opens
opening
opened
opener noun
openers
opening noun
openings
opera noun
operas
operate verb
operates
operating
operated
operatic
operation noun
operations
operator noun
operators
opinion noun
opinions
opium
opponent noun
opponents
opportunity noun
opportunities
oppose verb
opposes
opposing
opposed

opposite adjective
opposite noun
opposites
opposition
oppress verb
oppresses
oppressing
oppressed
oppression
oppressive adjective
oppressively
oppressor noun
oppressors
opt verb
opts
opting
opted
optical adjective
optically
optician noun
opticians
optimism
optimist noun
optimists
optimistic adjective
optimistically
option noun
options
optional adjective
optionally
opulence
opulent adjective
opulently
★ **or** conjunction
☆ **oral** adjective
orally
orange adjective and noun
oranges
orangeade noun
orangeades

orang-utan noun
orang-utans
oration noun
orations
orator noun
orators
oratorical
oratorio noun
oratorios
oratory
orbit noun
orbits
orbit verb
orbits
orbiting
orbited
orbital
orchard noun
orchards
orchestra noun
orchestras
orchestral
orchid noun
orchids
ordeal noun
ordeals
order noun
orders
order verb
orders
ordering
ordered
orderliness
orderly
ordinal number noun
ordinal numbers
ordinary adjective
ordinarily
⊙ **ore** noun
ores

· ·

★ You use or in e.g. Do you want a cake or a biscuit? ! oar, ore.
☆ Oral means spoken aloud. ! aural.
⊙ Ore is rock with metal in it. ! oar, or.

organ noun
organs

organic adjective
organically

organism noun
organisms

organist noun
organists

organization noun
organizations

organize verb
organizes
organizing
organized

organizer noun
organizers

oriental

orienteering

origami

origin noun
origins

original adjective
originally

originality

originate verb
originates
originating
originated

origination

originator noun
originators

ornament noun
ornaments

ornamental
adjective
ornamentally

ornamentation

ornithological

ornithologist

ornithology

orphan noun
orphans

orphanage noun
orphanages

orthodox

Orthodox Church

orthodoxy

oscillate verb
oscillates
oscillating
oscillated

oscillation noun
oscillations

ostrich noun
ostriches

other adjective and
noun
others

otherwise

otter noun
otters

ought

ounce noun
ounces

ours

ourselves

outback

outboard motor
noun
outboard motors

outbreak noun
outbreaks

outburst noun
outbursts

outcast noun
outcasts

outcome noun
outcomes

outcry noun
outcries

outdated

outdo verb
outdoes
outdoing
outdid
outdone

outdoor adjective

outdoors adverb

outer

outfit noun
outfits

outgrow verb
outgrows
outgrowing
outgrew
outgrown

outhouse noun
outhouses

outing noun
outings

outlast verb
outlasts
outlasting
outlasted

outlaw noun
outlaws

outlaw verb
outlaws
outlawing
outlawed

outlet noun
outlets

outline noun
outlines

outline verb
outlines
outlining
outlined

outlook noun
outlooks

outlying

outnumber verb
  outnumbers
  outnumbering
  outnumbered
outpatient noun
  outpatients
outpost noun
  outposts
output verb
  outputs
  outputting
  output
output noun
  outputs
outrage noun
  outrages
outrage verb
  outrages
  outraging
  outraged
outrageous adjective
  outrageously
outright
outset
outside adverb and
  preposition
outside noun
  outsides
outsider noun
  outsiders
outskirts plural noun
outspoken
outstanding
  adjective
  outstandingly
outward adjective
  outwardly
outwards adverb
outweigh verb
  outweighs
  outweighing
  outweighed

outwit verb
  outwits
  outwitting
  outwitted
oval adjective and
  noun
  ovals
ovary noun
  ovaries
oven noun
  ovens
over adverb and
  preposition
over noun
  overs

over-
over- makes words
meaning 'too' or 'too
much', e.g. **overactive**
and **overcook**. You do
not need a hyphen,
except in some words
beginning with e, e.g.
over-eager.

overall adjective
overalls plural noun
overarm adjective
overboard
overcast
overcoat noun
  overcoats
overcome verb
  overcomes
  overcoming
  overcame
  overcome
overdo verb
  overdoes
  overdoing
  overdid
  overdone

overdose noun
  overdoses
overdue
overflow verb
  overflows
  overflowing
  overflowed
overgrown
overhang verb
  overhangs
  overhanging
  overhung
overhaul verb
  overhauls
  overhauling
  overhauled
overhead adjective
overheads plural
  noun
overhear verb
  overhears
  overhearing
  overheard
overland adjective
overlap verb
  overlaps
  overlapping
  overlapped
overlook verb
  overlooks
  overlooking
  overlooked
overnight
overpower verb
  overpowers
  overpowering
  overpowered
overrun verb
  overruns
  overrunning
  overran
  overrun

overseas *adjective*
and *adverb*

oversight *noun*
oversights

oversleep *verb*
oversleeps
oversleeping
overslept

overtake *verb*
overtakes
overtaking
overtook
overtaken

overthrow *verb*
overthrows
overthrowing
overthrew
overthrown

overthrow *noun*
overthrows

overtime

overture *noun*
overtures

overturn *verb*
overturns
overturning
overturned

overwhelm *verb*
overwhelms
overwhelming
overwhelmed

overwork *verb*
overworks
overworking
overworked

overwork *noun*

ovum *noun*
ova

owe *verb*
owes
owing
owed

owl *noun*
owls

own *adjective*

own *verb*
owns
owning
owned

owner *noun*
owners

ownership

ox *noun*
oxen

oxidation

oxide *noun*
oxides

oxidize *verb*
oxidizes
oxidizing
oxidized

oxygen

oyster *noun*
oysters

oz. *abbreviation*

ozone

Pp

pa *noun*
pas

pace *noun*
paces

pace *verb*
paces
pacing
paced

pacemaker *noun*
pacemakers

pacification

pacifism

pacifist *noun*
pacifists

pacify *verb*
pacifies
pacifying
pacified

pack *verb*
packs
packing
packed

pack *noun*
packs

package *noun*
packages

packet *noun*
packets

pad *noun*
pads

pad *verb*
pads
padding
padded

padding

paddle *verb*
paddles
paddling
paddled

paddle *noun*
paddles

paddock *noun*
paddocks

paddy *noun*
paddies

padlock *noun*
padlocks

pagan *adjective* and
noun
pagans

page *noun*
pages

pageant *noun*
pageants

pageantry

pagoda *noun*
pagodas

paid *see* pay

★ pail *noun*
pails

☆ pain *noun*
pains

pain *verb*
pains
paining
pained

painful *adjective*
painfully

painkiller *noun*
painkillers

painless *adjective*
painlessly

painstaking

paint *noun*
paints

paint *verb*
paints
painting
painted

paintbox *noun*
paintboxes

paintbrush *noun*
paintbrushes

painter *noun*
painters

painting *noun*
paintings

○ pair *noun*
pairs

pair *verb*
pairs
pairing
paired

pal *noun*
pals

palace *noun*
palaces

palate *noun*
palates

✻ pale *adjective*
paler
palest

paleness

palette *noun*
palettes

paling *noun*
palings

palisade *noun*
palisades

pall *verb*
palls
palling
palled

pallid

pallor

palm *noun*
palms

palm *verb*
palms
palming
palmed

palmistry

Palm Sunday

paltry *adjective*
paltrier
paltriest

pampas *plural noun*

pamper *verb*
pampers
pampering
pampered

pamphlet *noun*
pamphlets

pan *noun*
pans

pancake *noun*
pancakes

panda *noun*
pandas

pandemonium

pander *verb*
panders
pandering
pandered

✳ pane *noun*
panes

panel *noun*
panels

pang *noun*
pangs

panic

panic *verb*
panics
panicking
panicked

panicky

pannier *noun*
panniers

panorama *noun*
panoramas

panoramic *adjective*
panoramically

pansy *noun*
pansies

pant *verb*
pants
panting
panted

. . . .

★ A pail is a bucket. ! pale.
☆ A pain is an unpleasant feeling caused by injury or disease. ! pane.
○ A pair is a set of two. ! pear.
✻ Pale means 'almost white'. ! pail.
✳ A pane is a piece of glass in a window. ! pain.

panther *noun*
panthers

panties *plural noun*

pantomime *noun*
pantomimes

pantry *noun*
pantries

pants *plural noun*

paper *noun*
papers

paper *verb*
papers
papering
papered

paperback *noun*
paperbacks

papier mâché

papyrus *noun*
papyri

parable *noun*
parables

parachute *noun*
parachutes

parachutist

parade *noun*
parades

parade *verb*
parades
parading
paraded

paradise

paradox *noun*
paradoxes

paradoxical
adjective
paradoxically

paraffin

paragraph *noun*
paragraphs

parallel

parallelogram *noun*
parallelograms

paralyse *verb*
paralyses
paralysing
paralysed

paralysis *noun*
paralyses

paralytic *adjective*
paralytically

parapet *noun*
parapets

paraphernalia

paraphrase *verb*
paraphrases
paraphrasing
paraphrased

parasite *noun*
parasites

parasitic *adjective*
parasitically

parasol *noun*
parasols

paratrooper

paratroops *plural
noun*

parcel *noun*
parcels

parched

parchment

pardon *verb*
pardons
pardoning
pardoned

pardon *noun*
pardons

pardonable

parent *noun*
parents

parentage

parental

parenthood

parenthesis *noun*
parentheses

parish *noun*
parishes

parishioner *noun*
parishioners

park *noun*
parks

park *verb*
parks
parking
parked

parka *noun*
parkas

parliament *noun*
parliaments

parliamentary

parody *noun*
parodies

parole

parrot *noun*
parrots

parsley

parsnip *noun*
parsnips

parson *noun*
parsons

parsonage *noun*
parsonages

part *noun*
parts

part *verb*
parts
parting
parted

partial *adjective*
partially

partiality

participant noun
participants

participate verb
participates
participating
participated

participation

participle noun
participles

particle noun
particles

particular adjective
particularly

particulars plural noun

parting noun
partings

partition noun
partitions

partly

partner noun
partners

partnership

partridge noun
partridges

part-time adjective

party noun
parties

pass verb
passes
passing
passed

pass noun
passes

passable

passage noun
passages

passageway noun
passageways

★ **passed** see **pass**

passenger noun
passengers

passer-by noun
passers-by

passion noun
passions

passionate adjective
passionately

passive adjective
passively

Passover

passport noun
passports

password noun
passwords

☆ **past** noun, adjective, and preposition

pasta noun
pastas

paste noun
pastes

paste verb
pastes
pasting
pasted

pastel noun
pastels

pasteurization

pasteurize verb
pasteurizes
pasteurizing
pasteurized

pastille noun
pastilles

pastime noun
pastimes

pastoral

pastry noun
pastries

pasture noun
pastures

pasty noun
pasties

pasty adjective
pastier
pastiest

pat verb
pats
patting
patted

pat noun
pats

patch noun
patches

patch verb
patches
patching
patched

patchwork

patchy adjective
patchier
patchiest

patent adjective
patently

patent verb
patents
patenting
patented

patent noun
patents

paternal adjective
paternally

path noun
paths

pathetic adjective
pathetically

patience

patient adjective
patiently

★ You use passed in e.g. We *passed the house*. **! past.**
☆ You use past in e.g. We *went past the house*. **! passed.**

patient noun
  patients

patio noun
  patios

patriot noun
  patriots

patriotic adjective
  patriotically

patriotism

patrol verb
  patrols
  patrolling
  patrolled

patrol noun
  patrols

patron noun
  patrons

patronage

patronize verb
  patronizes
  patronizing
  patronized

patter verb
  patters
  pattering
  pattered

patter noun
  patters

pattern noun
  patterns

pause verb
  pauses
  pausing
  paused

pause noun
  pauses

pave verb
  paves
  paving
  paved

pavement noun
  pavements

pavilion noun
  pavilions

paw noun
  paws

paw verb
  paws
  pawing
  pawed

pawn noun
  pawns

pawn verb
  pawns
  pawning
  pawned

pawnbroker noun
  pawnbrokers

pay verb
  pays
  paying
  paid

pay noun

payment noun
  payments

pea noun
  peas

★ **peace**

peaceful adjective
  peacefully

peach noun
  peaches

peacock noun
  peacocks

☆ **peak** noun
  peaks

○ **peak** verb
  peaks
  peaking
  peaked

peaked

✴ **peal** verb
  peals
  pealing
  pealed

✴ **peal** noun
  peals

peanut noun
  peanuts

✳ **pear** noun
  pears

pearl noun
  pearls

pearly adjective
  pearlier
  pearliest

peasant noun
  peasants

peasantry

peat

pebble noun
  pebbles

pebbly adjective
  pebblier
  pebbliest

peck verb
  pecks
  pecking
  pecked

peck noun
  pecks

peckish

peculiar adjective
  peculiarly

peculiarity noun
  peculiarities

pedal noun
  pedals

pedal verb
  pedals
  pedalling
  pedalled

. . . .

★ **Peace** is a time when there is no war. ! **piece.**
☆ A **peak** is the top of something. ! **peek.**
○ To **peak** is to reach the highest point. ! **peek.**
✴ To **peal** is to make a ringing sound of bells. ! **peel.**
✴ A **peal** is a ringing of bells. ! **peel.**
✳ A **pear** is a fruit. ! **pair.**

★ **peddle** *verb*
peddles
peddling
peddled

pedestal *noun*
pedestals

pedestrian *noun*
pedestrians

pedestrian *adjective*

pedigree *noun*
pedigrees

pedlar *noun*
pedlars

☆ **peek** *verb*
peeks
peeking
peeked

◎ **peel** *noun*
peels

✲ **peel** *verb*
peels
peeling
peeled

peep *verb*
peeps
peeping
peeped

peep *noun*
peeps

✱ **peer** *verb*
peers
peering
peered

peer *noun*
peers

peerless

peewit *noun*
peewits

peg *noun*
pegs

peg *verb*
pegs
pegging
pegged

Pekinese *noun*
Pekinese

pelican *noun*
pelicans

pellet *noun*
pellets

pelt *verb*
pelts
pelting
pelted

pelt *noun*
pelts

pen *noun*
pens

penalize *verb*
penalizes
penalizing
penalized

penalty *noun*
penalties

pence see **penny**

pencil *noun*
pencils

pencil *verb*
pencils
pencilling
pencilled

pendant *noun*
pendants

pendulum *noun*
pendulums

penetrate *verb*
penetrates
penetrating
penetrated

penetration

penfriend *noun*
penfriends

penguin *noun*
penguins

penicillin

peninsula *noun*
peninsulas

peninsular

penis *noun*
penises

penitence

penitent

penknife *noun*
penknives

pennant *noun*
pennants

penniless

penny *noun*
pennies *or* pence

pension *noun*
pensions

pensioner *noun*
pensioners

pentagon *noun*
pentagons

pentathlon *noun*
pentathlons

peony *noun*
peonies

people *plural noun*

people *noun*
peoples

pepper *noun*
peppers

peppermint *noun*
peppermints

peppery

perceive *verb*
perceives
perceiving
perceived

per cent

· ·

★ To **peddle** is to sell things on the street. ! **pedal.**
☆ To **peek** is to look secretly at something. ! **peak.**
◎ **Peel** is the skin of fruit and vegetables. ! **peal.**
✲ To **peel** something is to take the skin off it. ! **peal.**
✱ To **peer** is to look closely at something. ! **pier.**

percentage noun
  percentages
perceptible adjective
  perceptibly
perception noun
  perceptions
perceptive adjective
  perceptively
perch verb
  perches
  perching
  perched
perch noun
  perch
percolator noun
  percolators
percussion
percussive
perennial adjective
  perennially
perennial noun
  perennials
perfect adjective
  perfectly
perfect verb
  perfects
  perfecting
  perfected
perfection
perforate verb
  perforates
  perforating
  perforated
perforation noun
  perforations
perform verb
  performs
  performing
  performed
performance noun
  performances

performer noun
  performers
perfume noun
  perfumes
perhaps
peril noun
  perils
perilous adjective
  perilously
perimeter noun
  perimeters
period noun
  periods
periodic adjective
  periodically
periodical noun
  periodicals
periscope noun
  periscopes
perish verb
  perishes
  perishing
  perished
perishable
perm noun
  perms
perm verb
  perms
  perming
  permed
permanence
permanent adjective
  permanently
permissible
permission
permissive adjective
  permissively
permissiveness
permit verb
  permits
  permitting
  permitted

permit noun
  permits
perpendicular
perpetual
  adjective
  perpetually
perpetuate verb
  perpetuates
  perpetuating
  perpetuated
perplex verb
  perplexes
  perplexing
  perplexed
perplexity
persecute verb
  persecutes
  persecuting
  persecuted
persecution noun
  persecutions
persecutor noun
  persecutors
perseverance
persevere verb
  perseveres
  persevering
  persevered
persist verb
  persists
  persisting
  persisted
persistence
persistent adjective
  persistently
★ **person** noun
  persons or people
personal adjective
  personally
personality noun
  personalities

★ The normal plural is **people**: *three people came.* **Persons** is formal, e.g. in
  official reports.

personnel *plural noun*

perspective *noun*
perspectives

perspiration

perspire *verb*
perspires
perspiring
perspired

persuade *verb*
persuades
persuading
persuaded

persuasion

persuasive *adjective*
persuasively

perverse *adjective*
perversely

perversion *noun*
perversions

perversity

pervert *verb*
perverts
perverting
perverted

pervert *noun*
perverts

★ **Pesach**

pessimism

pessimist *noun*
pessimists

pessimistic *adjective*
pessimistically

pest *noun*
pests

pester *verb*
pesters
pestering
pestered

pesticide *noun*
pesticides

pestle *noun*
pestles

pet *noun*
pets

petal *noun*
petals

petition *noun*
petitions

petrify *verb*
petrifies
petrifying
petrified

petrochemical *noun*
petrochemicals

petrol

petroleum

petticoat *noun*
petticoats

pettiness

petty *adjective*
pettier
pettiest
pettily

pew *noun*
pews

pewter

pharmacy *noun*
pharmacies

phase *noun*
phases

phase *verb*
phases
phasing
phased

pheasant *noun*
pheasants

phenomenal *adjective*
phenomenally

phenomenon *noun*
phenomena

philatelist *noun*
philatelists

philately

philosopher *noun*
philosophers

philosophical *adjective*
philosophically

philosophy *noun*
philosophies

phobia *noun*
phobias

-phobia
-phobia makes words meaning 'a strong fear or dislike', e.g. **xenophobia** (= a dislike of strangers'). It comes from a Greek word and is only used with other Greek or Latin words.

phoenix *noun*
phoenixes

phone *noun*
phones

phone *verb*
phones
phoning
phoned

-phone
-phone makes words to do with sound, e.g. **telephone, saxophone**. You can sometimes make adjectives by using *-phonic*, e.g. **telephonic**, and nouns by using *-phony*, e.g. **telephony**.

★ The Hebrew name for Passover.

ph - pi

phonecard noun
phonecards

phone-in noun
phone-ins

phosphorescence

phosphorescent

phosphoric

phosphorus

photo noun
photos

photo-
photo- makes words
to do with light, e.g.
photograph,
photocopy. It is also
used in more
technical words such
as **photochemistry** (=
the chemistry of light)
and as a separate
word in **photo** (=
photograph) and
photo finish (= close
finish to a race).

photocopier noun
photocopiers

photocopy noun
photocopies

photocopy verb
photocopies
photocopying
photocopied

photoelectric

photograph noun
photographs

photograph verb
photographs
photographing
photographed

photographer noun
photographers

photographic
adjective
photographically

photography

phrase noun
phrases

phrase verb
phrases
phrasing
phrased

physical adjective
physically

physician noun
physicians

physicist noun
physicists

physics

physiological
adjective
physiologically

physiologist noun
physiologists

physiology

★ **pi**

pianist noun
pianists

piano noun
pianos

piccolo noun
piccolos

pick verb
picks
picking
picked

pick noun
picks

pickaxe noun
pickaxes

picket noun
pickets

picket verb
pickets
picketing
picketed

pickle noun
pickles

pickle verb
pickles
pickling
pickled

pickpocket noun
pickpockets

pick-up noun
pick-ups

picnic noun
picnics

picnic verb
picnics
picnicking
picnicked

picnicker noun
picnickers

pictogram noun
pictograms

pictorial adjective
pictorially

picture noun
pictures

picture verb
pictures
picturing
pictured

picturesque

☆ **pie** noun
pies

○ **piece** noun
pieces

piece verb
pieces
piecing
pieced

. . . .

★ **Pi** is a Greek letter, used in mathematics. ! **pie**.
☆ A **pie** is a food with pastry. ! **pi**.
○ You use **piece** in e.g. *a piece of cake*. ! **peace**.

piecemeal
pie chart noun
  pie charts
★ **pier** noun
  piers
pierce verb
  pierces
  piercing
  pierced
pig noun
  pigs
pigeon noun
  pigeons
pigeon-hole noun
  pigeon-holes
piggy noun
  piggies
piggyback noun
  piggybacks
piglet noun
  piglets
pigment noun
  pigments
pigmy noun
  use pygmy
pigsty noun
  pigsties
pigtail noun
  pigtails
pike noun
  pikes
pilchard noun
  pilchards
pile noun
  piles
pile verb
  piles
  piling
  piled

pilfer verb
  pilfers
  pilfering
  pilfered
pilgrim noun
  pilgrims
pilgrimage noun
  pilgrimages
pill noun
  pills
pillage verb
  pillages
  pillaging
  pillaged
pillar noun
  pillars
pillion noun
  pillions
pillow noun
  pillows
pillowcase noun
  pillowcases
pilot noun
  pilots
pilot verb
  pilots
  piloting
  piloted
pimple noun
  pimples
pimply adjective
  pimplier
  pimpliest
pin noun
  pins
pin verb
  pins
  pinning
  pinned
pinafore noun
  pinafores

pincer noun
  pincers
pinch verb
  pinches
  pinching
  pinched
pinch noun
  pinches
pincushion noun
  pincushions
pine noun
  pines
pine verb
  pines
  pining
  pined
pineapple noun
  pineapples
ping-pong
pink adjective
  pinker
  pinkest
pink noun
  pinks
pint noun
  pints
pioneer noun
  pioneers
pious adjective
  piously
pip noun
  pips
pipe noun
  pipes
pipe verb
  pipes
  piping
  piped
pipeline noun
  pipelines

• •

★ A **pier** is a long building on stilts going into the sea. **! peer.**

piper *noun*
pipers
piracy
pirate *noun*
pirates
★ **pistil** *noun*
pistils
★ **pistol** *noun*
pistols
piston *noun*
pistons
pit *noun*
pits
pit *verb*
pits
pitting
pitted
pitch *noun*
pitches
pitch *verb*
pitches
pitching
pitched
pitch-black
pitcher *noun*
pitchers
pitchfork *noun*
pitchforks
pitfall *noun*
pitfalls
pitiful *adjective*
pitifully
pitiless *adjective*
pitilessly
pity *verb*
pities
pitying
pitied
pity *noun*

pivot *noun*
pivots
pivot *verb*
pivots
pivoting
pivoted
pixie *noun*
pixies
pizza *noun*
pizzas
pizzicato
placard *noun*
placards
☆ **place** *noun*
places
place *verb*
places
placing
placed
placid *adjective*
placidly
plague *noun*
plagues
plague *verb*
plagues
plaguing
plagued
⊙ **plaice** *noun*
plaice
plaid *noun*
plaids
✳ **plain** *adjective*
plainer
plainest
plainly
plain *noun*
plains
plain clothes
plainness

plaintiff *noun*
plaintiffs
plaintive
plaintively
plait *noun*
plaits
plait *verb*
plaits
plaiting
plaited
plan *noun*
plans
plan *verb*
plans
planning
planned
✲ **plane** *noun*
planes
✲ **plane** *verb*
planes
planing
planed
planet *noun*
planets
planetary
plank *noun*
planks
plankton
planner *noun*
planners
plant *noun*
plants
plant *verb*
plants
planting
planted
plantation *noun*
plantations
planter *noun*
planters

· ·

★ A **pistil** is a part of a flower and a **pistol** is a gun.
☆ You use **place** in e.g. *a place in the country*. ! **plaice**.
⊙ A **plaice** is a fish. ! **place**.
✳ **Plain** means 'not pretty or decorated'. ! **plane**.
✲ A **plane** is an aeroplane, a level surface, a tool, or a tree. ! **plain**.
✲ To **plane** wood is to make it smooth with a tool. ! **plain**.

plaque *noun*
plaques
plasma
plaster *noun*
plasters
plaster *verb*
plasters
plastering
plastered
plasterer *noun*
plasterers
plaster of Paris
plastic *adjective* and
noun
plastics
Plasticine
plate *noun*
plates
plate *verb*
plates
plating
plated
plateau *noun*
plateaux
plateful *noun*
platefuls
platform *noun*
platforms
platinum
platoon *noun*
platoons
platypus *noun*
platypuses
play *verb*
plays
playing
played
play *noun*
plays
playback *noun*
playbacks

player *noun*
players
playful *adjective*
playfully
playfulness
playground *noun*
playgrounds
playgroup *noun*
playgroups
playmate *noun*
playmates
play-off *noun*
play-offs
playtime *noun*
playtimes
playwright *noun*
playwrights
plea *noun*
pleas
plead *verb*
pleads
pleading
pleaded
pleasant *adjective*
pleasanter
pleasantest
pleasantly
please *verb*
pleases
pleasing
pleased
pleasurable
adjective
pleasurably
pleasure *noun*
pleasures
pleat *noun*
pleats
pleated

pledge *verb*
pledges
pledging
pledged
pledge *noun*
pledges
plentiful *adjective*
plentifully
plenty
pliable
pliers *plural noun*
plight *noun*
plights
plod *verb*
plods
plodding
plodded
plodder *noun*
plodders
plop *verb*
plops
plopping
plopped
plop *noun*
plops
plot *noun*
plots
plot *verb*
plots
plotting
plotted
plotter *noun*
plotters
plough *noun*
ploughs
plough *verb*
ploughs
ploughing
ploughed
ploughman *noun*
ploughmen

plover noun
plovers

pluck verb
plucks
plucking
plucked

pluck noun

plucky adjective
pluckier
pluckiest
pluckily

plug noun
plugs

plug verb
plugs
plugging
plugged

★ **plum** noun
plums

plumage

☆ **plumb** verb
plumbs
plumbing
plumbed

plumber noun
plumbers

plumbing

plume noun
plumes

plumed

plump adjective
plumper
plumpest

plump verb
plumps
plumping
plumped

plunder verb
plunders
plundering
plundered

plunder noun

plunderer noun
plunderers

plunge verb
plunges
plunging
plunged

plunge noun
plunges

plural adjective and noun
plurals

plus preposition

plus noun
pluses

plutonium

plywood

pneumatic

pneumonia

poach verb
poaches
poaching
poached

poacher noun
poachers

pocket noun
pockets

pocket verb
pockets
pocketing
pocketed

pocketful noun
pocketfuls

pod noun
pods

podgy adjective
podgier
podgiest

poem noun
poems

poet noun
poets

poetic adjective
poetically

poetry

point noun
points

point verb
points
pointing
pointed

point-blank adjective

pointed adjective
pointedly

pointer noun
pointers

pointless adjective
pointlessly

poise noun

poise verb
poises
poising
poised

poison noun
poisons

poison verb
poisons
poisoning
poisoned

poisoner noun
poisoners

poisonous adjective
poisonously

poke verb
pokes
poking
poked

poke noun
pokes

poker noun
pokers

. . . .

★ A plum is a fruit. **! plumb.**
☆ To **plumb** water is to see how deep it is. **! plum.**

polar
Polaroid
★ pole *noun*
  poles
police *plural noun*
policeman *noun*
  policemen
police officer *noun*
  police officers
policewoman *noun*
  policewomen
policy *noun*
  policies
polio
poliomyelitis
polish *verb*
  polishes
  polishing
  polished
polish *noun*
  polishes
polished
polite *adjective*
  politer
  politest
  politely
politeness
political *adjective*
  politically
politician *noun*
  politicians
politics
polka *noun*
  polkas
☆ poll *noun*
  polls
pollen
pollute *verb*
  pollutes
  polluting
  polluted

pollution
polo
polo neck *noun*
  polo necks
poltergeist *noun*
  poltergeists
polygon *noun*
  polygons
polystyrene
polythene
pomp
pomposity
pompous *adjective*
  pompously
pond *noun*
  ponds
ponder *verb*
  ponders
  pondering
  pondered
ponderous *adjective*
  ponderously
pony *noun*
  ponies
ponytail *noun*
  ponytails
pony-trekking
poodle *noun*
  poodles
pool *noun*
  pools
pool *verb*
  pools
  pooling
  pooled
poor *adjective*
  poorer
  poorest
  poorly

poorly *adjective* and
  adverb
pop *verb*
  pops
  popping
  popped
pop *noun*
  pops
popcorn
Pope *noun*
  Popes
poplar *noun*
  poplars
poppadom *noun*
  poppadoms
poppy *noun*
  poppies
popular *adjective*
  popularly
popularity
popularize *verb*
  popularizes
  popularizing
  popularized
populated
population *noun*
  populations
populous
porcelain
porch *noun*
  porches
porcupine *noun*
  porcupines
pore *noun*
  pores
○ pore *verb*
  pores
  poring
  pored
pork

★ A **pole** is a long thin stick. ! **poll.**
☆ A **poll** is a vote in an election. ! **pole.**
○ To **pore** over something is to study it closely. ! **pour.**

pornographic
pornography
porosity
porous
porpoise *noun*
  porpoises
porridge
port *noun*
  ports
portable
portcullis *noun*
  portcullises
porter *noun*
  porters
porthole *noun*
  portholes
portion *noun*
  portions
portliness
portly *adjective*
  portlier
  portliest
portrait *noun*
  portraits
portray *verb*
  portrays
  portraying
  portrayed
portrayal *noun*
  portrayals
pose *verb*
  poses
  posing
  posed
pose *noun*
  poses
poser *noun*
  posers
posh *adjective*
  posher
  poshest

position *noun*
  positions
positive *adjective*
  positively
positive *noun*
  positives
posse *noun*
  posses
possess *verb*
  possesses
  possessing
  possessed
possession *noun*
  possessions
possessive *adjective*
  possessively
possessor *noun*
  possessors
possibility *noun*
  possibilities
possible *adjective*
  possibly
post *verb*
  posts
  posting
  posted
post *noun*
  posts
postage
postal
postbox *noun*
  postboxes
postcard *noun*
  postcards
postcode *noun*
  postcodes
poster *noun*
  posters
postman *noun*
  postmen

postmark *noun*
  postmarks
post-mortem *noun*
  post-mortems
postpone *verb*
  postpones
  postponing
  postponed
postponement *noun*
  postponements
postscript *noun*
  postscripts
posture *noun*
  postures
posy *noun*
  posies
pot *noun*
  pots
pot *verb*
  pots
  potting
  potted
potassium
potato *noun*
  potatoes
potency
potent *adjective*
  potently
potential *adjective*
  potentially
potential *noun*
  potentials
pothole *noun*
  potholes
potholer *noun*
  potholer
potholing
potion *noun*
  potions
potter *noun*
  potters

potter verb
potters
pottering
pottered

pottery noun
potteries

potty adjective
pottier
pottiest
pottily

potty noun
potties

pouch noun
pouches

poultry

pounce verb
pounces
pouncing
pounced

pound noun
pounds

pound verb
pounds
pounding
pounded

★ **pour** verb
pours
pouring
poured

pout verb
pouts
pouting
pouted

poverty

powder noun
powders

powder verb
powders
powdering
powdered

powdery

power noun
powers

powered

powerful adjective
powerfully

powerhouse noun
powerhouses

powerless

practicable

practical adjective
practically

practice noun
practices

practise verb
practises
practising
practised

prairie noun
prairies

praise verb
praises
praising
praised

praise noun
praises

pram noun
prams

prance verb
prances
prancing
pranced

prank noun
pranks

prawn noun
prawns

☆ **pray** verb
prays
praying
prayed

prayer noun
prayers

pre-
pre- makes words
meaning 'before', e.g.
pre-date (= to exist
before something
else), **prefabricated**
(= made in advance).
Many are spelt joined
up, but not all.

preach verb
preaches
preaching
preached

preacher noun
preachers

precarious adjective
precariously

precaution noun
precautions

precede verb
precedes
preceding
preceded

precedence

precedent noun
precedents

precinct noun
precincts

precious adjective
preciously

precipice noun
precipices

précis noun
précis

precise adjective
precisely

precision

predator noun
predators

predatory

. . . .

★ To **pour** a liquid is to tip it from a jug etc. ! **pore**.
☆ To **pray** is to say prayers. ! **prey**.

predecessor noun
predecessors

predict verb
predicts
predicting
predicted

predictable adjective
predictably

prediction noun
predictions

predominance

predominant
adjective
predominantly

predominate verb
predominates
predominating
predominated

preface noun
prefaces

prefect noun
prefects

prefer verb
prefers
preferring
preferred

preferable adjective
preferably

preference noun
preferences

prefix noun
prefixes

pregnancy noun
pregnancies

pregnant

prehistoric

prehistory

prejudice noun
prejudices

prejudiced

preliminary
adjective and noun
preliminaries

prelude noun
preludes

premier noun
premiers

première noun
premières

premises plural noun

premium noun
premiums

Premium Bond noun
Premium Bonds

preoccupation noun
preoccupations

preoccupied

prep

preparation noun
preparations

preparatory

prepare verb
prepares
preparing
prepared

preposition noun
prepositions

prescribe verb
prescribes
prescribing
prescribed

prescription noun
prescriptions

presence

present adjective
presently

present noun
presents

present verb
presents
presenting
presented

presentation noun
presentations

presenter noun
presenters

preservation

preservative noun
preservatives

preserve verb
preserves
preserving
preserved

preside verb
presides
presiding
presided

presidency noun
presidencies

president noun
presidents

presidential
adjective
presidentially

press verb
presses
pressing
pressed

press noun
presses

press-up noun
press-ups

pressure noun
pressures

pressurize verb
pressurizes
pressurizing
pressurized

prestige

prestigious adjective
prestigiously

presumably

presume *verb*
presumes
presuming
presumed
presumption *noun*
presumptions
presumptuous
adjective
presumptuously
pretence *noun*
pretences
pretend *verb*
pretends
pretending
pretended
pretender *noun*
pretenders
prettiness
pretty *adjective* and
adverb
prettier
prettiest
prettily
prevail *verb*
prevails
prevailing
prevailed
prevalent
prevent *verb*
prevents
preventing
prevented
prevention
preventive
preview *noun*
previews
previous *adjective*
previously
★ **prey** *verb*
preys
preying
preyed

prey *noun*
price *noun*
prices
price *verb*
prices
pricing
priced
priceless
prick *verb*
pricks
pricking
pricked
prick *noun*
pricks
prickle *noun*
prickles
prickly *adjective*
pricklier
prickliest
pride *noun*
prides
priest *noun*
priests
priestess *noun*
priestesses
priesthood
prig *noun*
prigs
priggish *adjective*
priggishly
prim *adjective*
primmer
primmest
primly
primness
primary *adjective*
primarily
primate *noun*
primates

prime *adjective*
prime *verb*
primes
priming
primed
prime *noun*
primes
prime minister
noun
prime ministers
primer *noun*
primers
primeval
primitive *adjective*
primitively
primrose *noun*
primroses
prince *noun*
princes
princely
princess *noun*
princesses
☆ **principal** *adjective*
principally
○ **principal** *noun*
principals
✳ **principle** *noun*
principles
print *verb*
prints
printing
printed
print *noun*
prints
printer *noun*
printers
printout *noun*
printouts
priority *noun*
priorities

- -

★ To **prey** on animals is to hunt and kill them. ! **pray.**
☆ **Principal** means 'chief' or 'main'. ! **principle.**
○ A **principal** is a head of a college. ! **principle.**
✳ A **principle** is a rule or belief. ! **principal.**

★ **prise** *verb*
prises
prising
prised

prism *noun*
prisms

prison *noun*
prisons

prisoner *noun*
prisoners

privacy

private *adjective*
privately

private *noun*
privates

privatization

privatize *verb*
privatizes
privatizing
privatized

privet

privilege *noun*
privileges

privileged

prize *noun*
prizes

☆ **prize** *verb*
prizes
prizing
prized

pro *noun*
pros

pro-
pro- makes words meaning 'in favour of', e.g. **pro-choice**. In this type of word you use a hyphen.

probability *noun*
probabilities

probable *adjective*
probably

probation

probationary

probe *verb*
probes
probing
probed

probe *noun*
probes

problem *noun*
problems

procedure *noun*
procedures

proceed *verb*
proceeds
proceeding
proceeded

proceedings *plural noun*

proceeds *plural noun*

process *noun*
processes

process *verb*
processes
processing
processed

procession *noun*
processions

proclaim *verb*
proclaims
proclaiming
proclaimed

proclamation *noun*
proclamations

prod *verb*
prods
prodding
prodded

prodigal *adjective*
prodigally

produce *verb*
produces
producing
produced

produce *noun*

producer *noun*
producers

product *noun*
products

production *noun*
productions

productive *adjective*
productively

productivity

profession *noun*
professions

professional *adjective*
professionally

professional *noun*
professionals

professor *noun*
professors

proficiency

proficient *adjective*
proficiently

profile *noun*
profiles

○ **profit** *noun*
profits

profit *verb*
profits
profiting
profited

profitable *adjective*
profitably

profound *adjective*
profoundly

profundity

profuse *adjective*
profusely

. . . .

★ To **prise** something is to open it. **!** prize.
☆ To **prize** something is to value it highly. **!** prise.
○ A **profit** is extra money made by selling something. **!** prophet.

profusion

★ **program** noun
programs

program verb
programs
programming
programmed

★ **programme** noun
programmes

progress noun

progress verb
progresses
progressing
progressed

progression

progressive adjective
progressively

prohibit verb
prohibits
prohibiting
prohibited

prohibition noun
prohibitions

project noun
projects

project verb
projects
projecting
projected

projection noun
projections

projectionist noun
projectionists

projector noun
projectors

prologue noun
prologues

prolong verb
prolongs
prolonging
prolonged

promenade noun
promenades

prominence

prominent adjective
prominently

promise verb
promises
promising
promised

promise noun
promises

promontory noun
promontories

promote verb
promotes
promoting
promoted

promoter noun
promoter

promotion noun
promotions

prompt adjective
prompter
promptest
promptly

prompt verb
prompts
prompting
prompted

prompter noun
prompters

promptness

prone

prong noun
prongs

pronoun noun
pronouns

pronounce verb
pronounces
pronouncing
pronounced

pronouncement noun
pronouncements

pronunciation noun
pronunciations

proof adjective and noun
proofs

prop verb
props
propping
propped

prop noun
props

propaganda

propel verb
propels
propelling
propelled

propellant noun
propellants

propeller noun
propellers

proper adjective
properly

property noun
properties

prophecy noun
prophecies

prophesy verb
prophesies
prophesying
prophesied

☆ **prophet** noun
prophets

prophetic adjective
prophetically

proportion noun
proportions

★ You use **program** when you are talking about computers. In other meanings you use **programme**.
☆ A **prophet** is someone who makes predictions about the future. ! **profit**.

proportional adjective
  proportionally
proportionate adjective
  proportionately
propose verb
  proposes
  proposing
  proposed
proposal noun
  proposals
proprietor noun
  proprietors
propulsion
prose
prosecute verb
  prosecutes
  prosecuting
  prosecuted
prosecution noun
  prosecutions
prosecutor noun
  prosecutors
prospect noun
  prospects
prospect verb
  prospects
  prospecting
  prospected
prospector noun
  prospectors
prosper verb
  prospers
  prospering
  prospered
prosperity
prosperous adjective
  prosperously
prostitute noun
  prostitutes

protect verb
  protects
  protecting
  protected
protection
protective adjective
  protectively
protector noun
  protectors
protein noun
  proteins
protest verb
  protests
  protesting
  protested
protest noun
  protests
protester noun
  protesters
Protestant noun
  Protestants
proton noun
  protons
protoplasm
prototype noun
  prototypes
protractor noun
  protractors
protrude verb
  protrudes
  protruding
  protruded
protrusion noun
  protrusions
proud adjective
  prouder
  proudest
  proudly
prove verb
  proves
  proving
  proved

proverb noun
  proverbs
proverbial adjective
  proverbially
provide verb
  provides
  providing
  provided
province noun
  provinces
provincial
provision noun
  provisions
provisional adjective
  provisionally
provocative adjective
  provocatively
provoke verb
  provokes
  provoking
  provoked
provocation noun
  provocations
prow noun
  prows
prowl verb
  prowls
  prowling
  prowled
prowler noun
  prowlers
prudence
prudent adjective
  prudently
prune noun
  prunes
prune verb
  prunes
  pruning
  pruned

pry verb
pries
prying
pried

psalm noun
psalms

pseudonym noun
pseudonyms

psychiatric

psychiatrist noun
psychiatrists

psychiatry

psychic

psychological adjective
psychologically

psychologist noun
psychologists

psychology

pub noun
pubs

puberty

public adjective and noun
publicly

publication noun
publications

publicity

publicize verb
publicizes
publicizing
publicized

publish verb
publishes
publishing
published

publisher noun
publishers

puck noun
pucks

pucker verb
puckers
puckering
puckered

pudding noun
puddings

puddle noun
puddles

puff verb
puffs
puffing
puffed

puff noun
puffs

puffin noun
puffins

pull verb
pulls
pulling
pulled

pull noun
pulls

pulley noun
pulleys

pullover noun
pullovers

pulp noun
pulps

pulp verb
pulps
pulping
pulped

pulpit noun
pulpits

pulse noun
pulses

pulverize verb
pulverizes
pulverizing
pulverized

puma noun
pumas

pumice

pump verb
pumps
pumping
pumped

pump noun
pumps

pumpkin noun
pumpkins

pun noun
puns

pun verb
puns
punning
punned

punch verb
punches
punching
punched

punch noun
punches

punch noun
punches

punchline noun
punchlines

punch-up noun
punch-ups

punctual adjective
punctually

punctuality

punctuate verb
punctuates
punctuating
punctuated

punctuation

puncture noun
punctures

punish verb
punishes
punishing
punished

punishment noun
punishments

punk noun
punks

punt noun
punts

punt verb
punts
punting
punted

puny adjective
punier
puniest

pup noun
pups

pupa noun
pupae

pupil noun
pupils

puppet noun
puppets

puppy noun
puppies

purchase verb
purchases
purchasing
purchased

purchase noun
purchases

purchaser noun
purchasers

purdah

pure adjective
purer
purest
purely

purge verb
purges
purging
purged

purge noun
purges

purification

purifier noun
purifiers

purify verb
purifies
purifying
purified

★ **Puritan** noun
Puritans

puritan noun
puritans

puritanical adjective
puritanically

purity

purple noun

purpose noun
purposes

purposely

purr verb
purrs
purring
purred

purse noun
purses

pursue verb
pursues
pursuing
pursued

pursuer noun
pursuers

pursuit noun
pursuits

☆ **pus** noun

push verb
pushes
pushing
pushed

push noun
pushes

pushchair noun
pushchairs

○ **puss** or **pussy** noun
pusses or pussies

✳ **put** verb
puts
putting
put

❋ **putt** verb
putts
putting
putted

putter noun
putters

putty

puzzle verb
puzzles
puzzling
puzzled

puzzle noun
puzzles

pygmy noun
pygmies

pyjamas

pylon noun
pylons

pyramid noun
pyramids

pyramidal

python noun
pythons

Qq

quack verb
quacks
quacking
quacked

quack noun
quacks

★ You use a capital P when you are talking about people in history, and a small p
when you mean anyone who is morally strict.

☆ **Pus** is yellow stuff produced in sore places on the body. ! **puss.**

○ **Puss** is a word for a cat. ! **pus.**

✳ To **put** something somewhere is to place it there. ! **putt.**

❋ To **putt** a ball is to tap it gently. ! **put.**

quad noun
quads

quadrangle noun
quadrangles

quadrant noun
quadrants

quadrilateral noun
quadrilaterals

quadruple adjective
and noun

quadruple verb
quadruples
quadrupling
quadrupled

quadruplet noun
quadruplets

quail verb
quails
quailing
quailed

quail noun
quail or quails

quaint adjective
quainter
quaintest
quaintly

quaintness noun

quake verb
quakes
quaking
quaked

Quaker noun
Quakers

qualification noun
qualifications

qualify verb
qualifies
qualifying
qualified

quality noun
qualities

quantity noun
quantities

quarantine

quarrel noun
quarrels

quarrel verb
quarrels
quarrelling
quarrelled

quarrelsome

quarry noun
quarries

quart noun
quarts

quarter noun
quarters

quartet noun
quartets

quartz

quaver verb
quavers
quavering
quavered

quaver noun
quavers

★ **quay** noun
quays

queasy adjective
queasier
queasiest

queen noun
queens

queer adjective
queerer
queerest

quench verb
quenches
quenching
quenched

query verb
queries
querying
queried

query noun
queries

quest noun
quests

question noun
questions

question verb
questions
questioning
questioned

questionable
adjective
questionably

questioner noun
questioner

questionnaire noun
questionnaires

☆ **queue** noun
queues

queue verb
queues
queueing
queued

quibble verb
quibbles
quibbling
quibbled

quibble noun
quibbles

quiche noun
quiches

quick adjective
quicker
quickest
quickly

quicken verb
quickens
quickening
quickened

. . . .

★ A **quay** is a place where ships tie up. **! key.**
☆ A **queue** is a line of people waiting for something. **! cue.**

quicksand noun
quicksands

quid noun
quid

quiet adjective
quieter
quietest
quietly

quieten verb
quietens
quietening
quietened

quill noun
quills

quilt noun
quilts

quintet noun
quintets

quit verb
quits
quitting
quitted
quit

quitter noun
quitters

quite

quiver verb
quivers
quivering
quivered

quiver noun
quivers

quiz noun
quizzes

quiz verb
quizzes
quizzing
quizzed

quoit noun
quoits

quota noun
quotas

quotation noun
quotations

quote verb
quotes
quoting
quoted

quotient noun
quotients

Rr

rabbi noun
rabbis

rabbit noun
rabbits

rabid

rabies

raccoon noun
raccoons

race noun
races

race verb
races
racing
raced

race noun
races

racecourse noun
racecourses

racer noun
racers

racial adjective
racially

racism

racist noun
racists

rack noun
racks

rack verb
racks
racking
racked

racket noun
rackets

radar

radial adjective
radially

radiance

radiant adjective
radiantly

radiate verb
radiates
radiating
radiated

radiation

radiator noun
radiators

radical adjective
radically

radical noun
radicals

radii see **radius**

radio noun
radios

radioactive

radioactivity

radish noun
radishes

radium

radius noun
radii

raffle noun
raffles

raffle verb
raffles
raffling
raffled

raft noun
rafts

rafter noun
rafters

rag noun
rags

rage noun
rages

rage verb
rages
raging
raged

ragged

ragtime

raid noun
raids

raid verb
raids
raiding
raided

raider noun
raiders

rail noun
rails

railings plural noun

railway noun
railways

rain verb
rains
raining
rained

rain noun
rains

rainbow noun
rainbows

raincoat noun
raincoats

raindrop noun
raindrops

rainfall

rainforest noun
rainforests

raise verb
raises
raising
raised

raisin noun
raisins

rake verb
rakes
raking
raked

rake noun
rakes

rally verb
rallies
rallying
rallied

rally noun
rallies

ram verb
rams
ramming
rammed

ram noun
rams

Ramadan

ramble noun
rambles

ramble verb
rambles
rambling
rambled

rambler noun
ramblers

ramp noun
ramps

rampage verb
rampages
rampaging
rampaged

rampage noun

ran see run

ranch noun
ranches

random

rang see ring

range noun
ranges

range verb
ranges
ranging
ranged

★ **ranger** noun
rangers

rank noun
ranks

rank verb
ranks
ranking
ranked

ransack verb
ransacks
ransacking
ransacked

ransom verb
ransoms
ransoming
ransomed

ransom noun
ransoms

☆ **rap** verb
raps
rapping
rapped

rap noun
raps

rapid adjective
rapidly

rapidity

rapids plural noun

. . . .

★ You use a capital R when you mean a senior Guide.
☆ To **rap** is to knock loudly. ! **wrap**.

rare adjective
rarer
rarest
rarely

rarity noun
rarities

rascal noun
rascals

rash adjective
rasher
rashest
rashly

rash noun
rashes

rasher noun
rashers

raspberry noun
raspberries

Rastafarian noun
Rastafarians

rat noun
rats

rate noun
rates

rate verb
rates
rating
rated

rather

ratio noun
ratios

ration noun
rations

ration verb
rations
rationing
rationed

rational adjective
rationally

rationalize verb
rationalizes
rationalizing
rationalized

rattle verb
rattles
rattling
rattled

rattle noun
rattles

rattlesnake noun
rattlesnakes

rave verb
raves
raving
raved

rave noun
raves

raven noun
ravens

ravenous adjective
ravenously

ravine noun
ravines

raw adjective
rawer
rawest

ray noun
rays

razor noun
razors

re-
re- makes words
meaning 'again', e.g.
reproduce. These
words are normally
spelt joined up, but a
few need a hyphen so
you don't confuse
them with other
words, e.g. **re-cover**
(= to put a new cover
on); **recover** has
another meaning. You
also need a hyphen in
words beginning with
e, e.g. **re-enter**.

reach verb
reaches
reaching
reached

reach noun
reaches

react verb
reacts
reacting
reacted

reaction noun
reactions

reactor noun
reactors

★ **read** verb
reads
reading
read

readable

reader noun
readers

readily

readiness

reading noun
readings

ready adjective
readier
readiest

☆ **real** adjective

realism

realist noun
realists

realistic adjective
realistically

reality noun
realities

realization

realize verb
realizes
realizing
realized

★ To **read** is to look at something written or printed. ! **reed**.
☆ **Real** means 'true' or 'existing'. ! **reel**.

really

realm noun
realms

reap verb
reaps
reaping
reaped

reaper noun
reapers

reappear verb
reappears
reappearing
reappeared

reappearance noun
reappearances

rear adjective and
noun
rears

rear verb
rears
rearing
reared

rearrange verb
rearranges
rearranging
rearranged

rearrangement noun
rearrangements

reason noun
reasons

reason verb
reasons
reasoning
reasoned

reasonable adjective
reasonably

reassurance noun
reassurances

reassure verb
reassures
reassuring
reassured

rebel verb
rebels
rebelling
rebelled

rebel noun
rebels

rebellion noun
rebellions

rebellious adjective
rebelliously

rebound verb
rebounds
rebounding
rebounded

rebuild verb
rebuilds
rebuilding
rebuilt

recall verb
recalls
recalling
recalled

recap verb
recaps
recapping
recapped

recapture verb
recaptures
recapturing
recaptured

recede verb
recedes
receding
receded

receipt noun
receipts

receive verb
receives
receiving
received

receiver noun
receivers

recent adjective
recently

receptacle noun
receptacles

reception noun
receptions

receptionist noun
receptionists

recess noun
recesses

recession noun
recessions

recipe noun
recipes

reciprocal adjective
reciprocally

reciprocal noun
reciprocals

recital noun
recitals

recitation noun
recitations

recite verb
recites
reciting
recited

reckless adjective
recklessly

recklessness

reckon verb
reckons
reckoning
reckoned

reclaim verb
reclaims
reclaiming
reclaimed

reclamation noun
reclamations

recline verb
reclines
reclining
reclined

recognition

recognizable adjective
recognizably

recognize verb
recognizes
recognizing
recognized

recoil verb
recoils
recoiling
recoiled

recollect verb
recollects
recollecting
recollected

recollection noun
recollections

recommend verb
recommends
recommending
recommended

recommendation noun
recommendations

reconcile verb
reconciles
reconciling
reconciled

reconciliation noun
reconciliations

reconstruction noun
reconstructions

record noun
records

record verb
records
recording
recorded

recorder noun
recorders

recover verb
recovers
recovering
recovered

recovery noun
recoveries

recreation noun
recreations

recreational adjective
recreationally

recruit noun
recruits

recruit verb
recruits
recruiting
recruited

rectangle noun
rectangles

rectangular

recur verb
recurs
recurring
recurred

recurrence noun
recurrences

recycle verb
recycles
recycling
recycled

red adjective
redder
reddest

red noun
reds

redden verb
reddens
reddening
reddened

reddish

redeem verb
redeems
redeeming
redeemed

redeemer noun
redeemers

redemption noun
redemptions

redhead noun
redheads

reduce verb
reduces
reducing
reduced

reduction noun
reductions

redundancy noun
redundancies

redundant adjective
redundantly

★ **reed** noun
reeds

reedy

reef noun
reefs

reef knot noun
reef knots

reek verb
reeks
reeking
reeked

☆ **reel** noun
reels

reel verb
reels
reeling
reeled

★ A **reed** is a plant or a thin strip. ! **read**.
☆ A **reel** is a cylinder on which something is wound. ! **real**.

refer verb
  refers
  referring
  referred

referee noun
  referees

referee verb
  referees
  refereeing
  refereed

reference noun
  references

referendum noun
  referendums

refill verb
  refills
  refilling
  refilled

refill noun
  refills

refine verb
  refines
  refining
  refined

refinement noun
  refinements

refinery noun
  refineries

reflect verb
  reflects
  reflecting
  reflected

reflective adjective
  reflectively

reflex noun
  reflexes

reflexive adjective
  reflexively

reform verb
  reforms
  reforming
  reformed

reform noun
  reforms

reformation noun
  reformations

★ **Reformation**

reformer noun
  reformers

refract verb
  refracts
  refracting
  refracted

refraction

refrain verb
  refrains
  refraining
  refrained

refrain noun
  refrains

refresh verb
  refreshes
  refreshing
  refreshed

refreshment noun
  refreshments

refrigerate verb
  refrigerates
  refrigerating
  refrigerated

refrigeration

refrigerator noun
  refrigerators

refuel verb
  refuels
  refuelling
  refuelled

refuge noun
  refuges

refugee noun
  refugees

refund verb
  refunds
  refunding
  refunded

refund noun
  refunds

refusal

refuse verb
  refuses
  refusing
  refused

refuse

regain verb
  regains
  regaining
  regained

regard verb
  regards
  regarding
  regarded

regard noun
  regards

regarding
  preposition

regardless

regatta noun
  regattas

reggae

regiment noun
  regiments

regimental

region noun
  regions

regional adjective
  regionally

register noun
  registers

register verb
  registers
  registering
  registered

registration noun
  registrations

★ You use a capital R when you mean the historical religious movement.

regret noun
regrets

regret verb
regrets
regretting
regretted

regretful adjective
regretfully

regrettable adjective
regrettably

regular adjective
regularly

regularity

regulate verb
regulates
regulating
regulated

regulation noun
regulations

regulator noun
regulators

rehearsal noun
rehearsals

rehearse verb
rehearses
rehearsing
rehearsed

★ **reign** verb
reigns
reigning
reigned

reign noun
reigns

☆ **rein** noun
reins

reindeer noun
reindeer

reinforce verb
reinforces
reinforcing
reinforced

reinforcement noun
reinforcements

reject verb
rejects
rejecting
rejected

reject noun
rejects

rejection noun
rejections

rejoice verb
rejoices
rejoicing
rejoiced

relate verb
relates
relating
related

relation noun
relations

relationship noun
relationships

relative adjective
relatively

relative noun
relatives

relax verb
relaxes
relaxing
relaxed

relaxation

relay verb
relays
relaying
relayed

relay noun
relays

release verb
releases
releasing
released

release noun
releases

relegate verb
relegates
relegating
relegated

relegation

relent verb
relents
relenting
relented

relentless adjective
relentlessly

relevance

relevant adjective
relevantly

reliability

reliable adjective
reliably

reliance

reliant

relic noun
relics

relief noun
reliefs

relieve verb
relieves
relieving
relieved

religion noun
religions

religious adjective
religiously

reluctance

reluctant adjective
reluctantly

rely verb
relies
relying
relied

★ To **reign** is to rule as a king or queen. ! **rein**.
☆ A **rein** is a strap used to guide a horse. ! **reign**.

remain verb
remains
remaining
remained

remainder noun
remainders

remains

remark verb
remarks
remarking
remarked

remark noun
remarks

remarkable
adjective
remarkably

remedial adjective
remedially

remedy noun
remedies

remember verb
remembers
remembering
remembered

remembrance

remind verb
reminds
reminding
reminded

reminder noun
reminders

reminisce verb
reminisces
reminiscing
reminisced

reminiscence noun
reminiscences

reminiscent

remnant noun
remnants

remorse

remorseful adjective
remorsefully

remorseless
adjective
remorselessly

remote adjective
remoter
remotest
remotely

remoteness

removal noun
removals

remove verb
removes
removing
removed

★ **Renaissance**

render verb
renders
rendering
rendered

rendezvous noun
rendezvous

renew verb
renews
renewing
renewed

renewable

renewal noun
renewals

renown

renowned

rent noun
rents

rent verb
rents
renting
rented

repair verb
repairs
repairing
repaired

repair noun
repairs

repay verb
repays
repaying
repaid

repayment noun
repayments

repeat verb
repeats
repeating
repeated

repeat noun
repeats

repeatedly

repel verb
repels
repelling
repelled

repellent

repent verb
repents
repenting
repented

repentance

repentant

repetition noun
repetitions

repetitive adjective
repetitively

replace verb
replaces
replacing
replaced

replacement noun
replacements

replay noun
replays

replica noun
replicas

★ You use a capital R when you mean the historical period.

reply *verb*
replies
replying
replied

reply *noun*
replies

report *verb*
reports
reporting
reported

report *noun*
reports

reporter *noun*
reporters

repossess *verb*
repossesses
repossessing
repossessed

represent *verb*
represents
representing
represented

representation
noun
representations

representative
adjective and *noun*
representatives

repress *verb*
represses
repressing
repressed

repression *noun*
repressions

repressive *adjective*
repressively

reprieve *verb*
reprieves
reprieving
reprieved

reprieve *noun*
reprieves

reprimand *verb*
reprimands
reprimanding
reprimanded

reprisal *noun*
reprisals

reproach *verb*
reproaches
reproaching
reproached

reproduce *verb*
reproduces
reproducing
reproduced

reproduction *noun*
reproduction

reproductive
adjective
reproductively

reptile *noun*
reptiles

republic *noun*
republics

republican *adjective*
and *noun*
republicans

★ **Republican** *adjective*
and *noun*
Republicans

repulsion

repulsive *adjective*
repulsively

reputation *noun*
reputations

request *verb*
requests
requesting
requested

request *noun*
requests

require *verb*
requires
requiring
required

requirement *noun*
requirements

reread *verb*
rereads
rereading
reread

rescue *verb*
rescues
rescuing
rescued

rescue *noun*
rescues

rescuer *noun*
rescuers

research *noun*
researches

researcher *noun*
researchers

resemblance *noun*
resemblances

resemble *verb*
resembles
resembling
resembled

resent *verb*
resents
resenting
resented

resentful *adjective*
resentfully

resentment

reservation *noun*
reservations

reserve *verb*
reserves
reserving
reserved

★ You use a capital R when you mean the political party in the USA.

reserve noun
reserves

reservoir noun
reservoirs

reshuffle noun
reshuffles

reside verb
resides
residing
resided

residence noun
residences

resident noun
residents

resign verb
resigns
resigning
resigned

resignation noun
resignations

resin noun
resins

resinous

resist verb
resists
resisting
resisted

resistance noun
resistances

resistant

resolute adjective
resolutely

resolution noun
resolutions

resolve verb
resolves
resolving
resolved

resort noun
resorts

resort verb
resorts
resorting
resorted

resound verb
resounds
resounding
resounded

resource noun
resources

respect verb
respects
respecting
respected

respect noun
respects

respectability

respectable
adjective
respectably

respectful adjective
respectfully

respective adjective
respectively

respiration

respirator noun
respirators

respiratory

respond verb
responds
responding
responded

response noun
responses

responsibility noun
responsibilities

responsible adjective
responsibly

rest verb
rests
resting
rested

rest noun
rests

restaurant noun
restaurants

restful adjective
restfully

restless adjective
restlessly

restlessness

restoration noun
restorations

restore verb
restores
restoring
restored

restrain verb
restrains
restraining
restrained

restraint noun
restraints

restrict verb
restricts
restricting
restricted

restriction noun
restrictions

restrictive adjective
restrictively

result verb
results
resulting
resulted

result noun
results

resume verb
resumes
resuming
resumed

resumption noun
resumptions

resuscitate verb
resuscitates
resuscitating
resuscitated

retail verb
retails
retailing
retailed

retail noun

retain verb
retains
retaining
retained

retina noun
retinas

retire verb
retires
retiring
retired

retirement

retort verb
retorts
retorting
retorted

retort noun
retorts

retrace verb
retraces
retracing
retraced

retreat verb
retreats
retreating
retreated

retrievable
adjective
retrievably

retrieval noun
retrievals

retrieve verb
retrieves
retrieving
retrieved

retriever noun
retrievers

return verb
returns
returning
returned

return noun
returns

reunion noun
reunions

rev verb
revs
revving
revved

rev noun
revs

reveal verb
reveals
revealing
revealed

revelation noun
revelations

revenge

revenue noun
revenues

revere verb
reveres
revering
revered

reverence

★ **Reverend**

★ **reverent** adjective
reverently

reversal noun
reversals

reverse verb
reverses
reversing
reversed

reverse noun
reverses

reversible adjective
reversibly

review verb
reviews
reviewing
reviewed

☆ **review** noun
reviews

reviewer noun
reviewers

revise verb
revises
revising
revised

revision noun
revisions

revival noun
revivals

revive verb
revives
reviving
revived

revolt verb
revolts
revolting
revolted

revolt noun
revolts

revolution noun
revolutions

revolutionary
adjective and noun
revolutionaries

revolutionize verb
revolutionizes
revolutionizing
revolutionized

. . . .

★ You use **Reverend** as a title of a member of the clergy, and **reverent** as an ordinary word meaning 'showing respect'.

☆ A **review** is a piece of writing about a film, play, etc. ! revue.

revolve verb
revolves
revolving
revolved

revolver noun
revolvers

★ **revue** noun
revues

reward verb
rewards
rewarding
rewarded

reward noun
rewards

rewind verb
rewinds
rewinding
rewound

rewrite verb
rewrites
rewriting
rewrote
rewritten

rheumatic

rheumatism

rhinoceros noun
rhinoceroses or
rhinoceros

rhododendron noun
rhododendrons

rhombus noun
rhombuses

rhubarb

rhyme verb
rhymes
rhyming
rhymed

rhyme noun
rhymes

rhythm noun
rhythms

rhythmic or
rhythmical adjective
rhythmically

rib noun
ribs

ribbon noun
ribbons

rice

rich adjective
richer
richest
richly

riches plural noun

richness

rick noun
ricks

rickety

rickshaw noun
rickshaws

ricochet verb
ricochets
ricocheting
ricocheted

rid verb
rids
ridding
rid

riddance

riddle noun
riddles

ride verb
rides
riding
rode
ridden

ride noun
rides

rider noun
riders

ridge noun
ridges

ridicule verb
ridicules
ridiculing
ridiculed

ridiculous adjective
ridiculously

rifle noun
rifles

rift noun
rifts

rig verb
rigs
rigging
rigged

rigging

right adjective
rightly

☆ **right** noun
rights

✪ **right** verb
rights
righting
righted

righteous adjective
righteously

righteousness

rightful adjective
rightfully

right-handed

rightness

rigid adjective
rigidly

rigidity

rim noun
rims

rind noun
rinds

ring noun
rings

- -

★ A **revue** is an entertainment of short sketches. ! **review**.

☆ A **right** is something you are entitled to. ! **rite, write**.

✪ To **right** something is to make it right. ! **rite, write**.

★ **ring** verb
rings
ringing
rang
rung

☆ **ring** verb
rings
ringing
ringed

ring noun
rings

ringleader noun
ringleaders

ringlet noun
ringlets

ringmaster noun
ringmasters

rink noun
rinks

rinse verb
rinses
rinsing
rinsed

rinse noun
rinses

riot verb
riots
rioting
rioted

riot noun
riots

riotous adjective
riotously

rip verb
rips
ripping
ripped

rip noun
rips

ripe adjective
riper
ripest

ripen verb
ripens
ripening
ripened

ripeness

rip-off noun
rip-offs

ripple noun
ripples

ripple verb
ripples
rippling
rippled

rise verb
rises
rising
rose
risen

rise noun
rises

risk verb
risks
risking
risked

risk noun
risks

risky adjective
riskier
riskiest
riskily

risotto noun
risottos

rissole noun
rissoles

○ **rite** noun
rites

ritual noun
rituals

rival noun
rivals

rival verb
rivals
rivalling
rivalled

rivalry noun
rivalries

river noun
rivers

rivet noun
rivets

rivet verb
rivets
riveting
riveted

✳ **road** noun
roads

roadroller noun
roadrollers

roadside noun
roadsides

roadway noun
roadways

roam verb
roams
roaming
roamed

roar verb
roars
roaring
roared

roar noun
roars

roast verb
roasts
roasting
roasted

rob verb
robs
robbing
robbed

· ·

★ The past tense is **rang** and the past participle is **rung** when you mean 'to make a sound like a bell'. ! **wring**.

☆ The past tense and past participle is **ringed** when you mean 'to put a ring round something'. ! **wring**.

○ A **rite** is a ceremony or ritual. ! **right, write**.

✳ A **road** is a hard surface for traffic to use. ! **rode**.

robber noun
robbers

robbery noun
robberies

robe noun
robes

robin noun
robins

robot noun
robots

robust adjective
robustly

rock verb
rocks
rocking
rocked

rock noun
rocks

rocker noun
rockers

rockery noun
rockeries

rocket noun
rockets

rocky adjective
rockier
rockiest
rockily

rod noun
rods

★ **rode** see ride

rodent noun
rodents

rodeo noun
rodeos

rogue noun
rogues

roguish adjective
roguishly

☆ **role** noun
roles

roll verb
rolls
rolling
rolled

○ **roll** noun
rolls

roller noun
rollers

Roman adjective and
noun
Romans

Roman Catholic
noun
Roman Catholics

romance noun
romances

Roman numeral

romantic adjective
romantically

Romany

romp verb
romps
romping
romped

romp noun
romps

rompers plural noun

roof noun
roofs

rook noun
rooks

room noun
rooms

roomful adjective
roomfuls

roomy adjective
roomier
roomiest
roomily

roost noun
roosts

✳ **root** noun
roots

root verb
roots
rooting
rooted

rope noun
ropes

rose noun
roses

rose see rise

rosette noun
rosettes

rosy adjective
rosier
rosiest
rosily

rot verb
rots
rotting
rotted

rot noun

rota noun
rotas

rotary

rotate verb
rotates
rotating
rotated

rotation noun
rotations

rotor noun
rotors

rotten

rottenness

rottweiler noun
rottweilers

. . . .

★ **Rode** is the past tense of **ride**. ! **road.**
☆ A **role** is a part in a play or film. ! **roll.**
○ A **roll** is a small loaf of bread or an act of rolling. ! **role.**
✳ A **root** is the part of a plant that grows underground. ! **route.**

rough adjective
rougher
roughest
roughly

roughness

roughage

roughen verb
roughens
roughening
roughened

round adjective,
adverb, and
preposition
rounder
roundest
roundly

round noun
rounds

round verb
rounds
rounding
rounded

roundabout
adjective and noun
roundabouts

rounders noun

Roundhead noun
Roundheads

rouse verb
rouses
rousing
roused

rout verb
routs
routing
routed

rout noun
routs

★ **route** noun
routes

routine noun
routines

routine adjective
routinely

rove verb
roves
roving
roved

rover noun
rovers

☆ **row** noun
rows

◉ **row** verb
rows
rowing
rowed

rowdiness

rowdy adjective
rowdier
rowdiest
rowdily

rower noun
rowers

rowlock noun
rowlocks

royal adjective
royally

royalty

rub verb
rubs
rubbing
rubbed

rub noun
rubs

rubber noun
rubbers

rubbery

rubbish

rubble

ruby noun
rubies

rucksack noun
rucksacks

rudder noun
rudders

ruddy adjective
ruddier
ruddiest

rude adjective
ruder
rudest
rudely

rudeness

ruffian noun
ruffians

ruffle verb
ruffles
ruffling
ruffled

rug noun
rugs

✱ **rugby**

rugged adjective
ruggedly

rugger

ruin verb
ruins
ruining
ruined

ruin noun
ruins

ruinous adjective
ruinously

rule noun
rules

rule verb
rules
ruling
ruled

ruler noun
rulers

ruling noun
rulings

. . . .

★ A **route** is the way you go to get to a place. ! **root**.

☆ A **row** is a line of people or things and rhymes with 'go'. A **row** is also a noise or
argument and rhymes with 'cow'.

◉ To **row** means to use oars to make a boat move and rhymes with 'go'.

✱ You can use a small r when you mean the game.

rum *noun*
rums

rumble *verb*
rumbles
rumbling
rumbled

rumble *noun*
rumbles

rummage *verb*
rummages
rummaging
rummaged

rummy

rumour *noun*
rumours

rump *noun*
rumps

run *verb*
runs
running
ran
run

run *noun*
runs

runaway *noun*
runaways

rung *noun*
rungs

rung see ring

runner *noun*
runners

runner-up *noun*
runners-up

runny *adjective*
runnier
runniest
runnily

runway *noun*
runways

rural

rush *verb*
rushes
rushing
rushed

rush *noun*
rushes

rusk *noun*
rusks

rust *noun*

rust *verb*
rusts
rusting
rusted

rustic

rustle *verb*
rustles
rustling
rustled

rustler *noun*
rustlers

rusty *adjective*
rustier
rustiest
rustily

rut *noun*
ruts

ruthless *adjective*
ruthlessly

ruthlessness

rutted

★ **rye** *noun*

Ss

sabbath *noun*
sabbaths

sabotage *noun*

sabotage *verb*
sabotages
sabotaging
sabotaged

saboteur *noun*
saboteurs

☆ **sac** *noun*
sacs

saccharin

sachet *noun*
sachets

○ **sack** *noun*
sacks

sack *verb*
sacks
sacking
sacked

sacred

sacrifice *noun*
sacrifices

sacrificial *adjective*
sacrificially

sacrifice *verb*
sacrifices
sacrificing
sacrificed

sad *adjective*
sadder
saddest
sadly

sadness

sadden *verb*
saddens
saddening
saddened

saddle *noun*
saddles

saddle *verb*
saddles
saddling
saddled

. . . .

★ **Rye** is a type of cereal or bread. ! **wry.**
☆ A **sac** is a bag-like part of an animal or plant. ! **sack.**
○ A **sack** is a large bag. ! **sac.**

sadist *noun*
sadists

sadism

sadistic *adjective*
sadistically

safari *noun*
safaris

safe *adjective*
safer
safest
safely

safe *noun*
safes

safeguard *noun*
safeguards

safety

sag *verb*
sags
sagging
sagged

saga *noun*
sagas

sago

said *see* say

sail *verb*
sails
sailing
sailed

★ sail *noun*
sails

sailboard *noun*
sailboards

sailor *noun*
sailors

saint *noun*
saints

saintly *adjective*
saintlier
saintliest

sake

salaam *interjection*

salad *noun*
salads

salami *noun*
salamis

salary *noun*
salaries

☆ sale *noun*
sales

salesman *noun*
salesmen

salesperson *noun*
salespersons

saleswoman *noun*
saleswomen

saline

saliva

sally *verb*
sallies
sallying
sallied

salmon *noun*
salmon

salon *noun*
salons

saloon *noun*
saloons

salt *noun*

salt *verb*
salts
salting
salted

salty *adjective*
saltier
saltiest

salute *verb*
salutes
saluting
saluted

salute *noun*
salutes

salvage *verb*
salvages
salvaging
salvaged

salvation

same

samosa *noun*
samosas

sample *noun*
samples

sample *verb*
samples
sampling
sampled

sanctuary *noun*
sanctuaries

sand *noun*
sands

sand *verb*
sands
sanding
sanded

sander *noun*
sanders

sandal *noun*
sandals

sandbag *noun*
sandbags

sandpaper

sands *plural noun*

sandstone

sandwich *noun*
sandwiches

sandy *adjective*
sandier
sandiest

sane *adjective*
saner
sanest
sanely

. . . .

★ A **sail** is a sheet that catches the wind to make a boat go. ! **sale**.
☆ You use **sale** in e.g. *The house is for sale.* ! **sail**.

sang see sing
sanitary
sanitation
sanity
sank see sink
Sanskrit
sap noun
sap verb
  saps
  sapping
  sapped
sapling noun
  saplings
sapphire noun
  sapphires
sarcasm
sarcastic adjective
  sarcastically
sardine noun
  sardines
sari noun
  saris
sash noun
  sashes
sat see sit
satchel noun
  satchels
satellite noun
  satellites
satin
satire noun
  satires
satirical adjective
  satirically
satirist noun
  satirists
satisfaction
satisfactory adjective
  satisfactorily

satisfy verb
  satisfies
  satisfying
  satisfied
saturate verb
  saturates
  saturating
  saturated
saturation
Saturday noun
  Saturdays
★ **sauce** noun
  sauces
saucepan noun
  saucepans
saucer noun
  saucers
saucy adjective
  saucier
  sauciest
  saucily
sauna noun
  saunas
saunter verb
  saunters
  sauntering
  sauntered
sausage noun
  sausages
savage adjective
  savagely
savage noun
  savages
savage verb
  savages
  savaging
  savaged
savagery
savannah noun
  savannahs

save verb
  saves
  saving
  saved
saver noun
  savers
savings plural noun
saviour noun
  saviours
savoury
saw noun
  saws
saw verb
  saws
  sawing
  sawed
  sawn
saw see see
sawdust
saxophone noun
  saxophones
say verb
  says
  saying
  said
say noun
saying noun
  sayings
scab noun
  scabs
scabbard noun
  scabbards
scaffold noun
  scaffolds
scaffolding
scald verb
  scalds
  scalding
  scalded

★ A sauce is a liquid you put on food. ! source.

SC

scale noun
scales

scale verb
scales
scaling
scaled

scales plural noun

scaly adjective
scalier
scaliest

scalp noun
scalps

scalp verb
scalps
scalping
scalped

scamper verb
scampers
scampering
scampered

scampi plural noun

scan verb
scans
scanning
scanned

scan noun
scans

scandal noun
scandals

scandalous adjective
scandalous

scanner noun
scanners

scanty adjective
scantier
scantiest
scantily

scapegoat noun
scapegoats

scar noun
scars

scar verb
scars
scarring
scarred

scarce adjective
scarcer
scarcest
scarcely

scarcity noun
scarcities

scare verb
scares
scaring
scared

scare noun
scares

scarecrow noun
scarecrows

scarf noun
scarves

scarlet

scary adjective
scarier
scariest
scarily

scatter verb
scatters
scattering
scattered

★ **scene** noun
scenes

scenery

☆ **scent** noun
scents

scent verb
scents
scenting
scented

sceptic noun
sceptics

sceptical adjective
sceptically

scepticism

schedule noun
schedules

scheme noun
schemes

scheme verb
schemes
scheming
schemed

schemer noun
schemers

scholar noun
scholars

scholarly

scholarship noun
scholarships

school noun
schools

schoolboy noun
schoolboys

schoolchild noun
schoolchildren

schoolgirl noun
schoolgirls

schoolteacher noun
schoolteachers

schooner noun
schooners

science

scientific adjective
scientifically

scientist noun
scientists

scissors plural noun

scoff verb
scoffs
scoffing
scoffed

★ A **scene** is a place or part of a play. ! **seen**.
☆ A **scent** is a smell or perfume. ! **cent**, **sent**.

scold verb
scolds
scolding
scolded

scone noun
scones

scoop noun
scoops

scoop verb
scoops
scooping
scooped

scooter noun
scooters

scope

scorch verb
scorches
scorching
scorched

score noun
scores

score verb
scores
scoring
scored

scorer noun
scorers

scorn noun

scorn verb
scorns
scorning
scorned

scorpion noun
scorpions

Scot noun
Scots

scoundrel noun
scoundrels

scour verb
scours
scouring
scoured

★ **Scout** noun
Scouts

scout noun
scouts

scowl verb
scowls
scowling
scowled

scramble verb
scrambles
scrambling
scrambled

scramble noun
scrambles

scrap verb
scraps
scrapping
scrapped

scrap noun
scraps

scrape verb
scrapes
scraping
scraped

scrape noun
scrapes

scraper noun
scrapers

scrappy adjective
scrappier
scrappiest
scrappily

scratch verb
scratches
scratching
scratched

scratch noun
scratches

scrawl verb
scrawls
scrawling
scrawled

scrawl noun
scrawls

scream verb
screams
screaming
screamed

scream noun
screams

screech verb
screeches
screeching
screeched

screech noun
screeches

screen noun
screens

screen verb
screens
screening
screened

screw noun
screws

screw verb
screws
screwing
screwed

screwdriver noun
screwdrivers

scribble verb
scribbles
scribbling
scribbled

scribble noun
scribbles

scribbler noun
scribblers

script noun
scripts

scripture noun
scriptures

★ You use a capital S when you mean a member of the Scout Association.

scroll noun
scrolls

scrotum noun
scrotums or scrota

scrounge verb
scrounges
scrounging
scrounged

scrounger noun
scroungers

scrub verb
scrubs
scrubbing
scrubbed

scrub noun

scruffy adjective
scruffier
scruffiest
scruffily

scrum noun
scrums

scrummage noun
scrummages

scrutinize verb
scrutinizes
scrutinizing
scrutinized

scrutiny noun
scrutinies

scuba diving

scuffle noun
scuffles

scuffle verb
scuffles
scuffling
scuffled

scullery noun
sculleries

sculptor noun
sculptors

sculpture noun
sculptures

scum

scurry verb
scurries
scurrying
scurried

scurvy

scuttle verb
scuttles
scuttling
scuttled

scuttle noun
scuttles

scythe noun
scythes

★ **sea** noun
seas

seabed

seafarer noun
seafarers

seafaring

seafood

seagull noun
seagulls

sea horse noun
sea horses

seal verb
seals
sealing
sealed

seal noun
seals

sea lion noun
sea lions

☆ **seam** noun
seams

seaman noun
seamen

seamanship

seaplane noun
seaplanes

seaport noun
seaports

search verb
searches
searching
searched

search noun
searches

searcher noun
searchers

searchlight noun
searchlights

seashore noun
seashores

seasick

seasickness

seaside

season noun
seasons

season verb
seasons
seasoning
seasoned

seasonal adjective
seasonally

seasoning noun
seasonings

seat noun
seats

seat verb
seats
seating
seated

seat belt noun
seat belts

seaward adjective
and adverb

· ·

★ A **sea** is an area of salt water. **! see.**
☆ A **seam** is a line of stitching in cloth. **! seem.**

seawards adverb
seaweed noun
seaweeds
secateurs plural
noun
secluded
seclusion
second adjective
secondly
second noun
seconds
second verb
seconds
seconding
seconded
secondary
second-hand
adjective
secrecy
secret adjective
secretly
secret noun
secrets
secretary noun
secretaries
secrete verb
secretes
secreting
secreted
secretion noun
secretions
secretive adjective
secretively
secretiveness
sect noun
sects
section noun
sections
sectional
sector noun
sectors

secure adjective
securer
securest
securely
secure verb
secures
securing
secured
security
sedate adjective
sedately
sedation
sedative noun
sedatives
sediment
sedimentary
★ **see** verb
sees
seeing
saw
seen
seed noun
seeds
seedling noun
seedlings
seek verb
seeks
seeking
sought
☆ **seem** verb
seems
seeming
seemed
seemingly
✪ **seen** see see
seep verb
seeps
seeping
seeped
seepage

see-saw noun
see-saws
seethe verb
seethes
seething
seethed
segment noun
segments
segmented
segregate verb
segregates
segregating
segregated
segregation
seismograph noun
seismographs
seize verb
seizes
seizing
seized
seizure noun
seizures
seldom
select verb
selects
selecting
selected
select adjective
self noun
selves
self-confidence
self-confident
adjective
self-confidently
self-conscious
adjective
self-consciously
self-contained
selfish adjective
selfishly

. . . .

★ You use see in e.g. *I can't see anything.* **!** sea.
☆ You use seem in e.g. *they seem tired.* **!** seam.
✪ **Seen** is the past participle of see. **!** scene.

selfishness

selfless *adjective*
selflessly

self-service

★ **sell** *verb*
sells
selling
sold

semaphore

semen

semi-
semi- makes words
meaning 'half', e.g.
**semi-automatic,
semi-skimmed.**
A few words are spelt
joined up, e.g.
**semicircle,
semicolon,** but most
of them have hyphens.

semibreve *noun*
semibreves

semicircle *noun*
semicircles

semicircular

semicolon *noun*
semicolons

semi-detached

semi-final *noun*
semi-finals

semi-finalist *noun*
semi-finalists

semitone *noun*
semitones

semolina

senate

senator *noun*
senators

send *verb*
sends
sending
sent

senior *adjective* and
noun
seniors

seniority

sensation *noun*
sensations

sensational *adjective*
sensationally

sense *noun*
senses

sense *verb*
senses
sensing
sensed

senseless *adjective*
senselessly

sensible *adjective*
sensibly

sensitive *adjective*
sensitively

sensitivity *noun*
sensitivities

sensitize *verb*
sensitizes
sensitizing
sensitized

sensor *noun*
sensors

☆ **sent** see **send**

sentence *noun*
sentences

sentence *verb*
sentences
sentencing
sentenced

sentiment *noun*
sentiments

sentimental
adjective
sentimentally

sentimentality

sentinel *noun*
sentinels

sentry *noun*
sentries

separable

separate *adjective*
separately

separate *verb*
separates
separating
separated

separation *noun*
separations

September *noun*
Septembers

septic

sequel *noun*
sequels

sequence *noun*
sequences

sequin *noun*
sequins

serene *adjective*
serenely

serenity

sergeant *noun*
sergeants

sergeant major
noun
sergeant majors

○ **serial** *noun*
serials

series *noun*
series

serious *adjective*
seriously

★ To **sell** something means 'to exchange it for money'. ! **cell.**
☆ You use **sent** in e.g. *he was sent home.* ! **cent, scent.**
○ A **serial** is a story or programme in separate parts. ! **cereal.**

seriousness

sermon *noun*
sermons

serpent *noun*
serpents

servant *noun*
servants

serve *verb*
serves
serving
served

server *noun*
servers

serve *noun*
serves

service *noun*
services

service *verb*
services
servicing
serviced

serviette *noun*
serviettes

session *noun*
sessions

set *verb*
sets
setting
set

set *noun*
sets

set square *noun*
set squares

★ **sett** *noun*
setts

settee *noun*
settees

setting *noun*
settings

settle *verb*
settles
settling
settled

settlement *noun*
settlements

settler *noun*
settlers

set-up *noun*
set-ups

seven

seventeen

seventeenth

seventh *adjective* and *noun*
seventhly

seventieth

seventy *adjective* and *noun*
seventies

sever *verb*
severs
severing
severed

several *adjective*
severally

severe *adjective*
severer
severest
severely

severity

☆ **sew** *verb*
sews
sewing
sewed
sewn

sewage

sewer *noun*
sewers

sex *noun*
sexes

sexism

sexist *adjective* and *noun*
sexists

sextet *noun*
sextets

sexual *adjective*
sexually

sexuality

sexy *adjective*
sexier
sexiest
sexily

shabbiness

shabby *adjective*
shabbier
shabbiest
shabbily

shack *noun*
shacks

shade *noun*
shades

shade *verb*
shades
shading
shaded

shadow *noun*
shadows

shadow *verb*
shadows
shadowing
shadowed

shadowy

shady *adjective*
shadier
shadiest

shaft *noun*
shafts

shaggy *adjective*
shaggier
shaggiest
shaggily

★ A **sett** is a badger's burrow.
☆ To **sew** is to work with a needle and thread. **! sow.**

shake *verb*
shakes
shaking
shook
shaken

★ **shake** *noun*
shakes

shaky *adjective*
shakier
shakiest
shakily

shall *verb*
should

shallow *adjective*
shallower
shallowest
shallowly

sham *noun*
shams

shamble *verb*
shambles
shambling
shambled

shambles *noun*

shame *verb*
shames
shaming
shamed

shame *noun*

shameful *adjective*
shamefully

shameless *adjective*
shamelessly

shampoo *noun*
shampoos

shampoo *verb*
shampoos
shampooing
shampooed

shamrock

shandy *noun*
shandies

shan't *verb*

shanty *noun*
shanties

shape *noun*
shapes

shape *verb*
shapes
shaping
shaped

shapeless *adjective*
shapelessly

shapely *adjective*
shapelier
shapeliest

share *noun*
shares

share *verb*
shares
sharing
shared

shark *noun*
sharks

sharp *adjective*
sharper
sharpest
sharply

sharp *noun*
sharps

sharpen *verb*
sharpens
sharpening
sharpened

sharpener *noun*
sharpeners

sharpness

shatter *verb*
shatters
shattering
shattered

shave *verb*
shaves
shaving
shaved

shave *noun*
shaves

shaver *noun*
shavers

shavings *plural noun*

shawl *noun*
shawls

she

sheaf *noun*
sheaves

☆ **shear** *verb*
shears
shearing
sheared
shorn

shearer *noun*
shearers

shears *plural noun*

sheath *noun*
sheaths

sheathe *verb*
sheathes
sheathing
sheathed

shed *noun*
sheds

shed *verb*
sheds
shedding
shed

she'd *verb*

sheen

sheep *noun*
sheep

sheepdog *noun*
sheepdogs

- -

★ To **shake** is to tremble or quiver. **!** sheikh.
☆ To **shear** is to cut wool from a sheep. **!** **sheer.**

sheepish adjective
sheepishly

★ **sheer** adjective
sheerer
sheerest

sheet noun
sheets

sheikh noun
sheikhs

shelf noun
shelves

shell noun
shells

shell verb
shells
shelling
shelled

she'll verb

shellfish noun
shellfish

shelter noun
shelters

shelter verb
shelters
sheltering
sheltered

shelve verb
shelves
shelving
shelved

shepherd noun
shepherds

sherbet noun
sherbets

sheriff noun
sheriffs

sherry noun
sherries

she's verb

shield noun
shields

shield verb
shields
shielding
shielded

shift noun
shifts

shift verb
shifts
shifting
shifted

shilling noun
shillings

shimmer verb
shimmers
shimmering
shimmered

shin noun
shins

shine verb
shines
shining
shone
shined

shine noun

shingle

shiny adjective
shinier
shiniest

-ship
-ship makes nouns,
e.g. friendship. Other
noun suffixes are
-dom, -hood, -ment,
and -ness.

ship noun
ships

ship verb
ships
shipping
shipped

shipping

shipwreck noun
shipwrecks

shipwrecked

shipyard noun
shipyards

shire noun
shires

shirk verb
shirks
shirking
shirked

shirt noun
shirts

shiver verb
shivers
shivering
shivered

shiver noun
shivers

shivery

shoal noun
shoals

shock verb
shocks
shocking
shocked

shock noun
shocks

shoddy adjective
shoddier
shoddiest
shoddily

shoe noun
shoes

shoelace noun
shoelaces

shoestring noun
shoestrings

shone see **shine**
shook see **shake**

- -

★ You use **sheer** in e.g. *sheer joy.* ! **shear.**

shoot verb
shoots
shooting
shot
★ **shoot** noun
shoots
shop noun
shops
shop verb
shops
shopping
shopped
shopkeeper noun
shopkeepers
shoplifter noun
shoplifters
shopper noun
shoppers
shopping
shore noun
shores
shorn see **shear**
short adjective
shorter
shortest
shortly
shortness
shortage noun
shortages
shortbread
shortcake noun
shortcakes
shortcoming noun
shortcomings
shorten verb
shortens
shortening
shortened
shorthand

short-handed
shortly
shorts plural noun
short-sighted
shot noun
shots
shot see **shoot**
shotgun noun
shotguns
should
shoulder noun
shoulders
shoulder verb
shoulders
shouldering
shouldered
shout verb
shouts
shouting
shouted
shout noun
shouts
shove verb
shoves
shoving
shoved
shovel noun
shovels
shovel verb
shovels
shovelling
shovelled
show verb
shows
showing
showed
shown
show noun
shows
shower noun
showers

shower verb
showers
showering
showered
showery
showjumper noun
showjumpers
showjumping
showman noun
showmen
showmanship
showroom noun
showrooms
showiness
showy adjective
showier
showiest
showily
shrank see **shrink**
shrapnel
shred noun
shreds
shred verb
shreds
shredding
shredded
shrew noun
shrews
shrewd adjective
shrewder
shrewdest
shrewdly
shrewdness
shriek verb
shrieks
shrieking
shrieked
shriek noun
shrieks

. . . .

★ To **shoot** is to fire at someone with a gun. ! **chute**.

shrill *adjective*
shriller
shrillest
shrilly
shrillness
shrimp *noun*
shrimps
shrine *noun*
shrines
shrink *verb*
shrinks
shrinking
shrank
shrunk
shrinkage
shrivel *verb*
shrivels
shrivelling
shrivelled
shroud *noun*
shrouds
shroud *verb*
shrouds
shrouding
shrouded
Shrove Tuesday
shrub *noun*
shrubs
shrubbery *noun*
shrubberies
shrug *verb*
shrugs
shrugging
shrugged
shrug *noun*
shrugs
shrunk see **shrink**
shrunken *adjective*
shudder *verb*
shudders
shuddering
shuddered

shudder *noun*
shudders
shuffle *verb*
shuffles
shuffling
shuffled
shuffle *noun*
shuffles
shunt *verb*
shunts
shunting
shunted
shunter *noun*
shunters
shut *verb*
shuts
shutting
shut
shutter *noun*
shutters
shuttle *noun*
shuttles
shuttlecock *noun*
shuttlecocks
shy *adjective*
shyer
shyest
shyly
Siamese
sick *adjective*
sicker
sickest
sicken *verb*
sickens
sickening
sickened
sickly *adjective*
sicklier
sickliest
sickness *noun*
sicknesses

side *noun*
sides
side *verb*
sides
siding
sided
sideboard *noun*
sideboards
sidecar *noun*
sidecars
sideline *noun*
sidelines
sideshow *noun*
sideshows
sideways
siding *noun*
sidings
siege *noun*
sieges
sieve *noun*
sieves
sift *verb*
sifts
sifting
sifted
sigh *verb*
sighs
sighing
sighed
sigh *noun*
sighs
★ **sight** *noun*
sights
sight *verb*
sights
sighting
sighted
sightseer *noun*
sightseers
sightseeing

★ A **sight** is something you see. ! **site**.

sign verb
signs
signing
signed

sign noun
signs

signal noun
signals

signal verb
signals
signalling
signalled

signaller noun
signallers

signalman noun
signalmen

signature noun
signatures

★ **signet** noun
signets

significance

significant adjective
significantly

signify verb
signifies
signifying
signified

signing

signpost noun
signposts

Sikh noun
Sikhs

silence noun
silences

silence verb
silences
silencing
silenced

silencer noun
silencers

silent adjective
silently

silhouette noun
silhouettes

silicon

silk

silken

silkworm noun
silkworms

silky adjective
silkier
silkiest
silkily

sill noun
sills

silliness

silly adjective
sillier
silliest
sillily

silver

silvery

similar adjective
similarly

similarity

simile noun
similes

simmer verb
simmers
simmering
simmered

simple adjective
simpler
simplest

simplicity

simplification

simplify verb
simplifies
simplifying
simplified

simply

simulate verb
simulates
simulating
simulated

simulation noun
simulations

simulator noun
simulators

simultaneous adjective
simultaneously

sin noun
sins

sin verb
sins
sinning
sinned

since preposition, adverb, and conjunction

sincere adjective
sincerer
sincerest
sincerely

sincerity

sinew noun
sinews

sinful adjective
sinfully

sinfulness

sing verb
sings
singing
sang
sung

singer noun
singers

singe verb
singes
singeing
singed

★ A **signet** is a seal worn in a ring. ! **cygnet.**

single adjective
singly
single noun
singles
single verb
singles
singling
singled
single-handed
singular adjective
singularly
singular noun
singulars
sinister adjective
sinisterly
sink verb
sinks
sinking
sank or sunk
sunk
sink noun
sinks
sinner noun
sinners
sinus noun
sinuses
sip verb
sips
sipping
sipped
siphon noun
siphons
siphon verb
siphons
siphoning
siphoned
sir
siren noun
sirens
sister noun
sisters

sisterly
sister-in-law noun
sisters-in-law
sit verb
sits
sitting
sat
sitter noun
sitters
★ **site** noun
sites
site verb
sites
siting
sited
sit-in noun
sit-ins
situated
situation noun
situations
six noun
sixes
sixpence noun
sixpences
sixteen noun
sixteens
sixteenth
sixth
sixthly
sixtieth
sixty noun
sixties
size noun
sizes
size verb
sizes
sizing
sized
sizeable

sizzle verb
sizzles
sizzling
sizzled
skate verb
skates
skating
skated
☆ **skate** noun
skates or skate
skateboard noun
skateboards
skater noun
skaters
skeletal adjective
skeletally
skeleton noun
skeletons
sketch noun
sketches
sketch verb
sketches
sketching
sketched
sketchy adjective
sketchier
sketchiest
sketchily
skewer noun
skewers
ski verb
skis
skiing
skied
ski'd
ski noun
skis

. . . .

★ A **site** is a place where something will be built. **! sight.**
☆ The plural is **skate** when you mean the fish.

skid verb
 skids
 skidding
 skidded

skid noun
 skids

skier noun
 skiers

skilful adjective
 skilfully

skill noun
 skills

skilled

skim verb
 skims
 skimming
 skimmed

skimp verb
 skimps
 skimping
 skimped

skimpy adjective
 skimpier
 skimpiest
 skimpily

skin noun
 skins

skin verb
 skins
 skinning
 skinned

skinny adjective
 skinnier
 skinniest

skint

skip verb
 skips
 skipping
 skipped

skip noun
 skips

skipper noun
 skippers

skirt noun
 skirts

skirt verb
 skirts
 skirting
 skirted

skirting noun
 skirtings

skit noun
 skits

skittish adjective
 skittishly

skittle noun
 skittles

skull noun
 skulls

skunk noun
 skunks

sky noun
 skies

skylark noun
 skylarks

skylight noun
 skylights

skyscraper noun
 skyscrapers

slab noun
 slabs

slack adjective
 slacker
 slackest
 slackly

slacken verb
 slackens
 slackening
 slackened

slackness

slacks plural noun

slag heap noun
 slag heaps

slain see slay

slam verb
 slams
 slamming
 slammed

slang

slant verb
 slants
 slanting
 slanted

slant noun
 slants

slap verb
 slaps
 slapping
 slapped

slap noun
 slaps

slapstick

slash verb
 slashes
 slashing
 slashed

slash noun
 slashes

slat noun
 slats

slate noun
 slates

slaty adjective
 slatier
 slatiest

slaughter verb
 slaughters
 slaughtering
 slaughtered

slaughter noun

slaughterhouse
noun
slaughterhouses

slave noun
slaves

slave verb
slaves
slaving
slaved

slavery

★ **slay** verb
slays
slaying
slew
slain

sled noun
sleds

sledge noun
sledges

sledgehammer
noun
sledgehammers

sleek adjective
sleeker
sleekest
sleekly

sleep verb
sleeps
sleeping
slept

sleep noun

sleeper noun
sleepers

sleepiness

sleepless

sleepwalker noun
sleepwalkers

sleepwalking

sleepy adjective
sleepier
sleepiest
sleepily

sleet

sleeve noun
sleeves

sleeveless

☆ **sleigh** noun
sleighs

slender adjective
slenderer
slenderest

slept see sleep
slew see slay

slice noun
slices

slice verb
slices
slicing
sliced

slick adjective
slicker
slickest
slickly

slick noun
slicks

slide verb
slides
sliding
slid

slide noun
slides

slight adjective
slighter
slightest
slightly

slim adjective
slimmer
slimmest
slimly

slim verb
slims
slimming
slimmed

slime

slimmer noun
slimmers

slimy adjective
slimier
slimiest

sling verb
slings
slinging
slung

sling noun
slings

slink verb
slinks
slinking
slunk

slip verb
slips
slipping
slipped

slip noun
slips

slipper noun
slippers

slippery

slipshod

slit noun
slits

slit verb
slits
slitting
slit

slither verb
slithers
slithering
slithered

sliver noun
slivers

slog verb
slogs
slogging
slogged

. . . .

★ To **slay** people is to kill them. **!** **sleigh**.
☆ A **sleigh** is a vehicle for sliding on snow. **!** **slay**.

slog *noun*
slogs

slogan *noun*
slogans

slop *verb*
slops
slopping
slopped

slope *verb*
slopes
sloping
sloped

slope *noun*
slopes

sloppiness

sloppy *adjective*
sloppier
sloppiest
sloppily

slops *plural noun*

slosh *verb*
sloshes
sloshing
sloshed

slot *noun*
slots

sloth *noun*
sloths

slouch *verb*
slouches
slouching
slouched

slovenly

slow *adjective*
slower
slowest
slowly

slow *verb*
slows
slowing
slowed

slowcoach *noun*
slowcoaches

slowness

sludge

slug *noun*
slugs

slum *noun*
slums

slumber

slumber *verb*
slumbers
slumbering
slumbered

slump *verb*
slumps
slumping
slumped

slump *noun*
slumps

slung see sling
slunk see slink
slur *noun*
slurs

slush

slushy *adjective*
slushier
slushiest
slushily

sly *adjective*
slyer
slyest
slyly

slyness

smack *verb*
smacks
smacking
smacked

smack *noun*
smacks

small *adjective*
smaller
smallest

smallpox

smart *adjective*
smarter
smartest
smartly

smart *verb*
smarts
smarting
smarted

smarten *verb*
smartens
smartening
smartened

smartness

smash *verb*
smashes
smashing
smashed

smash *noun*
smashes

smashing

smear *verb*
smears
smearing
smeared

smear *noun*
smears

smell *verb*
smells
smelling
smelt *or* smelled

smell *noun*
smells

smelly *adjective*
smellier
smelliest

smelt *verb*
smelts
smelting
smelted

smile *noun*
smiles

smile *verb*
smiles
smiling
smiled

smith *noun*
smiths

smithereens *plural noun*

smock *noun*
smocks

smog

smoke *noun*

smoke *verb*
smokes
smoking
smoked

smokeless

smoker *noun*
smokers

smoky *adjective*
smokier
smokiest

smooth *adjective*
smoother
smoothest
smoothly

smooth *verb*
smooths
smoothing
smoothed

smoothness

smother *verb*
smothers
smothering
smothered

smoulder *verb*
smoulders
smouldering
smouldered

smudge *verb*
smudges
smudging
smudged

smudge *noun*
smudges

smuggle *verb*
smuggles
smuggling
smuggled

smuggler *noun*
smugglers

smut *noun*
smuts

smutty *adjective*
smuttier
smuttiest
smuttily

snack *noun*
snacks

snag *noun*
snags

snail *noun*
snails

snake *noun*
snakes

snaky *adjective*
snakier
snakiest

snap *verb*
snaps
snapping
snapped

snap *noun*
snaps

snappy *adjective*
snappier
snappiest
snappily

snapshot *noun*
snapshots

snare *noun*
snares

snare *verb*
snares
snaring
snared

snarl *verb*
snarls
snarling
snarled

snarl *noun*
snarls

snatch *verb*
snatches
snatching
snatched

snatch *noun*
snatches

sneak *verb*
sneaks
sneaking
sneaked

sneak *noun*
sneaks

sneaky *adjective*
sneakier
sneakiest
sneakily

sneer *verb*
sneers
sneering
sneered

sneeze *verb*
sneezes
sneezing
sneezed

sneeze *noun*
sneezes

sniff *verb*
sniffs
sniffing
sniffed

sniff noun
sniffs

snigger verb
sniggers
sniggering
sniggered

snigger noun
sniggers

snip verb
snips
snipping
snipped

snip noun
snips

snipe verb
snipes
sniping
sniped

sniper noun
snipers

snippet noun
snippets

snivel verb
snivels
snivelling
snivelled

snob noun
snobs

snobbery

snobbish adjective
snobbishly

snooker

snoop verb
snoops
snooping
snooped

snooper noun
snoopers

snore verb
snores
snoring
snored

snorkel noun
snorkels

snort verb
snorts
snorting
snorted

snort noun
snorts

snout noun
snouts

snow noun
snow verb
snows
snowing
snowed

snowball noun
snowballs

snowdrop noun
snowdrops

snowflake noun
snowflakes

snowman noun
snowmen

snowplough noun
snowploughs

snowshoe noun
snowshoes

snowstorm noun
snowstorms

snowy adjective
snowier
snowiest

snub verb
snubs
snubbing
snubbed

snuff

snug adjective
snugger
snuggest
snugly

snuggle verb
snuggles
snuggling
snuggled

soak verb
soaks
soaking
soaked

so-and-so noun
so-and-so's

soap noun
soaps

soapiness noun

soapy adjective
soapier
soapiest
soapily

★ **soar** verb
soars
soaring
soared

sob verb
sobs
sobbing
sobbed

sob noun
sobs

sober adjective
soberly

sobriety

so-called

soccer

sociability

sociable adjective
sociably

social adjective
socially

socialism

socialist noun
socialists

★ To **soar** is to rise or fly high. ! **sore**.

society noun
societies
sociological adjective
sociologically
sociologist noun
sociologists
sociology
sock noun
socks
sock verb
socks
socking
socked
socket noun
sockets
soda
sodium
sofa noun
sofas
soft adjective
softer
softest
softly
soften verb
softens
softening
softened
softness
software
soggy adjective
soggier
soggiest
soggily
soil noun
soil verb
soils
soiling
soiled

solar
sold see sell
solder noun
solder verb
solders
soldering
soldered
soldier noun
soldiers
★ **sole** noun
soles
sole adjective
solely
solemn adjective
solemnly
solemnity
solicitor noun
solicitors
solid adjective
solidly
solid noun
solids
solidify verb
solidifies
solidifying
solidified
solidity
soliloquy noun
soliloquies
solitary
solitude
solo noun
solos
soloist noun
soloists
solstice noun
solstices

solubility
soluble adjective
solubly
solution noun
solutions
solve verb
solves
solving
solved
solvent adjective and noun
solvents
sombre adjective
sombrely
☆ **some** adjective and pronoun
somebody
somehow
someone
somersault noun
somersaults
something
sometime
sometimes
somewhat
somewhere
♻ **son** noun
sons
sonar noun
sonars
song noun
songs
songbird noun
songbirds
sonic adjective
sonically
sonnet noun
sonnets

. . . .

★ A **sole** is a fish or a part of a shoe. ! **soul.**
☆ You use **some** in e.g. *Have some cake.* ! **sum.**
♻ A **son** is a male child. ! **sun.**

soon adverb
sooner
soonest

soot

soothe verb
soothes
soothing
soothed

sooty adjective
sootier
sootiest

sophisticated

sophistication

sopping

soppy adjective
soppier
soppiest
soppily

soprano noun
sopranos

sorcerer noun
sorcerers

sorceress noun
sorceresses

sorcery

★ **sore** adjective
sorer
sorest
sorely

sore noun
sores

soreness

sorrow noun
sorrows

sorrowful adjective
sorrowfully

sorry adjective
sorrier
sorriest

sort noun
sorts

sort verb
sorts
sorting
sorted

sought see **seek**

☆ **soul** noun
souls

sound noun
sounds

sound verb
sounds
sounding
sounded

sound adjective
sounder
soundest
soundly

soundness

soundtrack noun
soundtracks

soup noun
soups

sour adjective
sourer
sourest
sourly

⊙ **source** noun
sources

sourness

south adjective and
adverb

✷ **south** noun

south-east noun and
adjective

southerly adjective
and noun
southerlies

southern adjective

southerner noun
southerners

southward adjective
and adverb

southwards adverb

south-west noun and
adjective

souvenir noun
souvenirs

sovereign noun
sovereigns

✱ **sow** verb
sows
sowing
sowed
sown

sow noun
sows

sower noun
sowers

soya bean noun
soya beans

space noun
spaces

space verb
spaces
spacing
spaced

spacecraft noun
spacecraft

spaceman noun
spacemen

spaceship noun
spaceships

spacewoman noun
spacewomen

spacious adjective
spaciously

. . . .

★ You use **sore** in e.g. *I've got a sore tooth.* ! **soar.**
☆ A **soul** is a person's spirit. ! **sole.**
⊙ The **source** is where something comes from. ! **sauce.**
✷ You use a capital S in the **South,** when you mean a particular region.
✱ To **sow** is to put seed in the ground. ! **sew.**

spaciousness

spade noun
  spades

spaghetti

span verb
  spans
  spanning
  spanned

span noun
  spans

spaniel noun
  spaniels

spank verb
  spanks
  spanking
  spanked

spanner noun
  spanners

spar noun
  spars

spar verb
  spars
  sparring
  sparred

spare verb
  spares
  sparing
  spared

spare adjective and
  noun
  spares

sparing adjective
  sparingly

spark noun
  sparks

spark verb
  sparks
  sparking
  sparked

sparkle verb
  sparkles
  sparkling
  sparkled

sparkler noun
  sparklers

sparrow noun
  sparrows

sparse adjective
  sparser
  sparsest
  sparsely

sparseness

spastic noun
  spastics

spat see **spit**

spatter verb
  spatters
  spattering
  spattered

spawn noun

spawn verb
  spawns
  spawning
  spawned

speak verb
  speaks
  speaking
  spoke
  spoken

speaker noun
  speakers

spear noun
  spears

spear verb
  spears
  spearing
  speared

special adjective
  specially

specialist noun
  specialists

speciality noun
  specialities

specialization

specialize verb
  specializes
  specializing
  specialized

species noun
  species

specific adjective
  specifically

specification noun
  specifications

specify verb
  specifies
  specifying
  specified

specimen noun
  specimens

speck noun
  specks

speckled

spectacle noun
  spectacles

spectacular
  adjective
  spectacularly

spectator noun
  spectators

spectre noun
  spectres

spectrum noun
  spectra

speech noun
  speeches

speechless

speed noun
speeds

★ **speed** verb
speeds
speeding
sped or speeded

speedboat noun
speedboats

speedometer noun
speedometers

speedway noun
speedways

speedy adjective
speedier
speediest
speedily

spell verb
spells
spelling
spelt
spelled

spell noun
spells

spelling noun
spellings

spend verb
spends
spending
spent

sperm noun
sperms or sperm

sphere noun
spheres

spherical adjective
spherically

spice noun
spices

spicy adjective
spicier
spiciest

spider noun
spiders

spied see spy

spike noun
spikes

spiky adjective
spikier
spikiest

☆ **spill** verb
spills
spilling
spilt or spilled

spill noun
spills

spin verb
spins
spinning
spun

spin noun
spins

spinach

spindle noun
spindles

spin-drier noun
spin-driers

spine noun
spines

spinal

spin-off noun
spin-offs

spinster noun
spinsters

spiny adjective
spiniest
spiniest

spiral adjective
spirally

spire noun
spires

spirit noun
spirits

spiritual adjective
spiritually

spiritual noun
spirituals

spiritualism

spiritualist noun
spiritualists

spit verb
spits
spitting
spat

spit noun
spits

spite

spiteful adjective
spitefully

spittle

splash verb
splashes
splashing
splashed

splash noun
splashes

splashdown noun
splashdowns

splendid adjective
splendidly

splendour

splint noun
splints

splinter noun
splinters

splinter verb
splinters
splintering
splintered

split verb
splits
splitting
split

split noun
splits

. . . .

★ You use **sped** in e.g. *Cars sped past* and **speeded** in e.g. *They speeded up the process.*

☆ You use **spilled** in e.g. *I spilled the milk.* You use **spilt** in e.g. *I can see spilt milk.* You use **spilled** or **spilt** in e.g. *I have spilled/spilt the milk.*

splutter verb
splutters
spluttering
spluttered

★ **spoil** verb
spoils
spoiling
spoilt or spoiled

spoils plural noun

spoilsport noun
spoilsports

spoke noun
spokes

spoke see speak

spoken see speak

spokesperson noun
spokespersons

sponge noun
sponges

sponge verb
sponges
sponging
sponged

sponger noun
spongers

sponginess noun

spongy adjective
spongier
spongiest
spongily

sponsor noun
sponsors

sponsorship noun
sponsorships

spontaneity

spontaneous
adjective
spontaneously

spooky adjective
spookier
spookiest
spookily

spool noun
spools

spoon noun
spoons

spoon verb
spoons
spooning
spooned

spoonful noun
spoonfuls

sport noun
sports

sporting

sportsman noun
sportsmen

sportsmanship

sportswoman noun
sportswomen

spot noun
spots

spot verb
spots
spotting
spotted

spotless adjective
spotlessly

spotlight noun
spotlights

spotter noun
spotters

spotty adjective
spottier
spottiest
spottily

spout noun
spouts

spout verb
spouts
spouting
spouted

sprain verb
sprains
spraining
sprained

sprain noun
sprains

sprang see spring

sprawl verb
sprawls
sprawling
sprawled

spray verb
sprays
spraying
sprayed

spray noun
sprays

spread verb
spreads
spreading
spread

spread noun
spreads

spreadsheet noun
spreadsheets

sprightliness

sprightly adjective
sprightlier
sprightliest

spring verb
springs
springing
sprang
sprung

spring noun
springs

springboard noun
springboards

. . . .

★ You use **spoiled** in e.g. *They spoiled the party.* You use **spoilt** in e.g. *a spoilt child.* You use **spoiled** or **spoilt** in e.g. *They have spoiled/spoilt the party.*

spring-clean verb
spring-cleans
spring-cleaning
spring-cleaned

springtime

springy adjective
springier
springiest

sprinkle verb
sprinkles
sprinkling
sprinkled

sprinkler noun
sprinklers

sprint verb
sprints
sprinting
sprinted

sprinter noun
sprinters

sprout verb
sprouts
sprouting
sprouted

sprout noun
sprouts

spruce noun
spruces

spruce adjective
sprucer
sprucest

sprung see **spring**

spud noun
spuds

spun see **spin**

spur noun
spurs

spur verb
spurs
spurring
spurred

spurt verb
spurts
spurting
spurted

spurt noun
spurts

spy noun
spies

spy verb
spies
spying
spied

squabble verb
squabbles
squabbling
squabbled

squabble noun
squabbles

squad noun
squads

squadron noun
squadrons

squalid adjective
squalidly

squall noun
squalls

squally adjective
squallier
squalliest

squalor

squander verb
squanders
squandering
squandered

square adjective
squarely

square noun
squares

square verb
squares
squaring
squared

squareness

squash verb
squashes
squashing
squashed

squash noun
squashes

squat verb
squats
squatting
squatted

squat adjective
squatter
squattest
squatly

squatter noun
squatters

squaw noun
squaws

squawk verb
squawks
squawking
squawked

squawk noun
squawks

squeak verb
squeaks
squeaking
squeaked

squeak noun
squeaks

squeaky adjective
squeakier
squeakiest
squeakily

squeal verb
squeals
squealing
squealed

squeal noun
squeals

squeeze verb
squeezes
squeezing
squeezed

squeeze noun
squeezes

squeezer noun
squeezers

squelch verb
squelches
squelching
squelched

squelch noun
squelches

squid noun
squid or squids

squint verb
squints
squinting
squinted

squint noun
squints

squire noun
squires

squirm verb
squirms
squirming
squirmed

squirrel noun
squirrels

squirt verb
squirts
squirting
squirted

stab verb
stabs
stabbing
stabbed

stab noun
stabs

stability

stabilize verb
stabilizes
stabilizing
stabilized

stabilizer noun
stabilizers

stable adjective
stabler
stablest
stably

stable noun
stables

stack verb
stacks
stacking
stacked

stack noun
stacks

stadium noun
stadiums or stadia

staff noun
staffs

stag noun
stags

stage noun
stages

stage verb
stages
staging
staged

stagecoach noun
stagecoaches

stagger verb
staggers
staggering
staggered

stagnant adjective
stagnantly

stain noun
stains

stain verb
stains
staining
stained

stainless

★ **stair** noun
stairs

staircase noun
staircases

☆ **stake** noun
stakes

stake verb
stakes
staking
staked

stalactite noun
stalactites

stalagmite noun
stalagmites

stale adjective
staler
stalest

stalk noun
stalks

stalk verb
stalks
stalking
stalked

stall noun
stalls

stall verb
stalls
stalling
stalled

stallion noun
stallions

stalls plural noun

stamen noun
stamens

stamina

· ·

★ A **stair** is one of a set of steps. ! stare.
☆ A **stake** is a pointed stick or post. ! steak.

stammer *verb*
stammers
stammering
stammered

stammer *noun*
stammers

stamp *noun*
stamps

stamp *verb*
stamps
stamping
stamped

stampede *noun*
stampedes

stand *verb*
stands
standing
stood

stand *noun*
stands

standard *adjective*
and *noun*
standards

standardize *verb*
standardizes
standardizing
standardized

standby *noun*
standbys

standstill *noun*
standstills

stank see **stink**

stanza *noun*
stanzas

staple *noun*
staples

staple *adjective*

stapler *noun*
staplers

star *noun*
stars

starry *adjective*
starrier
starriest
starrily

star *verb*
stars
starring
starred

starboard

starch *noun*
starches

starchy *adjective*
starchier
starchiest

★ **stare** *verb*
stares
staring
stared

starfish *noun*
starfish or starfishes

starling *noun*
starlings

start *verb*
starts
starting
started

start *noun*
starts

starter *noun*
starters

startle *verb*
startles
startling
startled

starvation

starve *verb*
starves
starving
starved

state *noun*
states

state *verb*
states
stating
stated

stateliness

stately *adjective*
statelier
stateliest

statement *noun*
statements

statesman *noun*
statesmen

statesmanship

stateswoman *noun*
stateswomen

static *adjective*
statically

station *noun*
stations

station *verb*
stations
stationing
stationed

☆ **stationary** *adjective*
◉ **stationery** *noun*
stationmaster *noun*
stationmasters

statistic *noun*
statistics

statistical *adjective*
statistically

statistician *noun*
statisticians

statistics

statue *noun*
statues

status *noun*
statuses

. . . .

★ To **stare** is to look at something without moving your eyes. ! **stair**.
☆ **Stationary** means 'not moving'. ! **stationery**.
◉ **Stationery** means 'paper and envelopes'. ! **stationary**.

staunch *adjective*
stauncher
staunchest
staunchly

stave *noun*
staves

stave *verb*
staves
staving
staved
stove

stay *verb*
stays
staying
stayed

stay *noun*
stays

steadiness

steady *adjective*
steadier
steadiest
steadily

steady *verb*
steadies
steadying
steadied

★ **steak** *noun*
steaks

☆ **steal** *verb*
steals
stealing
stole
stolen

stealth

stealthy *adjective*
stealthier
stealthiest
stealthily

steam *noun*

steam *verb*
steams
steaming
steamed

steamy *adjective*
steamier
steamiest
steamily

steamer *noun*
steamers

steamroller *noun*
steamrollers

steamship *noun*
steamships

steed *noun*
steeds

steel *noun*

○ **steel** *verb*
steels
steeling
steeled

steely *adjective*
steelier
steeliest

steep *adjective*
steeper
steepest
steeply

steepness

steeple *noun*
steeples

steeplechase *noun*
steeplechases

steeplejack *noun*
steeplejacks

steer *verb*
steers
steering
steered

steer *noun*
steers

stem *noun*
stems

stem *verb*
stems
stemming
stemmed

stench *noun*
stenches

stencil *noun*
stencils

✳ **step** *noun*
steps

step *verb*
steps
stepping
stepped

stepchild *noun*
stepchildren

stepfather *noun*
stepfathers

stepladder *noun*
stepladders

stepmother *noun*
stepmothers

✻ **steppe** *noun*
steppes

stereo *adjective* and *noun*
stereos

stereophonic *adjective*
stereophonically

sterile

sterility

sterilization

sterilize *verb*
sterilizes
sterilizing
sterilized

sterling

★ A steak is a thick slice of meat. **! stake.**
☆ To steal is to take something that is not yours. **! steel.**
○ To steel yourself is to find courage to do something hard. **! steal.**
✳ A step is a movement of the feet or part of a stair. **! steppe.**
✻ A steppe is a grassy plain. **! step.**

stern noun
  sterns

stern adjective
  sterner
  sternest
  sternly

sternness

stethoscope noun
  stethoscopes

stew verb
  stews
  stewing
  stewed

stew noun
  stews

steward noun
  stewards

stewardess noun
  stewardesses

stick verb
  sticks
  sticking
  stuck

stick noun
  sticks

sticker noun
  stickers

stickiness

stickleback noun
  sticklebacks

sticky adjective
  stickier
  stickiest
  stickily

stiff adjective
  stiffer
  stiffest
  stiffly

stiffen verb
  stiffens
  stiffening
  stiffened

stiffness

stifle verb
  stifles
  stifling
  stifled

stile noun
  stiles

still adjective
  stiller
  stillest

still adverb

still verb
  stills
  stilling
  stilled

stillness

stilts

stimulant noun
  stimulants

stimulate verb
  stimulates
  stimulating
  stimulated

stimulation

stimulus noun
  stimuli

sting noun
  stings

sting verb
  stings
  stinging
  stung

stingy adjective
  stingier
  stingiest
  stingily

stink noun
  stinks

stink verb
  stinks
  stinking
  stank
  stunk

stir verb
  stirs
  stirring
  stirred

stir noun
  stirs

stirrup noun
  stirrups

stitch noun
  stitches

stoat noun
  stoats

stock noun
  stocks

stock verb
  stocks
  stocking
  stocked

stockade noun
  stockades

stockbroker noun
  stockbrokers

stocking noun
  stockings

stockpile noun
  stockpiles

stocks plural noun

stocky adjective
  stockier
  stockiest
  stockily

stodgy adjective
  stodgier
  stodgiest
  stodgily

stoke verb
  stokes
  stoking
  stoked

stole noun
stoles

stole see steal

stolen see steal

stomach noun
stomachs

stomach verb
stomachs
stomaching
stomached

stone noun
stones or stone

stone verb
stones
stoning
stoned

stony adjective
stonier
stoniest

stood see stand

stool noun
stools

stoop verb
stoops
stooping
stooped

stop verb
stops
stopping
stopped

stop noun
stops

stoppage noun
stoppages

stopper noun
stoppers

stopwatch noun
stopwatches

storage

store verb
stores
storing
stored

store noun
stores

★ **storey** noun
storeys

stork noun
storks

storm noun
storms

storm verb
storms
storming
stormed

stormy adjective
stormier
stormiest
stormily

☆ **story** noun
stories

stout adjective
stouter
stoutest
stoutly

stoutness

stove noun
stoves

stove see stave

stow verb
stows
stowing
stowed

stowaway noun
stowaways

straddle verb
straddles
straddling
straddled

straggle verb
straggles
straggling
straggled

straggler noun
stragglers

straggly adjective
stragglier
straggliest

○ **straight** adjective
straighter
straightest

straighten verb
straightens
straightening
straightened

straightforward
adjective
straightforwardly

strain verb
strains
straining
strained

strain noun
strains

strainer noun
strainers

✳ **strait** noun
straits

✻ **straits** plural noun

strand noun
strands

stranded

strange adjective
stranger
strangest
strangely

strangeness

stranger noun
strangers

. . . .

★ A **storey** is a floor of a building. ! story.
☆ You use **story** in e.g. *read me a story*. ! storey.
○ **Straight** means 'not curving or bending'. ! strait.
✳ A **strait** is a narrow stretch of water. ! straight.
✻ You use **straits** in the phrase *in dire straits*.

strangle *verb*
strangles
strangling
strangled
strangler *noun*
stranglers
strangulation
strap *noun*
straps
strap *verb*
straps
strapping
strapped
strategic *adjective*
strategically
strategist *noun*
strategists
strategy *noun*
strategies
stratum *noun*
strata
straw *noun*
straws
strawberry *noun*
strawberries
stray *verb*
strays
straying
strayed
stray *adjective*
streak *noun*
streaks
streak *verb*
streaks
streaking
streaked
streaky *adjective*
streakier
streakiest
streakily
stream *noun*
streams

stream *verb*
streams
streaming
streamed
streamer *noun*
streamers
streamline *verb*
streamlines
streamlining
streamlined
street *noun*
streets
strength *noun*
strengths
strengthen *verb*
strengthens
strengthening
strengthened
strenuous *adjective*
strenuously
stress *noun*
stresses
stress *verb*
stresses
stressing
stressed
stretch *verb*
stretches
stretching
stretched
stretch *noun*
stretches
stretcher *noun*
stretchers
strew *verb*
strews
strewing
strewed
strewn
stricken

strict *adjective*
stricter
strictest
strictly
strictness
stride *verb*
strides
striding
strode
stridden
stride *noun*
strides
strife
strike *verb*
strikes
striking
struck
strike *noun*
strikes
striker *noun*
strikers
striking *adjective*
strikingly
string *noun*
strings
string *verb*
strings
stringing
strung
stringiness
stringy *adjective*
stringier
stringiest
stringily
strip *verb*
strips
stripping
stripped
strip *noun*
strips

stripe noun
  stripes
striped
stripy adjective
  stripier
  stripiest
strive verb
  strives
  striving
  strove
  striven
strobe noun
  strobes
strode see **stride**
stroke noun
  strokes
stroke verb
  strokes
  stroking
  stroked
stroll verb
  strolls
  strolling
  strolled
stroll noun
  strolls
strong adjective
  stronger
  strongest
  strongly
stronghold noun
  strongholds
strove see **strive**
struck see **strike**
structural adjective
  structurally
structure noun
  structures
struggle verb
  struggles
  struggling
  struggled

struggle noun
  struggles
strum verb
  strums
  strumming
  strummed
strung see **string**
strut verb
  struts
  strutting
  strutted
strut noun
  struts
stub verb
  stubs
  stubbing
  stubbed
stub noun
  stubs
stubble
stubborn adjective
  stubbornly
stubbornness
stuck see **stick**
stuck-up
stud noun
  studs
student noun
  students
studio noun
  studios
studious adjective
  studiously
study verb
  studies
  studying
  studied
study noun
  studies
stuff noun

stuff verb
  stuffs
  stuffing
  stuffed
stuffiness
stuffing noun
  stuffings
stuffy adjective
  stuffier
  stuffiest
  stuffily
stumble verb
  stumbles
  stumbling
  stumbled
stump noun
  stumps
stump verb
  stumps
  stumping
  stumped
stun verb
  stuns
  stunning
  stunned
stung see **sting**
stunk see **stink**
stunt noun
  stunts
stupendous adjective
  stupendously
stupid adjective
  stupider
  stupidest
  stupidly
stupidity
sturdiness
sturdy adjective
  sturdier
  sturdiest
  sturdily

stutter *verb*
stutters
stuttering
stuttered

stutter *noun*
stutters

★ **sty** *noun*
sties

style *noun*
styles

style *verb*
styles
styling
styled

stylish *adjective*
stylishly

stylus *noun*
styluses

subcontinent *noun*
subcontinents

subdivide *verb*
subdivides
subdividing
subdivided

subdivision *noun*
subdivisions

subdue *verb*
subdues
subduing
subdued

subject *adjective* and *noun*
subjects

subject *verb*
subjects
subjecting
subjected

subjective *adjective*
subjectively

submarine *noun*
submarines

submerge *verb*
submerges
submerging
submerged

submersion

submission *noun*
submissions

submissive *adjective*
submissively

submit *verb*
submits
submitting
submitted

subordinate *adjective* and *noun*
subordinates

subordinate *verb*
subordinates
subordinating
subordinated

subordination

subscribe *verb*
subscribes
subscribing
subscribed

subscriber *noun*
subscribers

subscription *noun*
subscriptions

subsequent *adjective*
subsequently

subside *verb*
subsides
subsiding
subsided

subsidence

subsidize *verb*
subsidizes
subsidizing
subsidized

subsidy *noun*
subsidies

substance *noun*
substances

substantial *adjective*
substantially

substitute *verb*
substitutes
substituting
substituted

substitute *noun*
substitutes

substitution *noun*
substitutions

subtle *adjective*
subtler
subtlest
subtly

subtlety *noun*
subtleties

subtract *verb*
subtracts
subtracting
subtracted

subtraction *noun*
subtractions

suburb *noun*
suburbs

suburban

suburbia

subway *noun*
subways

succeed *verb*
succeeds
succeeding
succeeded

success *noun*
successes

successful *adjective*
successfully

★ A sty is a place for pigs or a swelling on the eye. In the second meaning you
can also use *stye*, plural *styes*.

succession noun
  successions
successive adjective
  successively
successor noun
  successors
such
suck verb
  sucks
  sucking
  sucked
suck noun
  sucks
suction
sudden adjective
  suddenly
suddenness
suds plural noun
sue verb
  sues
  suing
  sued
suede
suet
suffer verb
  suffers
  suffering
  suffered
sufficiency
sufficient adjective
  sufficiently
suffix noun
  suffixes
suffocate verb
  suffocates
  suffocating
  suffocated
suffocation
sugar
sugary

suggest verb
  suggests
  suggesting
  suggested
suggestion noun
  suggestions
suicidal adjective
  suicidally
suicide noun
  suicides
★ **suit** noun
  suits
suit verb
  suits
  suiting
  suited
suitability
suitable adjective
  suitably
suitcase noun
  suitcases
☆ **suite** noun
  suites
suitor noun
  suitors
sulk verb
  sulks
  sulking
  sulked
sulkiness
sulky adjective
  sulkier
  sulkiest
  sulkily
sullen adjective
  sullenly
sullenness
sulphur
sulphuric acid
sultan noun
  sultans

sultana noun
  sultanas
○ **sum** noun
  sums
sum verb
  sums
  summing
  summed
summarize verb
  summarizes
  summarizing
  summarized
summary noun
  summaries
summer noun
  summers
summertime
summit noun
  summits
summon verb
  summons
  summoning
  summoned
summons noun
  summonses
✳ **sun** noun
  suns
sun verb
  suns
  sunning
  sunned
sunbathe verb
  sunbathes
  sunbathing
  sunbathed
sunburn
sunburned or
sunburnt
✻ **sundae** noun
  sundaes

. . . .

★ A suit is a set of matching clothes. ! suite.
☆ A suite is a set of furniture or a group of rooms. ! suit.
○ A sum is an amount or total. ! some.
✳ A sun is a large star. ! son.
✻ A sundae is a cocktail of fruit and ice cream. ! **Sunday**.

★ **Sunday** noun
  Sundays
sundial noun
  sundials
sunflower noun
  sunflowers
sung see **sing**
sunglasses
sunk see **sink**
sunlight
sunlit
sunny adjective
  sunnier
  sunniest
  sunnily
sunrise noun
  sunrises
sunset noun
  sunsets
sunshade noun
  sunshades
sunshine
sunspot noun
  sunspots
sunstroke
suntan noun
  suntans
suntanned
super

> **super-**
> super- makes words
> meaning 'very good'
> or 'extra', e.g.
> supermarket,
> supermodel. They
> are normally spelt
> joined up.

superb adjective
  superbly
superficial adjective
  superficially

superfluous adjective
  superfluously
superintend verb
  superintends
  superintending
  superintended
superintendent
  noun
  superintendents
superior adjective
  and noun
  superiors
superiority
superlative adjective
  superlatively
superlative noun
  superlatives
supermarket noun
  supermarkets
supernatural
  adjective
  supernaturally
supersonic adjective
  supersonically
superstition noun
  superstitions
superstitious
  adjective
  superstitiously
supervise verb
  supervises
  supervising
  supervised
supervision
supervisor
supper noun
  suppers
supple adjective
  suppler
  supplest
  supplely

supplement noun
  supplements
supplementary
suppleness
supply verb
  supplies
  supplying
  supplied
supplier noun
  suppliers
supply noun
  supplies
support verb
  supports
  supporting
  supported
support noun
  supports
supporter noun
  supporters
suppose verb
  supposes
  supposing
  supposed
supposedly
supposition noun
  suppositions
suppress verb
  suppresses
  suppressing
  suppressed
suppression
supremacy
supreme adjective
  supremely
sure adjective
  surer
  surest
  surely
surf noun

- -
★ **Sunday** is a day of the week. ! **sundae.**

surf *verb*
surfs
surfing
surfed

surface *noun*
surfaces

surface *verb*
surfaces
surfacing
surfaced

surfboard *noun*
surfboards

surfer *noun*
surfers

surge *verb*
surges
surging
surged

surge *noun*
surges

surgeon *noun*
surgeons

surgery *noun*
surgeries

surgical *adjective*
surgically

surname *noun*
surnames

surpass *verb*
surpasses
surpassing
surpassed

surplus *noun*
surpluses

surprise *verb*
surprises
surprising
surprised

surprise *noun*
surprises

surrender *verb*
surrenders
surrendering
surrendered

surrender *noun*
surrenders

surround *verb*
surrounds
surrounding
surrounded

surroundings *plural noun*

survey *noun*
surveys

survey *verb*
surveys
surveying
surveyed

surveyor *noun*
surveyors

survival

survive *verb*
survives
surviving
survived

survivor *noun*
survivors

suspect *verb*
suspects
suspecting
suspected

suspect *noun*
suspects

suspend *verb*
suspends
suspending
suspended

suspense

suspension *noun*
suspensions

suspicion *noun*
suspicions

suspicious *adjective*
suspiciously

sustain *verb*
sustains
sustaining
sustained

swagger *verb*
swaggers
swaggering
swaggered

swallow *verb*
swallows
swallowing
swallowed

swallow *noun*
swallows

swam see swim

swamp *verb*
swamps
swamping
swamped

swamp *noun*
swamps

swampy *adjective*
swampier
swampiest

swan *noun*
swans

swank *verb*
swanks
swanking
swanked

swap *verb*
swaps
swapping
swapped

swap *noun*
swaps

swarm *noun*
swarms

swarm *verb*
swarms
swarming
swarmed

swastika *noun*
swastikas

★ **swat** *verb*
swats
swatting
swatted

swatter *noun*
swatters

sway *verb*
sways
swaying
swayed

swear *verb*
swears
swearing
swore
sworn

sweat *verb*
sweats
sweating
sweated

sweat *noun*

sweater *noun*
sweaters

sweatshirt *noun*
sweatshirts

sweaty *adjective*
sweatier
sweatiest
sweatily

swede *noun*
swedes

sweep *verb*
sweeps
sweeping
swept

sweep *noun*
sweeps

sweeper *noun*
sweepers

sweet *adjective*
sweeter
sweetest
sweetly

sweet *noun*
sweets

sweetcorn

sweeten *verb*
sweetens
sweetening
sweetened

sweetener *noun*
sweeteners

sweetheart *noun*
sweethearts

sweetness

swell *verb*
swells
swelling
swelled
swollen

swell *noun*
swells

swelling *noun*
swellings

swelter *verb*
swelters
sweltering
sweltered

swept see **sweep**

swerve *verb*
swerves
swerving
swerved

swerve *noun*
swerves

swift *adjective*
swifter
swiftest
swiftly

swift *noun*
swifts

swiftness

swill *verb*
swills
swilling
swilled

swill *noun*

swim *verb*
swims
swimming
swam
swum

swim *noun*
swims

swimmer *noun*
swimmers

swimsuit *noun*
swimsuits

swindle *verb*
swindles
swindling
swindled

swindler *noun*
swindlers

swindle *noun*
swindles

swine *noun*
swine or swines

swing *verb*
swings
swinging
swung

swing *noun*
swings

swipe *verb*
swipes
swiping
swiped

★ To **swat** an insect is to hit it. ! **swot**.

swipe noun
swipes

swirl verb
swirls
swirling
swirled

swirl noun
swirls

swish verb
swishes
swishing
swished

swish noun
swishes

Swiss roll noun
Swiss rolls

switch verb
switches
switching
switched

switch noun
switches

switchboard noun
switchboards

swivel verb
swivels
swivelling
swivelled

swollen see **swell**

swoon verb
swoons
swooning
swooned

swoop verb
swoops
swooping
swooped

swoop noun
swoops

swop verb
swops
swopping
swopped

sword noun
swords

swore see **swear**

sworn see **swear**

★ **swot** verb
swots
swotting
swotted

swot noun
swots

swum see **swim**

swung see **swing**

sycamore noun
sycamores

syllabic adjective
syllabically

syllable noun
syllables

syllabus noun
syllabuses

symbol noun
symbols

symbolic adjective
symbolically

symbolism

symbolize verb
symbolizes
symbolizing
symbolized

symmetrical
adjective
symmetrically

symmetry

sympathetic
adjective
sympathetically

sympathize verb
sympathizes
sympathizing
sympathized

sympathy noun
sympathies

symphonic adjective
symphonically

symphony noun
symphonies

symptom noun
symptoms

symptomatic
adjective
symptomatically

synagogue noun
synagogues

synchronization

synchronize verb
synchronizes
synchronizing
synchronized

syncopated

synonym noun
synonyms

synonymous
adjective
synonymously

synthesis noun
syntheses

synthesize verb
synthesizes
synthesizing
synthesized

synthesizer noun
synthesizers

synthetic adjective
synthetically

syringe noun
syringes

· ·

★ To **swot** is to study hard. ! **swat.**

syrup noun
syrups

syrupy

system noun
systems

systematic adjective
systematically

Tt

-t
See the note at -ed.

tab noun
tabs

tabby noun
tabbies

table noun
tables

tablecloth noun
tablecloths

tablespoon noun
tablespoons

tablespoonful noun
tablespoonfuls

tablet noun
tablets

tack noun
tacks

tack verb
tacks
tacking
tacked

tackle verb
tackles
tackling
tackled

tackle noun
tackles

tacky adjective
tackier
tackiest
tackily

tact

tactful adjective
tactfully

tactical adjective
tactically

tactics plural noun

tactless adjective
tactlessly

tadpole noun
tadpoles

tag noun
tags

tag verb
tags
tagging
tagged

★ **tail** noun
tails

tail verb
tails
tailing
tailed

tailback noun
tailbacks

tailless

tailor noun
tailors

take verb
takes
taking
took
taken

takeaway noun
takeaways

takings plural noun

talc

talcum powder

☆ **tale** noun
tales

talent noun
talents

talented

talk verb
talks
talking
talked

talk noun
talks

talkative adjective
talkatively

talker noun
talkers

tall adjective
taller
tallest

tally verb
tallies
tallying
tallied

Talmud

talon noun
talons

tambourine noun
tambourines

tame adjective
tamer
tamest
tamely

tame verb
tames
taming
tamed

tameness

tamer noun
tamers

- -

★ A tail is a part at the back of an animal. ! tale.
☆ A tale is a story. ! tail.

tamper verb
tampers
tampering
tampered

tampon noun
tampons

tan noun
tans

tan verb
tans
tanning
tanned

tandem noun
tandems

tang noun
tangs

tangent noun
tangents

tangerine noun
tangerines

tangle verb
tangles
tangling
tangled

tangle noun
tangles

tank noun
tanks

tankard noun
tankards

tanker noun
tankers

tanner noun
tanners

tantalize verb
tantalizes
tantalizing
tantalized

tantrum noun
tantrums

tap noun
taps

tap verb
taps
tapping
tapped

tap dance noun
tap dances

tap dancer noun
tap dancers

tap dancing

tape noun
tapes

tape verb
tapes
taping
taped

tape-measure noun
tape-measures

taper verb
tapers
tapering
tapered

taper noun
tapers

tape recorder noun
tape recorders

tapestry noun
tapestries

tapeworm noun
tapeworms

tapioca

tar noun

tar verb
tars
tarring
tarred

tarantula noun
tarantulas

target noun
targets

target verb
targets
targeting
targeted

tarmac

tarmacadam

tarnish verb
tarnishes
tarnishing
tarnished

tarpaulin noun
tarpaulins

tarry adjective
tarrier
tarriest

tart noun
tarts

tart adjective
tarter
tartest
tartly

tartan noun
tartans

task noun
tasks

tassel noun
tassels

taste verb
tastes
tasting
tasted

taste noun
tastes

tasteful adjective
tastefully

tasteless adjective
tastelessly

tasty adjective
tastier
tastiest
tastily

tattered

tatters plural noun

tattoo noun
tattoos

tattoo verb
tattoos
tattooing
tattooed

tatty adjective
tattier
tattiest
tattily

taught see teach

taunt verb
taunts
taunting
taunted

taunt noun
taunts

taut adjective
tauter
tautest
tautly

tautness

tavern noun
taverns

tawny adjective
tawnier
tawniest

tax noun
taxes

tax verb
taxes
taxing
taxed

taxable

taxation

taxi noun
taxis

taxi verb
taxis
taxiing
taxied

taxpayer noun
taxpayers

★ **tea** noun
teas

teabag noun
teabags

teacake noun
teacakes

teach verb
teaches
teaching
taught

teacher noun
teachers

tea cloth or
tea towel noun
tea cloths or
tea towels

teacup noun
teacups

teak

☆ **team** noun
teams

teapot noun
teapots

tear verb
tears
tearing
tore
torn

○ **tear** noun
tears

tearful adjective
tearfully

tear gas

tease verb
teases
teasing
teased

teaspoon noun
teaspoons

teaspoonful noun
teaspoonfuls

teat noun
teats

tech noun
techs

technical adjective
technically

technicality noun
technicalities

technician noun
technicians

technique noun
techniques

technological
adjective
technologically

technology noun
technologies

teddy bear noun
teddy bears

tedious adjective
tediously

tediousness

tedium

✳ **tee** noun
tees

✱ **teem** verb
teems
teeming
teemed

teenage

teenager noun
teenagers

teens

teeth see tooth

teetotal

teetotaller noun
teetotallers

- -

★ Tea is a hot drink. ! tee.

☆ You use team in e.g. *a football team*. ! teem.

○ A tear is a drop of water from an eye and rhymes with 'here', or a split in
   something and rhymes with 'hair'.

✳ A tee is part of a golf course. ! tea.

✱ You use teem in e.g. *a place teeming with people*. ! team.

telecommunications plural noun

telegram noun
telegrams

telegraph noun
telegraphs

telegraphic adjective
telegraphically

telegraphy

telepathic adjective
telepathically

telepathy

telephone noun
telephones

telephone verb
telephones
telephoning
telephoned

telephonist noun
telephonists

telescope noun
telescopes

telescopic adjective
telescopically

teletext

televise verb
televises
televising
televised

television noun
televisions

tell verb
tells
telling
told

tell-tale adjective
and noun
tell-tales

telly noun
tellies

temper noun
tempers

temperate

temperature noun
temperatures

tempest noun
tempests

tempestuous
adjective
tempestuously

temple noun
temples

tempo noun
tempos

temporary adjective
temporarily

tempt verb
tempts
tempting
tempted

temptation noun
temptations

tempter noun
tempters

temptress noun
temptresses

ten noun
tens

tenancy noun
tenancies

tenant noun
tenants

tend verb
tends
tending
tended

tendency noun
tendencies

tender adjective
tenderer
tenderest
tenderly

tender noun
tenders

tender verb
tenders
tendering
tendered

tenderness

tendon noun
tendons

tendril noun
tendrils

tennis

tenor noun
tenors

tenpin bowling

tense adjective
tenser
tensest
tensely

tense noun
tenses

tension noun
tensions

tent noun
tents

tentacle noun
tentacles

tenth

tenthly

tepid

term noun
terms

term verb
terms
terming
termed

terminal noun
terminals

terminate verb
terminates
terminating
terminated

termination noun
terminations

terminus noun
termini

terrace noun
terraces

terrapin noun
terrapins

terrible adjective
terribly

terrier noun
terriers

terrific adjective
terrifically

terrify verb
terrifies
terrifying
terrified

territorial adjective
territorially

territory noun
territories

terror noun
terrors

terrorism

terrorist adjective
and noun
terrorists

terrorize verb
terrorizes
terrorizing
terrorized

tessellation noun
tessellations

test noun
tests

test verb
tests
testing
tested

testament noun
testaments

testicle noun
testicles

testify verb
testifies
testifying
testified

testimonial noun
testimonials

testimony noun
testimonies

testy adjective
testier
testiest

tether verb
tethers
tethering
tethered

tether noun
tethers

text noun
texts

textbook noun
textbooks

textile noun
textiles

texture noun
textures

than

thank verb
thanks
thanking
thanked

thankful adjective
thankfully

thankless adjective
thanklessly

thanks plural noun

that adjective,
pronoun, and
conjunction

thatch noun

thatch verb
thatches
thatching
thatched

thatcher noun
thatchers

thaw verb
thaws
thawing
thawed

theatre noun
theatres

theatrical adjective
theatrically

thee

theft noun
thefts

★ **their**

☆ **theirs**

them

theme noun
themes

theme park noun
theme parks

themselves

then

theologian noun
theologians

theological adjective
theologically

theology

theorem noun
theorems

theoretical adjective
theoretically

theory noun
theories

therapist noun
therapists

. . . .

★ You use **their** in e.g. *this is their house*. ! there, they're.

☆ You use **theirs** in e.g. *the house is theirs*. Note that there is no apostrophe in this word.

therapy noun
therapies

★ **there** adverb

thereabouts

therefore

thermal adjective
thermally

thermometer noun
thermometers

Thermos noun
Thermoses

thermostat noun
thermostats

thermostatic
adjective
thermostatically

thesaurus noun
thesauri or
thesauruses

these

they

they'd verb

they'll verb

☆ **they're** verb

they've verb

thick adjective
thicker
thickest
thickly

thicken verb
thickens
thickening
thickened

thicket noun
thickets

thickness noun
thicknesses

thief noun
thieves

thigh noun
thighs

thimble noun
thimbles

thin adjective
thinner
thinnest
thinly

thin verb
thins
thinning
thinned

thine

thing noun
things

think verb
thinks
thinking
thought

thinker noun
thinkers

thinness

third

thirdly

Third World

thirst

thirsty adjective
thirstier
thirstiest
thirstily

thirteen

thirteenth

thirtieth

thirty noun
thirties

this

thistle noun
thistles

thorn noun
thorns

thorny adjective
thornier
thorniest

thorough adjective
thoroughly

thoroughness

those

thou

though

thought noun
thoughts

thought see think

thoughtful adjective
thoughtfully

thoughtfulness

thoughtless adjective
thoughtlessly

thoughtlessness

thousand noun
thousands

thousandth

◦ **thrash** verb
thrashes
thrashing
thrashed

thread noun
threads

thread verb
threads
threading
threaded

threadbare

threat noun
threats

threaten verb
threatens
threatening
threatened

three noun
threes

- -

★ You use **there** in e.g. *Look over there*. ! their, they're.

☆ **They're** is short for *they are*. ! their, there.

◦ To **thrash** someone is to beat them. ! thresh.

three-dimensional
  adjective
  three-dimensionally
★ **thresh** verb
  threshes
  threshing
  threshed

threshold noun
  thresholds

threw see throw

thrift

thrifty adjective
  thriftier
  thriftiest
  thriftily

thrill noun
  thrills

thrill verb
  thrills
  thrilling
  thrilled

thriller noun
  thrillers

thrive verb
  thrives
  thriving
  thrived or throve or
  thriven

throat noun
  throats

throb verb
  throbs
  throbbing
  throbbed

throb noun
  throbs

throne noun
  thrones

throng noun
  throngs

throttle verb
  throttles
  throttling
  throttled

throttle noun
  throttles

through

throughout

throve see thrive

throw verb
  throws
  throwing
  threw
  thrown

throw noun
  throws

thrush noun
  thrushes

thrust verb
  thrusts
  thrusting
  thrust

thud noun
  thuds

thud verb
  thuds
  thudding
  thudded

thumb noun
  thumbs

thump verb
  thumps
  thumping
  thumped

thump noun
  thumps

thunder noun

thunder verb
  thunders
  thundering
  thundered

thunderous adjective
  thunderously

thunderstorm noun
  thunderstorms

Thursday noun
  Thursdays

thus

thy

tick verb
  ticks
  ticking
  ticked

tick noun
  ticks

ticket noun
  tickets

tickle verb
  tickles
  tickling
  tickled

ticklish adjective
  ticklishly

tidal

tiddler noun
  tiddlers

tiddlywink noun
  tiddlywinks

tide noun
  tides

tide verb
  tides
  tiding
  tided

tidiness

tidy adjective
  tidier
  tidiest
  tidily

tie verb
  ties
  tying
  tied

. . . .

★ To **thresh** corn is to beat it to separate the grain. ! **thrash**.

tie noun
ties

tie-break noun
tie-breaks

tiger noun
tigers

tight adjective
tighter
tightest
tightly

tighten verb
tightens
tightening
tightened

tightness

tightrope noun
tightropes

tights plural noun

tigress noun
tigresses

tile noun
tiles

tiled

till preposition and
conjunction

till noun
tills

till verb
tills
tilling
tilled

tiller noun
tillers

tilt verb
tilts
tilting
tilted

tilt noun
tilts

timber noun
timbers

time noun
times

time verb
times
timing
timed

timer noun
timers

times

timetable noun
timetables

timid adjective
timidly

timidity

timing

timpani plural noun

tin noun
tins

tin verb
tins
tinning
tinned

tingle verb
tingles
tingling
tingled

tingle noun
tingles

tinker verb
tinkers
tinkering
tinkered

tinker noun
tinkers

tinkle verb
tinkles
tinkling
tinkled

tinkle noun
tinkles

tinny adjective
tinnier
tinniest
tinnily

tinsel

tint noun
tints

tint verb
tints
tinting
tinted

tiny adjective
tinier
tiniest

tip verb
tips
tipping
tipped

tip noun
tips

tiptoe verb
tiptoes
tiptoeing
tiptoed

tiptoe noun
tiptoes

★ **tire** verb
tires
tiring
tired

tired

tireless adjective
tirelessly

tiresome adjective
tiresomely

tissue noun
tissues

tit noun
tits

titbit noun
titbits

· ·

★ To **tire** is to become tired. ! **tyre**.

ti - to

title noun
titles

titter verb
titters
tittering
tittered

★ **to** preposition

toad noun
toads

toadstool noun
toadstools

toast verb
toasts
toasting
toasted

toast noun
toasts

toaster noun
toasters

tobacco noun
tobaccos

tobacconist noun
tobacconists

toboggan noun
toboggans

tobogganing

today

toddler noun
toddlers

☆ **toe** noun
toes

toffee noun
toffees

toga noun
togas

together

toil verb
toils
toiling
toiled

toilet noun
toilets

token noun
tokens

told see tell

tolerable adjective
tolerably

tolerance

tolerant adjective
tolerantly

tolerate verb
tolerates
tolerating
tolerated

toll noun
tolls

toll verb
tolls
tolling
tolled

tomahawk noun
tomahawks

tomato noun
tomatoes

tomb noun
tombs

tomboy noun
tomboys

tombstone noun
tombstones

tomcat noun
tomcats

tommy-gun noun
tommy-guns

tomorrow

tom-tom noun
tom-toms

◉ **ton** noun
tons

tonal adjective
tonally

tone noun
tones

tone verb
tones
toning
toned

tone-deaf

tongs plural noun

tongue noun
tongues

tonic noun
tonics

tonight

✳ **tonne** noun
tonnes

tonsillitis

tonsils plural noun

✱ **too** adverb

took see take

tool noun
tools

tooth noun
teeth

toothache

toothbrush noun
toothbrushes

toothed

toothpaste noun
toothpastes

top noun
tops

top verb
tops
topping
topped

topic noun
topics

topical adjective
topically

topicality

★ You use to in e.g. *go to bed* or *I want to stay*. ! too, two.
☆ A toe is a part of a foot. ! tow.
◉ A ton is a non-metric unit of weight. ! tonne.
✳ A tonne is a metric unit of weight. ! ton.
✱ You use too in e.g. *it's too late* or *I want to come too*. ! to, two.

topless

topmost

topping *noun*
toppings

topple *verb*
topples
toppling
toppled

topsy-turvy

torch *noun*
torches

tore see **tear**

toreador *noun*
toreadors

torment *verb*
torments
tormenting
tormented

torment *noun*
torments

tormentor *noun*
tormentors

torn see **tear**

tornado *noun*
tornadoes

torpedo *noun*
torpedoes

torpedo *verb*
torpedoes
torpedoing
torpedoed

torrent *noun*
torrents

torrential *adjective*
torrentially

torso *noun*
torsos

tortoise *noun*
tortoises

torture *verb*
tortures
torturing
tortured

torture *noun*
tortures

torturer *noun*
torturers

Tory *noun*
Tories

toss *verb*
tosses
tossing
tossed

toss *noun*
tosses

total *noun*
totals

total *adjective*
totally

total *verb*
totals
totalling
totalled

totalitarian

totem pole *noun*
totem poles

totter *verb*
totters
tottering
tottered

touch *verb*
touches
touching
touched

touch *noun*
touches

touchy *adjective*
touchier
touchiest
touchily

tough *adjective*
tougher
toughest
toughly

toughen *verb*
toughens
toughening
toughened

toughness

tour *noun*
tours

tourism

tourist *noun*
tourists

tournament *noun*
tournaments

★ **tow** *verb*
tows
towing
towed

tow *noun*

toward *or* **towards**

towel *noun*
towels

towelling

tower *noun*
towers

tower *verb*
towers
towering
towered

town *noun*
towns

towpath *noun*
towpaths

toxic *adjective*
toxically

toy *noun*
toys

. . . .

★ To **tow** something is to pull it along. ! **toe**.

toy *verb*
toys
toying
toyed

toyshop *noun*
toyshops

trace *noun*
traces

trace *verb*
traces
tracing
traced

traceable

track *noun*
tracks

track *verb*
tracks
tracking
tracked

tracker *noun*
trackers

tracksuit *noun*
tracksuits

tract *noun*
tracts

traction

tractor *noun*
tractors

trade *noun*
trades

trade *verb*
trades
trading
traded

trademark *noun*
trademarks

trader *noun*
traders

tradesman *noun*
tradesmen

trade union *noun*
trade unions

tradition *noun*
traditions

traditional *adjective*
traditionally

traffic *noun*

traffic *verb*
traffics
trafficking
trafficked

tragedy *noun*
tragedies

tragic *adjective*
tragically

trail *noun*
trails

trail *verb*
trails
trailing
trailed

trailer *noun*
trailers

train *noun*
trains

train *verb*
trains
training
trained

trainer *noun*
trainers

traitor *noun*
traitors

tram *noun*
trams

tramp *noun*
tramps

tramp *verb*
tramps
tramping
tramped

trample *verb*
tramples
trampling
trampled

trampoline *noun*
trampolines

trance *noun*
trances

tranquil *adjective*
tranquilly

★ **tranquillity**

tranquillizer *noun*
tranquillizers

transact *verb*
transacts
transacting
transacted

transaction *noun*
transactions

transatlantic

transfer *verb*
transfers
transferring
transferred

transfer *noun*
transfers

transferable

transference

transform *verb*
transforms
transforming
transformed

transformation *noun*
transformations

transformer *noun*
transformers

transfusion *noun*
transfusions

transistor *noun*
transistors

★ Note that there are two ls in this word.

transition *noun*
transitions

transitional *adjective*
transitionally

transitive *adjective*
transitively

translate *verb*
translates
translating
translated

translation *noun*
translations

translator *noun*
translators

translucent

transmission *noun*
transmissions

transmit *verb*
transmits
transmitting
transmitted

transmitter *noun*
transmitters

transparency *noun*
transparencies

transparent
adjective
transparently

transpire *verb*
transpires
transpiring
transpired

transplant *verb*
transplants
transplanting
transplanted

transplant *noun*
transplants

transplantation
noun
transplantations

transport *verb*
transports
transporting
transported

transportation

transport

transporter *noun*
transporters

trap *verb*
traps
trapping
trapped

trap *noun*
traps

trapdoor *noun*
trapdoors

trapeze *noun*
trapezes

trapezium *noun*
trapeziums

trapezoid *noun*
trapezoids

trapper *noun*
trappers

trash

trashy *adjective*
trashier
trashiest
trashily

travel *verb*
travels
travelling
travelled

travel *noun*

traveller *noun*
travellers

traveller's cheque
noun
traveller's cheques

trawler *noun*
trawlers

tray *noun*
trays

treacherous
adjective
treacherously

treachery

treacle

tread *verb*
treads
treading
trod
trodden

tread *noun*
treads

treason

treasure *noun*
treasures

treasure *verb*
treasures
treasuring
treasured

treasurer *noun*
treasurers

treasury *noun*
treasuries

treat *verb*
treats
treating
treated

treat *noun*
treats

treatment *noun*
treatments

treaty *noun*
treaties

treble adjective and
noun
trebles

treble verb
trebles
trebling
trebled

tree noun
trees

trek verb
treks
trekking
trekked

trek noun
treks

trellis noun
trellises

tremble verb
trembles
trembling
trembled

tremble noun
trembles

tremendous
adjective
tremendously

tremor noun
tremors

trench noun
trenches

trend noun
trends

trendiness

trendy adjective
trendier
trendiest
trendily

trespass verb
trespasses
trespassing
trespassed

trespasser noun
trespassers

trestle noun
trestles

trial noun
trials

triangle noun
triangles

triangular

tribal adjective
tribally

tribe noun
tribes

tribesman noun
tribesmen

tributary noun
tributaries

tribute noun
tributes

trick noun
tricks

trick verb
tricks
tricking
tricked

trickery

trickster noun
tricksters

trickle verb
trickles
trickling
trickled

trickle noun
trickles

tricky adjective
trickier
trickiest
trickily

tricycle noun
tricycles

tried see **try**

trifle noun
trifles

trifle verb
trifles
trifling
trifled

trifling

trigger noun
triggers

trigger verb
triggers
triggering
triggered

trillion noun
trillions

trim adjective
trimmer
trimmest
trimly

trim verb
trims
trimming
trimmed

trim noun
trims

★ **Trinity**

trio noun
trios

trip verb
trips
tripping
tripped

trip noun
trips

tripe

triple adjective
triply

triple noun
triples

· ·

★ You use a capital T when you mean the three persons of God in Christianity.

triple verb
triples
tripling
tripled

triplet noun
triplets

tripod noun
tripods

triumph noun
triumphs

triumphant adjective
triumphantly

trivial adjective
trivially

triviality noun
trivialities

trod see tread
trodden see tread
troll noun
trolls

trolley noun
trolleys

trombone noun
trombones

troop noun
troops

troop verb
troops
trooping
trooped

troops plural noun
trophy noun
trophies

tropic noun
tropics

tropical adjective
trot verb
trots
trotting
trotted

trot noun
trots

trouble noun
troubles

trouble verb
troubles
troubling
troubled

troublesome
trough noun
troughs

trousers plural noun
trout noun
trout

trowel noun
trowels

truancy noun
truancies

truant noun
truants

truce noun
truces

truck noun
trucks

trudge verb
trudges
trudging
trudged

true adjective
truer
truest
truly

trump noun
trumps

trump verb
trumps
trumping
trumped

trumpet noun
trumpets

trumpet verb
trumpets
trumpeting
trumpeted

trumpeter noun
trumpeters

truncheon noun
truncheons

trundle verb
trundles
trundling
trundled

trunk noun
trunks

trunks plural noun
trust verb
trusts
trusting
trusted

trust
trustful adjective
trustfully

trustworthy
adjective
trustworthily

trusty adjective
trustier
trustiest
trustily

truth noun
truths

truthful adjective
truthfully

truthfulness
try verb
tries
trying
tried

try noun
tries

T-shirt noun
T-shirts

tub noun
tubs

tuba noun
tubas

tube noun
tubes

tuber noun
tubers

tubing

tubular

tuck verb
tucks
tucking
tucked

tuck noun
tucks

Tuesday noun
Tuesdays

tuft noun
tufts

tug noun
tugs

tug verb
tugs
tugging
tugged

tulip noun
tulips

tumble verb
tumbles
tumbling
tumbled

tumble noun
tumbles

tumble-drier noun
tumble-driers

tumbler noun
tumblers

tummy noun
tummies

tumour noun
tumours

tumult

tumultuous adjective
tumultuously

tuna noun
tuna or tunas

tundra

tune noun
tunes

tune verb
tunes
tuning
tuned

tuneful adjective
tunefully

tunic noun
tunics

tunnel noun
tunnels

tunnel verb
tunnels
tunnelling
tunnelled

turban noun
turbans

turbine noun
turbines

turbulence

turbulent adjective
turbulently

turf noun
turfs or turves

turkey noun
turkeys

Turkish bath noun
Turkish baths

Turkish delight

turmoil

turn verb
turns
turning
turned

turn
noun
turns

turncoat noun
turncoats

turnip noun
turnips

turnover noun
turnovers

turnstile noun
turnstiles

turntable noun
turntables

turpentine

turquoise

turret noun
turrets

turtle noun
turtles

tusk noun
tusks

tussle verb
tussles
tussling
tussled

tussle noun
tussles

tutor noun
tutors

tweak verb
tweaks
tweaking
tweaked

tweak noun
tweaks

tweed

tweezers plural noun

Uu

twelve noun
twelves

twelfth

twentieth

twenty noun
twenties

twice

twiddle verb
twiddles
twiddling
twiddled

twiddle noun
twiddles

twig noun
twigs

twig verb
twigs
twigging
twigged

twilight

twin noun
twins

twin verb
twins
twinning
twinned

twine

twinkle verb
twinkles
twinkling
twinkled

twinkle noun
twinkles

twirl verb
twirls
twirling
twirled

twirl noun
twirls

twist verb
twists
twisting
twisted

twist noun
twists

twister noun
twisters

twitch verb
twitches
twitching
twitched

twitch noun
twitches

twitter verb
twitters
twittering
twittered

★ **two** adjective and
noun
twos

tying see **tie**

type noun
types

type verb
types
typing
typed

typewriter noun
typewriters

typewritten

typhoon noun
typhoons

typical adjective
typically

typist noun
typists

tyranny noun
tyrannies

tyrannical adjective
tyrannically

tyrant noun
tyrants

☆ **tyre** noun
tyres

udder noun
udders

ugliness

ugly adjective
uglier
ugliest

ulcer noun
ulcers

ultimate adjective
ultimately

ultraviolet

umbilical cord noun
umbilical cords

umbrella noun
umbrellas

umpire noun
umpires

un-
un- makes words
meaning 'not', e.g.
unable, unhappiness.
Some of these words
have special
meanings, e.g.
unprofessional. See
the note at **non-**.

unable

unaided

unanimity

unanimous adjective
unanimously

unavoidable
adjective
unavoidably

unaware

★ You use **two** in e.g. *two people* or *there are two of them.* ! **to, too.**
☆ A **tyre** is a rubber cover for a wheel. ! **tire.**

unawares

unbearable *adjective*
unbearably

unbelievable
adjective
unbelievably

unblock *verb*
unblocks
unblocking
unblocked

unborn

uncalled for

uncanny *adjective*
uncannier
uncanniest

uncertain *adjective*
uncertainly

uncertainty

uncle *noun*
uncles

uncomfortable
adjective
uncomfortably

uncommon
adjective
uncommonly

unconscious
adjective
unconsciously

unconsciousness

uncontrollable
adjective
uncontrollably

uncountable

uncouth

uncover *verb*
uncovers
uncovering
uncovered

undecided

undeniable *adjective*
undeniably

under

underarm *adjective*

underclothes *plural noun*

underdeveloped

underdone

underfoot

undergo *verb*
undergoes
undergoing
underwent
undergone

undergraduate
noun
undergraduates

underground
adjective and noun
undergrounds

undergrowth

underhand

underlie *verb*
underlies
underlying
underlay
underlain

underline *verb*
underlines
underlining
underlined

undermine *verb*
undermines
undermining
undermined

underneath
preposition

underpants *plural noun*

underpass *noun*
underpasses

underprivileged

understand *verb*
understands
understanding
understood

understandable
adjective
understandably

understanding

undertake *verb*
undertakes
undertaking
undertook
undertaken

undertaker *noun*
undertakers

undertaking *noun*
undertakings

underwater

underwear

underworld

undesirable
adjective
undesirably

undeveloped

undo *verb*
undoes
undoing
undid
undone

undoubted *adjective*
undoubtedly

undress *verb*
undresses
undressing
undressed

unearth *verb*
unearths
unearthing
unearthed

unearthly

unease
uneasiness
uneasy *adjective*
 uneasier
 uneasiest
 uneasily
uneatable
unemployed
unemployment
uneven *adjective*
 unevenly
unevenness
unexpected *adjective*
 unexpectedly
unfair *adjective*
 unfairly
unfairness
unfaithful *adjective*
 unfaithfully
unfamiliar
unfamiliarity
unfasten *verb*
 unfastens
 unfastening
 unfastened
unfavourable
 adjective
 unfavourably
unfinished
unfit
unfold *verb*
 unfolds
 unfolding
 unfolded
unforgettable
 adjective
 unforgettably
unforgivable
 adjective
 unforgivably

unfortunate
 adjective
 unfortunately
unfreeze *verb*
 unfreezes
 unfreezing
 unfroze
 unfrozen
unfriendliness
unfriendly
ungrateful *adjective*
 ungratefully
unhappiness
unhappy *adjective*
 unhappier
 unhappiest
 unhappily
unhealthy *adjective*
 unhealthier
 unhealthiest
 unhealthily
unheard-of
unicorn *noun*
 unicorns
unification
uniform *noun*
 uniforms
uniform *adjective*
 uniformly
uniformed
uniformity
unify *verb*
 unifies
 unifying
 unified
unimportance
unimportant
uninhabited

unintentional
 adjective
 unintentionally
uninterested
uninteresting
union *noun*
 unions
unique *adjective*
 uniquely
uniqueness
unisex
unison
unit *noun*
 units
unite *verb*
 unites
 uniting
 united
unity *noun*
 unities
universal *adjective*
 universally
universe
university *noun*
 universities
unjust *adjective*
 unjustly
unkind *adjective*
 unkinder
 unkindest
 unkindly
unkindness
unknown
unleaded
unless
unlike
unlikely *adjective*
 unlikelier
 unlikeliest

unload *verb*
unloads
unloading
unloaded

unlock *verb*
unlocks
unlocking
unlocked

unlucky *adjective*
unluckier
unluckiest
unluckily

unmistakable
adjective
unmistakably

unnatural *adjective*
unnaturally

unnecessary
adjective
unnecessarily

unoccupied

unpack *verb*
unpacks
unpacking
unpacked

unpleasant *adjective*
unpleasantly

unpleasantness

unplug *verb*
unplugs
unplugging
unplugged

unpopular *adjective*
unpopularly

unpopularity

unravel *verb*
unravels
unravelling
unravelled

unreal

unreasonable
adjective
unreasonably

unrest

unroll *verb*
unrolls
unrolling
unrolled

unruliness

unruly *adjective*
unrulier
unruliest

unscrew *verb*
unscrews
unscrewing
unscrewed

unseemly

unseen

unselfish *adjective*
unselfishly

unselfishness

unsightly

unskilled

unsound *adjective*
unsoundly

unsteadiness

unsteady *adjective*
unsteadier
unsteadiest
unsteadily

unsuccessful
adjective
unsuccessfully

unsuitable *adjective*
unsuitably

unthinkable
adjective
unthinkably

untidiness

untidy *adjective*
untidier
untidiest
untidily

untie *verb*
unties
untying
untied

until

untimely

unto

untold

untoward

untrue *adjective*
untruly

untruthful *adjective*
untruthfully

unused

unusual *adjective*
unusually

unwanted

unwell

unwilling *adjective*
unwillingly

unwillingness

unwind *verb*
unwinds
unwinding
unwound

unwrap *verb*
unwraps
unwrapping
unwrapped

unzip *verb*
unzips
unzipping
unzipped

update *verb*
updates
updating
updated

upgrade *verb*
upgrades
upgrading
upgraded

upheaval *noun*
upheavals

uphill

uphold *verb*
upholds
upholding
upheld

upholstery

upkeep

uplands *plural noun*

upon

upper

upright *adjective*
uprightly

upright *noun*
uprights

uprising *noun*
uprisings

uproar *noun*
uproars

upset *verb*
upsets
upsetting
upset

upset *noun*
upsets

upshot

upside down

upstairs

upstart *noun*
upstarts

upstream *adjective*

uptake

uptight

upward *adjective* and
adverb

upwards *adverb*

uranium

urban

urbanization

urbanize *verb*
urbanizes
urbanizing
urbanized

urchin *noun*
urchins

Urdu

urge *verb*
urges
urging
urged

urge *noun*
urges

urgency

urgent *adjective*
urgently

urinary

urinate *verb*
urinates
urinating
urinated

urination

urine

urn *noun*
urns

-us
Most nouns ending in
-us come from Latin
words, e.g. bonus and
terminus. They
normally have plurals
ending in -uses, e.g.
bonuses and
terminuses. Some
more technical words
have plurals ending in
-i, e.g. nucleus -
nuclei.

usable

usage *noun*
usages

use *verb*
uses
using
used

use *noun*
uses

useful *adjective*
usefully

usefulness

useless *adjective*
uselessly

uselessness

user *noun*
users

user-friendly
adjective
user-friendlier
user-friendliest

usher *noun*
ushers

usher *verb*
ushers
ushering
ushered

usherette *noun*
usherettes

usual *adjective*
usually

usurp *verb*
usurps
usurping
usurped

usurper *noun*
usurpers

utensil *noun*
utensils

uterus *noun*
uteri

utilization
utilize verb
  utilizes
  utilizing
  utilized
utmost
utter adjective
utter verb
  utters
  uttering
  uttered
utterance noun
  utterances
utterly adverb
U-turn noun
  U-turns

Vv

vacancy noun
  vacancies
vacant adjective
  vacantly
vacate verb
  vacates
  vacating
  vacated
vacation noun
  vacations
vaccinate verb
  vaccinates
  vaccinating
  vaccinated
vaccination noun
  vaccinations
vaccine noun
  vaccines
vacuum noun
  vacuums

vagina noun
  vaginas
vague adjective
  vaguer
  vaguest
  vaguely
vagueness
★ **vain** adjective
  vainer
  vainest
  vainly
☆ **vale** noun
  vales
valentine noun
  valentines
valiant adjective
  valiantly
valid adjective
  validly
validity
valley noun
  valleys
valour
valuable adjective
  valuably
valuables plural
  noun
valuation noun
  valuations
value noun
  values
value verb
  values
  valuing
  valued
valueless
valuer noun
  valuers
valve noun
  valves

vampire noun
  vampires
van noun
  vans
vandal noun
  vandals
vandalism
◦ **vane** noun
  vanes
vanilla
vanish verb
  vanishes
  vanishing
  vanished
vanity
vanquish verb
  vanquishes
  vanquishing
  vanquished
vaporize verb
  vaporizes
  vaporizing
  vaporized
vapour noun
  vapours
variable adjective
  variably
variable noun
  variables
variation noun
  variations
varied
variety noun
  varieties
various adjective
  variously
varnish noun
  varnishes

. . . .

★ Vain means 'conceited' or 'proud'. ! vane, vein.
☆ A vale is a valley. ! veil.
◦ A vane is a pointer that shows which way the wind is blowing. ! vain, vein.

269

varnish *verb*
varnishes
varnishing
varnished

vary *verb*
varies
varying
varied

vase *noun*
vases

vast *adjective*
vastly

vastness

vat *noun*
vats

vault *verb*
vaults
vaulting
vaulted

vault *noun*
vaults

veal

vector *noun*
vectors

Veda

veer *verb*
veers
veering
veered

vegan *noun*
vegans

vegetable *noun*
vegetables

vegetarian *noun*
vegetarians

vegetate *verb*
vegetates
vegetating
vegetated

vegetation

vehicle *noun*
vehicles

★ **veil** *noun*
veils

veil *verb*
veils
veiling
veiled

☆ **vein** *noun*
veins

velocity *noun*
velocities

velvet

velvety

vendetta *noun*
vendettas

vendor *noun*
vendors

venerable *adjective*
venerably

venereal disease *noun*
venereal diseases

venetian blind *noun*
venetian blinds

vengeance

venison

Venn diagram *noun*
Venn diagrams

venom

venomous *adjective*
venomously

vent *noun*
vents

ventilate *verb*
ventilates
ventilating
ventilated

ventilation

ventilator *noun*
ventilators

ventriloquism

ventriloquist *noun*
ventriloquists

venture *verb*
ventures
venturing
ventured

venture *noun*
ventures

veranda *noun*
verandas

verb *noun*
verbs

verdict *noun*
verdicts

verge *verb*
verges
verging
verged

verge *noun*
verges

verification

verify *verb*
verifies
verifying
verified

vermin

verruca *noun*
verrucas

versatile

versatility

verse *noun*
verses

version *noun*
versions

versus

vertebra *noun*
vertebrae

vertebrate *noun*
vertebrates

vertex *noun*
vertices

. . . .

★ A **veil** is a covering for the face. ! **vale**.
☆ A **vein** carries blood to the heart. ! **vain**, **vane**.

vertical *adjective*
vertically

very

Vesak

vessel *noun*
vessels

vest *noun*
vests

vested *adjective*
vested

vestment *noun*
vestments

vestry *noun*
vestries

vet *noun*
vets

veteran *noun*
veterans

veterinary

veto *verb*
vetoes
vetoing
vetoed

veto *noun*
vetoes

vex *verb*
vexes
vexing
vexed

vexation

via

viaduct *noun*
viaducts

vibrate *verb*
vibrates
vibrating
vibrated

vibration *noun*
vibrations

vicar *noun*
vicars

vicarage *noun*
vicarages

vice *noun*
vices

vice-president *noun*
vice-presidents

vice versa

vicinity *noun*
vicinities

vicious *adjective*
viciously

viciousness

victim *noun*
victims

victimize *verb*
victimizes
victimizing
victimized

victor *noun*
victors

Victorian *adjective
and noun*
Victorians

victorious *adjective*
victoriously

victory *noun*
victories

video *noun*
videos

video *verb*
videoes
videoing
videoed

videotape *noun*
videotapes

view *noun*
views

view *verb*
views
viewing
viewed

viewer *noun*
viewers

vigilance

vigilant *adjective*
vigilantly

vigorous *adjective*
vigorously

vigour

Viking *noun*
Vikings

vile *adjective*
viler
vilest
vilely

villa *noun*
villas

village *noun*
villages

villager *noun*
villagers

villain *noun*
villains

villainous *adjective*
villainously

villainy

vine *noun*
vines

vinegar

vineyard *noun*
vineyards

vintage *noun*
vintages

vinyl

viola *noun*
violas

violate *verb*
violates
violating
violated

violation noun
violations

violator noun
violators

violence

violent adjective
violently

violet noun
violets

violin noun
violins

violinist noun
violinists

viper noun
vipers

virgin noun
virgins

virginity

virtual adjective
virtually

virtue noun
virtues

virtuous adjective
virtuously

virus noun
viruses

visa noun
visas

visibility

visible adjective
visibly

vision noun
visions

visit verb
visits
visiting
visited

visit noun
visits

visitor noun
visitors

visor noun
visors

visual adjective
visually

visualize verb
visualizes
visualizing
visualized

vital adjective
vitally

vitality

vitamin noun
vitamins

vivid adjective
vividly

vividness

vivisection noun
vivisections

vixen noun
vixens

vocabulary noun
vocabularies

vocal adjective
vocally

vocalist noun
vocalists

vocation noun
vocations

vocational adjective
vocationally

vodka noun
vodkas

voice noun
voices

voice verb
voices
voicing
voiced

volcanic

volcano noun
volcanoes

vole noun
voles

volley noun
volleys

volleyball

volt noun
volts

voltage noun
voltages

volume noun
volumes

voluntary adjective
voluntarily

volunteer verb
volunteers
volunteering
volunteered

volunteer noun
volunteers

vomit verb
vomits
vomiting
vomited

vote verb
votes
voting
voted

vote noun
votes

voter noun
voters

vouch verb
vouches
vouching
vouched

voucher noun
vouchers

vow noun
vows

vow verb
vows
vowing
vowed

vowel noun
vowels

voyage noun
voyages

voyager noun
voyagers

vulgar adjective
vulgarly

vulnerable adjective
vulnerably

vulture noun
vultures

vulva noun
vulvas

Ww

wad noun
wads

waddle verb
waddles
waddling
waddled

waddle noun
waddles

wade verb
wades
wading
waded

wafer noun
wafers

wag verb
wags
wagging
wagged

wag noun
wags

wage noun
wages

wage verb
wages
waging
waged

wager noun
wagers

wager verb
wagers
wagering
wagered

waggle verb
waggles
waggling
waggled

wagon noun
wagons

wagtail noun
wagtails

wail verb
wails
wailing
wailed

★ **wail** noun
wails

☆ **waist** noun
waists

waistcoat noun
waistcoats

◉ **wait** verb
waits
waiting
waited

wait noun
waits

waiter noun
waiters

waitress noun
waitresses

✳ **waive** verb
waives
waiving
waived

wake verb
wakes
waking
woke
woken

wake noun
wakes

waken verb
wakens
wakening
wakened

walk verb
walks
walking
walked

walk noun
walks

walkabout noun
walkabouts

walker noun
walkers

walkie-talkie noun
walkie-talkies

Walkman noun
Walkmans

wall noun
walls

wall verb
walls
walling
walled

wallaby noun
wallabies

. . . .

★ A **wail** is a loud sad cry. **!** **whale.**
☆ A person's **waist** is the narrow part around their middle. **!** **waste.**
◉ To **wait** is to delay, pause, or rest. **!** **weight.**
✳ To **waive** a right is to say you do not need it. **!** **wave.**

wallet noun
wallets

wallflower noun
wallflowers

wallop verb
wallops
walloping
walloped

wallow verb
wallows
wallowing
wallowed

wallpaper noun
wallpapers

walnut noun
walnuts

walrus noun
walruses

waltz noun
waltzes

waltz verb
waltzes
waltzing
waltzed

wand noun
wands

wander verb
wanders
wandering
wandered

wanderer noun
wanderers

wane verb
wanes
waning
waned

wangle verb
wangles
wangling
wangled

want verb
wants
wanting
wanted

want noun
wants

war noun
wars

warble verb
warbles
warbling
warbled

warble noun
warbles

warbler noun
warblers

ward noun
wards

ward verb
wards
warding
warded

warden noun
wardens

warder noun
warders

wardrobe noun
wardrobes

★ **ware** noun
wares

warehouse noun
warehouses

warfare

warhead noun
warheads

wariness

warlike

warm adjective
warmer
warmest
warmly

warm verb
warms
warming
warmed

warmth

warn verb
warns
warning
warned

warning noun
warnings

warp verb
warps
warping
warped

warp noun
warps

warrant noun
warrants

warrant verb
warrants
warranting
warranted

warren noun
warrens

warrior noun
warriors

warship noun
warships

wart noun
warts

wary adjective
warier
wariest
warily

was

wash verb
washes
washing
washed

wash noun
washes

. . . .

★ **Wares** are manufactured goods. ! wear, where.

washable

washbasin noun
washbasins

washer noun
washers

washing

washing-up

wash-out noun
wash-outs

wasn't verb

wasp noun
wasps

wastage

★ **waste** verb
wastes
wasting
wasted

waste adjective and
noun
wastes

wasteful adjective
wastefully

watch verb
watches
watching
watched

watch noun
watches

watchdog noun
watchdogs

watcher noun
watchers

watchful adjective
watchfully

watchfulness

watchman noun
watchmen

water noun
waters

water verb
waters
watering
watered

watercolour noun
watercolours

watercress

waterfall noun
waterfalls

waterlogged

watermark noun
watermarks

waterproof

water-skiing

watertight

waterway noun
waterways

waterworks noun
waterworks

watery

☆ **watt** noun
watts

◐ **wave** verb
waves
waving
waved

wave noun
waves

waveband noun
wavebands

wavelength noun
wavelengths

waver verb
wavers
wavering
wavered

wavy adjective
wavier
waviest
wavily

wax noun
waxes

wax verb
waxes
waxing
waxed

waxwork noun
waxworks

waxy adjective
waxier
waxiest

✱ **way** noun
ways

✱ **weak** adjective
weaker
weakest
weakly

weakness

weaken verb
weakens
weakening
weakened

weakling noun
weaklings

wealth

wealthy adjective
wealthier
wealthiest
wealthily

weapon noun
weapons

✱ **wear** verb
wears
wearing
wore
worn

wear noun

wearer noun
wearers

weariness

· ·

★ To **waste** something is to use more of it than is needed. ! **waist**.

☆ A **watt** is a unit of electricity. ! **what**.

◐ To **wave** is to move your arm in greeting. ! **waive**.

✱ You use **way** in e.g. *can you tell me the way?* ! **weigh, whey**.

✱ **Weak** means 'not strong'. ! **week**.

✱ To **wear** clothes is to be dressed in them. ! **ware, where**.

weary adjective
  wearier
  weariest
  wearily

weasel noun
  weasels

weather noun

weather verb
  weathers
  weathering
  weathered

weathercock noun
  weathercocks

★ **weave** verb
  weaves
  weaving
  weaved or wove
  woven

weaver noun
  weavers

web noun
  webs

webbed

website noun
  websites

wed verb
  weds
  wedding
  wedded or wed

we'd verb

wedding noun
  weddings

wedge noun
  wedges

wedge verb
  wedges
  wedging
  wedged

Wednesday noun
  Wednesdays

weed noun
  weeds

weed verb
  weeds
  weeding
  weeded

weedy adjective
  weedier
  weediest
  weedily

☆ **week** noun
  weeks

weekday noun
  weekdays

weekend noun
  weekends

weekly adjective and adverb

weep verb
  weeps
  weeping
  wept

weft

○ **weigh** verb
  weighs
  weighing
  weighed

✻ **weight** noun
  weights

weightless

weightlifting

weighty adjective
  weightier
  weightiest
  weightily

weir noun
  weirs

weird adjective
  weirder
  weirdest
  weirdly

weirdness

welcome noun
  welcomes

welcome verb
  welcomes
  welcoming
  welcomed

weld verb
  welds
  welding
  welded

welder noun
  welders

welfare

well noun
  wells

well adjective and adverb
  better
  best

we'll verb

well-being

wellington boots plural noun

well-known

went see go
wept see weep
were see are
we're verb
werewolf noun
  werewolves

west adjective and adverb

✻ **west** noun

westerly adjective and noun
  westerlies

western adjective

western noun
  westerns

★ The past tense is **weaved** in e.g. *she weaved her way through the crowd* and **wove** in e.g. *she wove a shawl*.
☆ A **week** is a period of seven days. ! weak.
○ You use **weigh** in e.g. *how much do you weigh?* ! way, whey.
✻ **Weight** is how heavy something is. ! wait.
✻ You use a capital W in the **West**, when you mean a particular region.

westward *adjective*
and *adverb*

westwards *adverb*

wet *adjective*
  wetter
  wettest

wet *verb*
  wets
  wetting
  wetted

wetness

we've *abbreviation*

whack *verb*
  whacks
  whacking
  whacked

whack *noun*
  whacks

★ **whale** *noun*
  whales

whaler *noun*
  whalers

whaling

wharf *noun*
  wharves *or* wharfs

☆ **what**

whatever

wheat

wheel *noun*
  wheels

wheel *verb*
  wheels
  wheeling
  wheeled

wheelbarrow *noun*
  wheelbarrows

wheelchair *noun*
  wheelchairs

wheeze *verb*
  wheezes
  wheezing
  wheezed

whelk *noun*
  whelks

when

whenever *conjunction*

◐ **where**

whereabouts

whereas

whereupon

wherever

whether *conjunction*

✻ **whey**

∗ **which**

whichever

whiff *noun*
  whiffs

while *adjective* and *noun*

while *verb*
  whiles
  whiling
  whiled

whilst *conjunction*

whimper *verb*
  whimpers
  whimpering
  whimpered

whimper *noun*
  whimpers

whine *verb*
  whines
  whining
  whined

✻ **whine** *noun*
  whines

whinny *verb*
  whinnies
  whinnying
  whinnied

whip *noun*
  whips

whip *verb*
  whips
  whipping
  whipped

whirl *verb*
  whirls
  whirling
  whirled

whirl *noun*
  whirls

whirlpool *noun*
  whirlpools

whirlwind *noun*
  whirlwinds

whirr *verb*
  whirrs
  whirring
  whirred

whirr *noun*
  whirrs

whisk *verb*
  whisks
  whisking
  whisked

whisk *noun*
  whisks

whisker *noun*
  whiskers

whisky *noun*
  whiskies

whisper *verb*
  whispers
  whispering
  whispered

whisper *noun*
  whispers

whist

- -

★ A whale is a large sea mammal. ! **wail**.

☆ You use what in e.g. *what are they doing?* or *I don't know what you mean.* ! **watt**.

◐ You use where in e.g. *where are you?* ! **ware, wear**.

✻ Whey is a watery liquid from milk. ! **way, weigh**.

∗ You use which in e.g. *which one is that?* ! **witch**.

✻ A whine is a high piercing sound. ! **wine**.

whistle *verb*
whistles
whistling
whistled

whistle *noun*
whistles

whistler *noun*
whistlers

white *adjective*
whiter
whitest

whiteness

whitish

white *noun*
whites

whiten *verb*
whitens
whitening
whitened

whitewash *noun*

whitewash *verb*
whitewashes
whitewashing
whitewashed

Whitsun

Whit Sunday

whiz *verb*
whizzes
whizzing
whizzed

who

whoever

★ **whole** *adjective*
wholly

whole *noun*
wholes

wholefood *noun*
wholefoods

wholemeal

wholesale *adjective*

wholesome

wholly

whom

whoop *noun*
whoops

whoopee *interjection*

whooping cough

☆ **who's** *verb*

✪ **whose** *adjective*

why

wick *noun*
wicks

wicked *adjective*
wickeder
wickedest
wickedly

wickedness

wicker

wickerwork

wicket *noun*
wickets

wicketkeeper *noun*
wicketkeepers

wide *adjective* and
adverb
wider
widest
widely

widen *verb*
widens
widening
widened

widespread

widow *noun*
widows

widower *noun*
widowers

width *noun*
widths

wield *verb*
wields
wielding
wielded

wife *noun*
wives

wig *noun*
wigs

wiggle *verb*
wiggles
wiggling
wiggled

wiggle *noun*
wiggles

wigwam *noun*
wigwams

wild *adjective*
wilder
wildest
wildly

wilderness *noun*
wildernesses

wildness

wildlife

wilful *adjective*
wilfully

wilfulness

wiliness

will *verb*
would

will *noun*
wills

willing *adjective*
willingly

willingness

willow *noun*
willows

wilt *verb*
wilts
wilting
wilted

. . . .

★ You use **whole** in e.g. *I saw the whole film.* **! hole.**

☆ You use **who's** in *who's* (= who is) *that?* and *I don't know who's* (= who has) *done it.* **! whose.**

✪ You use **whose** in *whose is this?* and *I don't know whose it is.* **! who's.**

wily *adjective*
wilier
wiliest

wimp *noun*
wimps

win *verb*
wins
winning
won

win *noun*
wins

wince *verb*
winces
wincing
winced

winch *noun*
winches

winch *verb*
winches
winching
winched

wind *noun*
winds

wind *verb*
winds
winding
wound

windfall *noun*
windfalls

windmill *noun*
windmills

window *noun*
windows

windpipe *noun*
windpipes

windscreen *noun*
windscreens

windsurfer

windsurfing

windward

windy *adjective*
windier
windiest
windily

★ **wine** *noun*
wines

wing *noun*
wings

wing *verb*
wings
winging
winged

winged

wingless

wingspan *noun*
wingspans

wink *verb*
winks
winking
winked

wink *noun*
winks

winkle *noun*
winkles

winkle *verb*
winkles
winkling
winkled

winner *noun*
winners

winnings *plural noun*

winter *noun*
winters

wintertime

wintry *adjective*
wintrier
wintriest

wipe *verb*
wipes
wiping
wiped

wipe *noun*
wipes

wiper *noun*
wipers

wire *noun*
wires

wire *verb*
wires
wiring
wired

wireless *noun*
wirelesses

wiring

wiry *adjective*
wirier
wiriest
wirily

wisdom

wise *adjective*
wiser
wisest
wisely

wish *verb*
wishes
wishing
wished

wish *noun*
wishes

wishbone *noun*
wishbones

wisp *noun*
wisps

wispy *adjective*
wispier
wispiest
wispily

wistful *adjective*
wistfully

wistfulness

wit *noun*
wits

. . . .

★ **Wine** is a drink. ! whine.

★ **witch** noun
  witches
witchcraft
with
withdraw verb
  withdraws
  withdrawing
  withdrew
  withdrawn
withdrawal noun
  withdrawals
wither verb
  withers
  withering
  withered
withhold verb
  withholds
  withholding
  withheld
within
without
withstand verb
  withstands
  withstanding
  withstood
witness noun
  witnesses
wittiness
witty adjective
  wittier
  wittiest
  wittily
wizard noun
  wizards
wizardry
wobble verb
  wobbles
  wobbling
  wobbled
wobble noun
  wobbles

wobbly adjective
  wobblier
  wobbliest
woe noun
  woes
woeful
  adjective
  woefully
wok noun
  woks
woke see wake
woken see wake
wolf noun
  wolves
woman noun
  women
womb noun
  wombs
☆ **won** see win
wonder noun
  wonders
wonder verb
  wonders
  wondering
  wondered
wonderful adjective
  wonderfully
won't verb
○ **wood** noun
  woods
wooded
wooden
woodland noun
  woodlands
woodlouse noun
  woodlice
woodpecker noun
  woodpeckers
woodwind
woodwork

woodworm noun
  woodworm or
  woodworms
woody adjective
  woodier
  woodiest
wool
woollen
woollens plural noun
woolliness
woolly adjective
  woollier
  woolliest
word noun
  words
word verb
  words
  wording
  worded
wording
wordy adjective
  wordier
  wordiest
wore see wear
work noun
  works
work verb
  works
  working
  worked
workable
worker noun
  workers
workforce noun
  workforces
workman noun
  workmen
workmanship
workout noun
  workouts

. . . .

★ A witch is someone who uses witchcraft. ! which.
☆ You use won in e.g. I won a prize. ! one.
○ Wood is material from trees or a lot of trees growing together. ! would.

works plural noun
worksheet noun
worksheets
workshop noun
workshops
world noun
worlds
worldliness
worldly adjective
worldlier
worldliest
worldwide adjective
worm noun
worms
worm verb
worms
worming
wormed
worn see wear
worry verb
worries
worrying
worried
worrier noun
worriers
worry noun
worries
worse adjective and
adverb
worsen verb
worsens
worsening
worsened
worship verb
worships
worshipping
worshipped
worship noun
worshipper noun
worshippers

worst adjective and
adverb
worth
worthiness
worthless adjective
worthlessly
worthwhile
worthy adjective
worthier
worthiest
worthily
★ **would** see will
wouldn't verb
wound noun
wounds
wound verb
wounds
wounding
wounded
wound see wind
wove see weave
woven see weave
☆ **wrap** verb
wraps
wrapping
wrapped
wrap noun
wraps
wrapper noun
wrappers
wrapping noun
wrappings
wrath
wrathful adjective
wrathfully
wreath noun
wreaths
wreathe verb
wreathes
wreathing
wreathed

wreck verb
wrecks
wrecking
wrecked
wreck noun
wrecks
wreckage noun
wreckages
wrecker noun
wreckers
wren noun
wrens
wrench verb
wrenches
wrenching
wrenched
wrench noun
wrenches
wrestle verb
wrestles
wrestling
wrestled
wrestler noun
wrestlers
wretch noun
wretches
wretched adjective
wretchedly
wriggle verb
wriggles
wriggling
wriggled
wriggle noun
wriggles
wriggly adjective
wrigglier
wriggliest
○ **wring** verb
wrings
wringing
wrung

- -

★ You use **would** in e.g. *would you like to come to tea?* ! **wood.**
☆ To **wrap** something is to cover it in paper etc. ! **rap.**
○ To **wring** something is to squeeze it hard. ! **ring.**

wrinkle noun
  wrinkles
wrinkle verb
  wrinkles
  wrinkling
  wrinkled
wrist noun
  wrists
wristwatch noun
  wristwatches
★ **write** verb
  writes
  writing
  wrote
  written
writer noun
  writers
writhe verb
  writhes
  writhing
  writhed
writing noun
  writings
written see write
wrong adjective and
  adverb
  wrongly
wrong noun
  wrongs
wrong verb
  wrongs
  wronging
  wronged
wrote see write
wrung see wring
☆ **wry** adjective
  wryer
  wryest

Xx

xenophobia
Xmas noun
  Xmases
X-ray noun
  X-rays
X-ray verb
  X-rays
  X-raying
  X-rayed
xylophone noun
  xylophones

Yy

-y and -ey
Nouns ending in -y
following a
consonant, e.g. **story**,
make plurals ending
in -ies, e.g. **stories**,
and verbs, e.g. **try**,
make forms in -ies
and -ied, e.g. **tries**,
tried. Nouns ending
in -ey, e.g. **journey**,
make plurals ending
in -eys, e.g. **journeys**.

yacht noun
  yachts
yachtsman noun
  yachtsmen
yachtswoman noun
  yachtswomen
yam noun
  yams

yank verb
  yanks
  yanking
  yanked
yap verb
  yaps
  yapping
  yapped
yap noun
  yaps
yard noun
  yards
yard noun
  yards
yarn noun
  yarns
yawn verb
  yawns
  yawning
  yawned
yawn noun
  yawns
year noun
  years
yearly adjective and
  adverb
yearn verb
  yearns
  yearning
  yearned
yeast
yell noun
  yells
yell verb
  yells
  yelling
  yelled
yellow adjective and
  noun
  yellower
  yellowest

★ You use **write** in e.g. to write a letter. ! right, rite.
☆ You use **wry** in e.g. a wry smile. ! rye.

yelp verb
yelps
yelping
yelped

yelp noun
yelps

★ **yen** noun
yens or yen

yeoman noun
yeomen

yesterday adjective
and noun
yesterdays

yet

yeti noun
yetis

☆ **yew** noun
yews

yield verb
yields
yielding
yielded

yield noun
yields

yippee

yodel verb
yodels
yodelling
yodelled

yodeller noun
yodellers

yoga

yoghurt noun
yoghurts

◎ **yoke** noun
yokes

yoke verb
yokes
yoking
yoked

✱ **yolk** noun
yolks

Yom Kippur

yonder

✱ **you**

you'd verb

you'll verb

young adjective
younger
youngest

young plural noun

youngster noun
youngsters

your

you're abbreviation

yours

yourself pronoun
yourselves

youth noun
youths

youthful adjective
youthfully

you've abbreviation

yo-yo noun
yo-yos

yuppie noun
yuppies

Zz

zany adjective
zanier
zaniest
zanily

zap verb
zaps
zapping
zapped

zeal

zealous adjective
zealously

zebra noun
zebras

zenith noun
zeniths

zero noun
zeros

zest

zigzag noun
zigzags

zigzag verb
zigzags
zigzagging
zigzagged

zinc

zip noun
zips

zip verb
zips
zipping
zipped

zodiac

zombie noun
zombies

zone noun
zones

zoo noun
zoos

zoological adjective
zoologically

zoologist noun
zoologists

zoology

zoom verb
zooms
zooming
zoomed

- -

★ The plural is **yens** when you mean 'a longing' and **yen** for Japanese money.
☆ A **yew** is a tree. ! ewe, you.
◎ A **yoke** is a piece of wood put across animals pulling a cart. ! yolk.
✱ A **yolk** is the yellow part of an egg. ! yoke.
✱ You use **you** in e.g. *I love you*. ! ewe, yew.